THE ACTOR'S SURVIVAL GUIDE

THE ACTOR'S SURVIVAL GUIDE

How to Make Your Way in Hollywood

Second Edition

Jon S. Robbins

methuen | drama

LONDON • NEW YORK • OXFORD • NEW DELHI • SYDNEY

METHUEN DRAMA
Bloomsbury Publishing Plc
50 Bedford Square, London, WC1B 3DP, UK
1385 Broadway, New York, NY 10018, USA

BLOOMSBURY, METHUEN DRAMA and the Methuen Drama logo
are trademarks of Bloomsbury Publishing Plc

First published in Great Britain 2008
This edition published 2019

Cover design by Jason Anscomb
Cover images © Shutterstock

A catalogue record for this book is available from the British Library.

Library of Congress Cataloging-in-Publication Data
Names: Robbins, Jon S., author.
Title: The actor's survival guide : how to make your way in
Hollywood / Jon S. Robbins.
Description: [Second edition] | London ; New York, NY : Methuen Drama, 2019.
Identifiers: LCCN 2018026302| ISBN 9781350039377 (hbk.) |
ISBN 9781350039384 (pbk.) | ISBN 9781350039360 (ePDF) |
ISBN 9781350039391 (ebk.)
Subjects: LCSH: Motion picture acting—Vocational guidance—California—Los Angeles.
Classification: LCC PN1995.9.P75 R62 2019 | DDC 791.4302/8/2379494—dc23 LC record
available at https://lccn.loc.gov/2018026302

ISBN:	HB:	978-1-350-03937-7
	PB:	978-1-350-03938-4
	ePDF:	978-1-350-03936-0
	eBook:	978-1-350-03939-1

Typeset by RefineCatch Limited, Bungay, Suffolk
Printed and bound in Great Britain

To find out more about our authors and books visit www.bloomsbury.com
and sign up for our newsletters.

CONTENTS

List of Illustrations   x
Preface   xi
Acknowledgments   xvi
List of Abbreviations   xvii

1   Moving to Los Angeles   2
What Should I Do Before I Move?   3
What Should I NOT Do When I Move?   10

2   Living in Los Angeles   13
What is the Difference Between Los Angeles County and the City
of Los Angeles?   15
Where Should I Live in Los Angeles?   16

**3   Surviving in Los Angeles: Employment, Housing and
Transportation**   33
How Should I Begin to Implement My Business Plan?   34

EMPLOYMENT   34
Who Hires Struggling Actors in Los Angeles?   34
Where Do I Look for Employment Notices?   38
Are There Jobs I Should Avoid?   39
What is Better, Employment or Entrepreneurship?   41

HOUSING   43
How Do I Rent an Apartment?   43
Should I Rent, Lease, Sublet, or Live With a Roommate?   43
Where Do I Look for Housing Notices?   44

What Should I Look for When I Inspect the Unit?   46
What Application Fees May I Be Charged to Rent/Lease an
Apartment?   47
Are There Additional Fees I Can Be Charged if I am Approved?   48
What Are My Renter's Rights?   50

TRANSPORTATION   51
Do I Really Need a Car in Los Angeles?   51
What Are Transportation Corridors?   51
What Is With the Freeway Names?   52
What Are My Public Transportation Options?   52
Public Transportation vs Private Vehicle?   53
Is Parking a Problem?   53

4   **The Business of Hollywood**   55
What Is Meant By the "Media and Entertainment Industry?"   56
Who Are the Players?   57
What Is the Product Being Bought and Sold?   60
How Well Do Minority Actors Do in Hollywood?   60
Is There a Gender Disparity in Casting?   63
Is There Bias Towards Disabled Actors?   64
Is There Bias Against the LGBT Community?   65
Can Senior Actors Still Find Work in Hollywood?   66

5   **Marketing Your Career**   69
What Marketing Materials Do I Need?   70
How Do I Find a Good Photographer?   71
How Do I Prepare for the Photo Shoot?   74
What Should I Expect During the Photo Shoot?   75
How Do I Choose a Headshot?   76
Where Do I Have Headshots Printed?   76

RESUME   77
What Should I Put On My Resume?   77
What if I Have No Professional Credits?   78
How Should I Organize My Resume?   78
What Should I NOT Put On My Resume?   80
Do All Actors Lie or Exaggerate on their Resume?   81
How Should I Format and Reproduce My Resume?   81

How Do I Get Clips of my Work?   82
What If I Have No Clips?   83

PERSONAL WEBSITE   83
How Do I Establish a Personal Website?   83

SOCIAL MEDIA   84
What Social Media Sites Should I Use for My Career?   84
What Social Media Etiquette Should I Maintain?   86
What Other Computer Software, Extensions, or Apps Will I Find Useful?   87

6   Talent Agents and Personal Managers   90

Why Do I Need a Talent Agent?   91
What Does a Talent Agent Do for an Actor?   91
Must an Actor Have a Talent Agent to Submit?   93
What is the Difference Between a Talent Agent and a Personal Manager?   93
How Do I Know a Manager or Management Company is Legitimate?   94
Are There Different Kinds of Talent Agents?   95
How Do You Become a Talent Agent?   95
What is Meant By a Union Franchised Talent Agent?   96
Are All Talent Agents SAG-AFTRA Franchised?   97
What is the Difference Between a SAG-AFTRA Agency Contract and a GSA?   97
Why Would an Actor Sign a GSA?   99
How Do I Find a Licensed Talent Agent?   100
What Should I Expect When I Meet with a Talent Agent?   101
How Do Talent Agents and Personal Managers Work Together?   101
What Scams Should I Watch Out For?   102

7   The Unions   106

A Brief History   108
What Led to the Merger Between SAG and AFTRA?   109
What Have Been the Results of this Merger?   109
What Are the Issues Still Before the Union?   110
Are There Other Unions I Should Join?   111
What Does a Union Do For an Actor?   112
How Do I Join SAG-AFTRA?   114

Do I Have to Join SAG-AFTRA?   117
Can I Continue to Do Nonunion Work if I am a Union Member?   118

8   The Casting Game   120

Who Are Casting Directors?   121
What Happens During the Casting Process?   121
Are Casting Directors Licensed?   122
Is the Casting Process the Same for All Projects?   123
How Does an Actor Get an Audition in Hollywood?   126
How Does An Actor Learn What Projects Are Being Cast?   127
Can Actors Subscribe to this Service?   127
Are There Legitimate Electronic Casting Websites an Actor Can
Subscribe To?   127
Are There Other Sources of Casting Notices?   129
What Information Do Casting Notices Provide?   129
How Do You Know if a Project is Legitimate?   131
If Everybody Uses Electronic Casting, Why Do I Need Hard Copy
Headshots?   132

9   Auditioning in Hollywood   135

What Information Should I Receive with an Audition Call?   136
How Should I Prepare for an Audition?   137
What Should I Do When I Arrive for the Audition?   139
What Happens During an Audition?   140
What Should I NOT Do During an Audition?   142
What Should NOT Happen During an Audition?   143
What Should I Do After an Audition?   144
Can I Self-Tape My Audition?   145
What Equipment Do I Need?   145
How Do I Self-Tape a Professional-Looking Audition?   146
Are There Audition Scams I Should Avoid?   147

10   Hollywood Contracts   151

What is the Difference Between a Union and a Nonunion Contract?   151
What Kind of Contract Information Will I Receive for a Booking?   152
What Should I Expect of a Union Contract?   153
What Changes Occurred With the New 2017 Theatrical/Television
Agreement?   160

What Are the Contractual Differences Within the Various Kinds of
Projects?   161
What About Background Actors?   168
Are There Other Legal Documents an Actor Must Know About?   169

11 **Working in Hollywood**   172

What Should I Bring with Me to the Set?   173
What Should I NOT Bring?   174
What Should I Do When I Arrive On the Set?   174
What Set Etiquette Should I Observe?   175
What Different Work Environments Will I Encounter?   175
What Can I Expect From Nonunion Projects?   178
What Kind of Nonunion Projects Will I Encounter?   179
What Workplace Issues Might I Encounter?   182

12 **Finance and Accounting**   186

Do Actors Have Any Special Tax Liabilities?   188
Does the IRS Offer Any Special Tax Incentives to an Actor?   189
What Deductions May Actors Take on Their Income Taxes as an
Employee?   189
The Cost of Looking For Employment   190
Unreimbursed Expenses   195
What Additional Deductions May Actors Take on Their Income Taxes
as an Independent Contractor?   197
What Should I Do if I Am Audited?   198
What Mistakes Should I Avoid?   199
What Items Are NOT Deductible?   199

13 **Professional Development**   202

Why Should I Continue With My Education Or Training?   203
What Are The Different Training Options for an Actor in Los Angeles?   204
What Other Kinds of Research Resources Will I Find in Los Angeles?   207

Appendix A: Los Angeles City Neighborhood Statistical Data   209
Appendix B: Los Angeles Extra Casting Agencies   214
Appendix C: Documents   216
An Actor's Film and Television Glossary   222
Bibliography   233

LIST OF ILLUSTRATIONS

Figures

1.1 Actor's Skills Checklist   5
1.2 Five-Year Career Action Plan Outline   7
5.1 Sample Resume   80

Charts

3.1 Professional Living Costs in Los Angeles   35
4.1 Percent of TV and Theatrical Roles   61
4.2 Percent of Theatrical Roles to Population   61
4.3 Share of TV and Theatrical Roles by Ethnicity   62
4.4 Share of Roles in 2016–2017 Scripted Projects by Race   63
4.5 Percent of Speaking Roles by Gender   64
4.6 Senior Characters by Gender and Year   67
10.1 SAG-AFTRA Contract Comparison   162
12.1 Simplified Option for Home Office Deduction   196

Maps

2.1 Entertainment Industry Zone   16
2.2 Satellite Map of Los Angeles   17
2.3 Los Angeles Neighborhoods   18

PREFACE

Ten years ago I wrote the first edition of the *Actor's Survival Guide* as an attempt to make academic lemonade out of the lemon I had been handed. My professional years in Hollywood had occurred years before, and my irrelevance as a theater arts professor had become as a headlight bearing down on a deer. My classes had become exercises in predictability, and only by toiling in the casting offices of Seattle had I maintained my bearings. My students were now skeptical of my sage advice and several had returned from Los Angeles broke and humbled. A failed job interview capped it all off.

As I listened to various students give accounts of their failed excursions to Hollywood to pursue a career in the film industry, I realized that these students had not failed for lack of talent, but for lack of business skills. The stories behind each student's move to Hollywood reflected bad business decisions that doomed their effort to failure long before boxes had been packed and addresses had been changed. Serious acting students must strategize entrepreneurially before transitioning to professional life. Having made this transition more than once in my own life, I understood its complexities, and as an educator, I also understood my inadequacy in preparing students for this experience. Hollywood had changed, as had I. At this juncture, all paths now pointed to a sabbatical; to regain my artistic soul and my professional center.

With no more than a chest or two of clothes, a computer, and a blow-up bed, I did move to Hollywood for one year, and one year only as I resurrected a long dormant career. That year I auditioned for sixty projects and was booked for twenty-four, including: commercials, episodic dramas, a reality program, music videos, films, stage plays, and print assignments. I experienced moments of success and applause followed by many more moments of rejection. Admittedly, I had several advantages over most. I had already earned my union membership, had a rent-free arrangement with my brother-in-law for the year, and had an understanding partner to tend the home fires. Financially, I only broke even for the year, which would be an average year for most union members. Sadly, less than one percent of union members make a living wage yearly.

I found out that time had moved on from the Hollywood world of the 1970s with showcases, answering services, and the black and white headshots that I had remembered. Casting workshops, cell phones and digital marketing services had taken their place, requiring a vastly different skillset in marketing, business, and technology. And the twentieth-century clichéd theatrical talent agent knocking on every casting director's door had long been replaced by a twenty-first-century, technologically connected jobber who bartered an actor's services in cyberspace. Everything had changed.

Exactly one year later, I returned to the teaching profession, convinced that the complexities of Hollywood now required entrepreneurial business skills on par with any small business owner. I developed the curriculum at my college to address this issue. And, I wrote the *Actor's Survival Guide.* The fact that I am now preparing its second edition for publication suggests that those efforts were successful. Over the ten years I had kept abreast of changes in the industry both as a professor and as an actor, but not until researching and gathering the notes for this revised edition did I discover how profoundly the entertainment industry has changed once again. The subtleties of new mergers, corporate acquisitions, contracts, digital platforms, weekly scandals, and changing trends had gotten lost in the milieu of everyday living. My return to Los Angeles this time, though shorter in duration, pivoted upon interviews with many industry professionals, agents, casting associates, and working actors of many stripes. I attended union workshops and listened to industry executives predict future trends, renewed old friendships at old haunts, and walked the well-worn sidewalks of Hollywood once again. Much less a homecoming, I, like Rip Van Winkle, had awakened to find a world I barely recognized.

Change 1. **Merger of the Screen Actors Guild and the American Federation of Television and Radio Artists**. This merger had seemed so logical, so necessary, and so impossible for so many years that most actors had resigned themselves to forever paying two annual union dues and forever coping with confusing contractual complications about union jurisdiction. The latest contractual negotiations with the producer's guild had exposed a divided membership between SAG and AFTRA. Like feuding sisters, their side-by-side contract negotiations with the guild had become adversarial and contradictory. And just when it seemed reconciliation between the two organizations was impossible, the impossible happened. On March 30, 2012, their respective members overwhelmingly approved a merger of the two unions. For those who doubted the merger's advisability, the subsequent contractual advances bear out this leap of faith.

Change 2. **New Media Contract**. The union sets the bar high for membership by requiring each actor to jump through a hoop by first securing employment. With its New Media Contract, SAG-AFTRA offers a new "hoop," a portal to union membership tailor-made for a millennial generation raised on video consumption and who define themselves more broadly as filmmakers. Actors now have the opportunity to self-produce themselves into union membership.

Change 3. **Cord-cutting**. The phenomenon now known as cord-cutting only reaffirms Adam Smith's marketplace "invisible hand." For decades television consumers have been captive audiences to programming, targeting society's lowest common denominators, controlled by corporate sponsors who paid the bills. But, a generation raised on video, demand their media anytime, anywhere, any place, and any way possible. Consumers have irrevocably changed the marketplace by embracing new delivery platforms and new business models. The year 2017's record offering of scripted series continues to increase and can be viewed as streaming video, on multiple devices, with an on-demand structure that now benefits actors with residuals.

Change 4. **Scandals.** From Cosby to Spacey, careers have been shattered in a digital second, as society recoils from the stories of women's exploitation and degradation. The media has already shone a bright light on the lack of diversity in Hollywood through several award seasons now, and each ensuing drama of the #MeToo movement serves only to increase the intensity. Multiple studies document the extent to which Hollywood remains a "good ol' boys club"; white, male, and ostensibly straight, though insiders know differently. Of course, all could change in a nanosecond if minority-produced, -written, -directed, and -performed projects suddenly rock the box office. Changes do seem afoot, and Hollywood ignores its consumers at its own peril.

Change 5. **Social media as a marketing tool**. In the past, A-list actors lived and died by their Q-Rating, an analytical measure of an actor's popularity. Today's top actors bow to the Top Actors Chart rankings published in *The Hollywood Reporter,* based on global data culled from Facebook, Instagram, Twitter, YouTube, and Google Plus. This chart's methodology blends data on social engagement on the platforms along with weekly additions of followers and subscribers. It has become a mainstay of casting, always mindful of the power of consumer engagement. The emergence of social media, not just as a marketing tool, but as a measure of an actor's profitability presents actors with a contradiction: requiring them to work publicly and live privately in a world where one must work privately and live publicly.

Change 6. **Self-taping auditions**. The digital revolution has democratized many facets of society. The possibility for actors in Biloxi, Idaho, or wherever, to compete for roles, on an equal footing with those in Hollywood has raised the question of "Why Hollywood?" Indeed, with much of filming now scattered regionally, I confronted the real possibility that a book facilitating an actor's pilgrimage to Hollywood was in itself irrelevant. But, while true actors have more flexibility in conducting a career, Hollywood still remains the center of decision-making and principal casting. But, whether one lives in Biloxi or right on Hollywood Boulevard, when faced with deciding between an audition and a job that pays the bills, self-taping removes one more burden from an actor.

Change 7. **New tax law**. The Tax Cuts and Jobs Act that Congress passed in 2017 throws an existential curveball to union actors who, as employees now, can deduct from their income taxes the enormous cost of marketing themselves that by estimates absorbs 35 percent of an actor's annual income (Karas, *2018: What can we expect?*). As of the tax year 2018, they can *do so* no longer. Ironically, nonunion actors, who work as independent contractors, can continue to deduct this cost of business. Only union actors will find themselves with a tax bill by some estimates three times higher. Time will tell if actors can find a work-around. Some have already suggested actors incorporate as a loan-out, S-Corporation, and many A-list actors do so already as a hedge against liability. The alternative, paying the significantly increased income tax, will adversely affect the rank and file who already shoulder a difficult financial burden before their investment pays off.

In many ways the changes I observed during this second sabbatical in Los Angeles points to a continuation of what I observed the first time: a technological revolution reordering a marketplace now under the control of its consumers. Undeniably, this market rebellion will continue, underscoring once again the importance of business skills in traversing the Hollywood landscape. Few college acting programs teach actors these skills and even college-trained actors with years in professional training fail in Hollywood, unprepared for the business reality of the industry. These chapters attempt to prepare the serious film and television actor for the *business* of Hollywood that few college programs teach and that would take Hollywood newcomers years to learn and master on their own. Each chapter has been organized sequentially from planning stage, to establishing a base of operations, to tackling career obstacles. Each chapter begins with an **Actor's Forum**, excerpts from interviews with three professional working actors who have forged careers in vastly different niches of the film industry.

Michael Gabiano—A veteran working professional, Michael represents the traditional Hollywood actor. His pathway from Western Connecticut State University led through the New York City stage and tours with the National Theatre for the Performing Arts and TheatreWorks USA. Now established in Los Angeles, Michael's credits include *General Hospital, Days of Our Lives* and *Sean Saves the World*.

Peter Lavin—A voice-over actor, Peter followed a more circuitous route, first moving from London's West End musicals to Washington DC and then to Hollywood. His versatile vocal talents, from welcoming Kate Winslet on board the Titanic to the latest Marvel feature, can be heard in hundreds of films, television, animation, and video game projects.

Richard Dorton—Known as the "Mocap Man," Richard has more hours in a mocap suit than anyone in over 100 video game projects, performing the characters of Shaggy, Darth Vader, Wolverine, Conan, and Peter Venkman, to name a few. Also hailing from Washington DC, a passion for all things theater led Richard to stunt work and eventually motion capture. Now teaching for Mocap Vaults, Richard brings his years of experience from advanced combat to specially movement to a new generation of performance capture actors.

Throughout this book I have endeavored to provide authoritative sources and voices to support my counsel. I culled data from the most recent studies on casting, collected demographic statistical data on Los Angeles' many eclectic neighborhoods, reread verbose government guides and reports, and trudged through the gobbledygook of contractual clauses. At the head of each chapter is a list of **Actor's Resources**, useful topical sources of information, including names, addresses, contact numbers, and web links. Finally, **In the Box**, a slang phrase referring to the audition room, provides personal anecdotes of my time in Hollywood.

This book's goal has always been to provide advice to actors from the perspective of working actors, not just from those who talk about acting and work in some other aspect of the industry. Their perspective is also important, but only other actors can attest to the business decisions necessary to sustain oneself for the at least three to five years needed to establish oneself in Hollywood. Newcomers will still find that Hollywood is like a minefield within a maze. I have tried to provide a guide, a road map through the pitfalls and wrong turns that derail too many promising careers and frustrate even the most dedicated actors. I point out the scams and frauds of those who prey upon artists, dazzling them with talk of the glitter of fame and fortune but with no other intention than to separate the artists from their money, and in doing so, make this business harder than it needs to be. I debunk some myths, issue a few warnings about strategies to avoid, and try to point toward more sustainable, low cost options for those with slim budgets.

This book, though, was not written to supplant or replace the training, discipline, and experience students acquire in formal training programs (whether college-based, or otherwise). This book does not teach acting and will certainly not guarantee success. No book can substitute for the hard work, solid training, and dedication to learning technique and craft that you need before others will take your acting career seriously. Now is an exciting time to launch a career in Hollywood as it glitters brighter than ever, and its allure draws actors, as moths to a flame. The smart ones survive by not getting burned.

ACKNOWLEDGMENTS

would like to thank fellow actors Dale Reynolds, Jacque Lynn Colton, Gera Hermann, and SAG-AFTRA local president Rik Deskin, for their support and help in researching this book. Also thanks to Oliver Hollis-Leick, co-founder of the Mocap Vaults, along with actors Richard Dorton, "Mocap Man," Peter Lavin, and Michael Gambiano for their candor and generosity of time and to Joan Messinger, talent agent at Pinnacle Commercial for her candor, Valerie Yaros, Historian and Archivist at SAG-AFTRA for her professional input, and the two refugees from *Mork and Mindy*, Donald and Ronald Welch for keeping me centered.

LIST OF ABBREVIATIONS

3D	three dimensional
AA	Associate of Arts
ABC	California Department of Alcoholic Beverage Control
ABC Television	American Broadcasting Corporation Television
AD	assistant director
ADR	automated dialogue replacement
AEA	Actors Equity Association
AFL	American Federation of Labor
AFTRA	American Federation of Television and Radio Artists
AGMA	American Guild of Musical Artists
AGVA	American Guild of Variety Artists
AMPTP	Alliance of Motion Picture and Television Producers
app.	application
ATA	Association of Talent Agents
CA	California
CAA	Creative Artists Agency
CBS	Columbia Broadcasting System
CD	compact disc
CDCA	California Department of Consumer Affairs
CGI	computer generated imagery
CIO	Congress of Industrial Organizations

CSLB	California Contractors State Licensing Board
CSA	Casting Society of America
DBA	doing business as
DCA	County of Los Angeles Department of Consumer Affairs
MV	California Department of Motor Vehicles
DSLR	digital single-lens reflex camera
DVD	digital video disc
FCC	Federal Communications Commission
FI-Core	financial core
GDP	Gross Domestic Product
GLAAD	Gay and Lesbian Alliance Against Defamation
GPS	Global Positioning System
GSA	General Services Agreement
HCIDLA	Housing and Community Investment Department of Los Angeles
HDR	high definition resolution
ICM	International Creative Management
ID.	identification
IMDb	Internet Movie Database
IMSDb	Internet Movie Script Database
IRS	Internal Revenue Service
LA	Los Angeles
LADOT	Los Angeles Department of Transportation
LA Metro	Los Angeles Metropolitan Transportation Authority
LAPD	Los Angeles Police Department
LAX	Los Angeles International Airport
LCD	liquid crystal diode
LEAD	Licensee Education on Alcohol and Drugs
LED	light emitting diode

LGBTQ	lesbian, gay, bisexual, transsexual, queer
LLC	limited liability company
LORT	League of Resident Theaters
OLED	organic light emitting diode
OSHA	Occupational Safety and Health Administration
MGM	Metro-Goldwyn-Mayer Studios
mm.	millimeter
NATR	National Association of Talent Representatives
NBC/Universal	National Broadcasting System/Universal Studios
PA	Production Assistant
PSA	public service announcement
RSO	Los Angeles Rent Stabilization Ordinance
SAG	Screen Actors Guild
SBS	Spanish Broadcasting System
SCEP	Systematic Code Enforcement Program
spec	speculation
SSI	Social Security Insurance
SVoD	subscription video-on-demand
TAA	Talent Agents Act of 1978
Taft–Hartley	The Labor Management Relations Act of 1947
tba	to be announced
temp.	temporary
UCLA	University of California—Los Angeles
USC	University of Southern California
WGA	Writer's Guild of America
VITA	Volunteer Income Tax Assistance
VOD	video-on-demand

ACTOR'S FORUM

I started making plans to come out, and by 2004 I was here [in Hollywood]. I had been here before as a tourist and touring, and with that you only get a flavor of Hollywood, West Hollywood, the mountains, the ocean, and all that. I was kind of blown away by the glitz of it all, but you live here for even a week and you learn that that's all a facade. It's still a very pretty place to live. The weather is really nice, but it's hard. It's hard! The reality just hits you right in the face. A friend of mine used to say, "There's something in Hollywood that you see, especially among actors. There's a desperation to it." I found myself going down that rabbit hole until I realized that you don't compare yourself to other people or other people's careers. Just stay on your course. That old saying, keep your eyes on your own paper. I take that advice seriously, though, and when I do that I find that good things happen, and I'm very happy to be here.

MICHAEL GABIANO

I moved here [Hollywood] from London in 1992, but circuitously because I went to Washington D.C. first. I loved it. I'm probably the minority. I've always loved big cities anyway. Back then it wasn't as big as it is now or as bustling as it is now, but it was a great city and, of course, the weather is fantastic, and the access to so many recreational opportunities is fantastic, so I really liked it. And I'm not frightened by diversity and hustle and bustle and noise. I kind of thrive on it . . . I got into voice-overs in 1996. Initially, like any young actor, I was pursuing commercials and co-star auditions for film and television and then lucked into some voice work on a feature film called *Rob Roy*, back in the day, and doing some additional voices, group ADR (Automated Dialogue Replacement).

PETER LAVIN

I moved here [Hollywood] in 2000. I lived in Maryland. I had a pretty good theater career in D.C. I went to theater school to try and learn everything. I wanted to work in the business wherever I could whether it was in stunts, makeup, or wardrobe. Anything. I was stunt coordinating a short film for a friend and somebody on the set saw me do a flip on a bike over the bike handles and said they needed stunt coordinators for *America's Most Wanted*, and did I want to come over? So, I started stunt coordinating for them. We were supposed to shoot an episode in D.C. but it snowed, and they were going to move the episode to Los Angeles. I wanted to do movies, so I moved out here with a job luckily enough. I knew this was the place to be, to be in the business. I loved it. So, when you come here, it's all your dreams. It's movies and TV. I wanted to be a stunt man. Motion capture found me because stunt people were doing a lot of motion capture. *Titanic* had just come out. They used motion capture for the stunts of people falling off the ship and things like that, so I thought, I'll go to Los Angeles and get into a stunt show. That's what I really wanted to do.

RICHARD DORTON

1 MOVING TO LOS ANGELES

I learned this, at least, by my experiment; that if one advanced confidently in the direction of his dreams, and endeavors to live the life which he has imagined, he will meet with a success unexpected in common hours.
HENRY DAVID THOREAU—*Walden*

ACTOR'S RESOURCES

Discover: Los Angeles—"Explore the Neighborhoods of Los Angeles"

The City of Los Angeles / Housing Department—Residential Housing Information

Bing Maps—Los Angeles—Detailed map of Los Angeles

Sigalert Traffic Map—Real-time traffic information

Los Angeles Metro—Public transportation and maps

The LA Beat—Entertainment, Dining, and the Arts

IMSDb—Internet Movie Script Database

Los Angeles Almanac—Reference Guide to Los Angeles

Okay, you have decided to move to Los Angeles to pursue a career in film and television. You have taken classes, trained, and paid your dues performing in the regional and community theater ecosphere that exists in whatever corner of the world you hail from. You are ready. You have the chops. No one can talk you out of it, and no one should; otherwise, you risk becoming one of the, what Thoreau identified as, "men who lead lives of quiet desperation" (Thoreau, *Walden*, 111). And, if you truly have the fire in your belly, then nothing will change your mind. But you do need to know that you will be one of thousands of "wannabe" professional actors who each year move to Los Angeles to follow that dream, nine out of ten of whom give up within their first year.

Dreamers fail for many reasons, but lack of planning ranks high among them. Los Angeles has grown to a megalopolis of over 12.9 million people, crammed into over 4,751 miles of suburban jungle. Dorothy Parker called it "seventy-two suburbs in search of a city." Raymond Chandler described it as "a big, hard-boiled city with no more personality than a paper cup." You will probably invent your own epithet, but before you can call it "home," you will need to do some serious planning. To maximize your efforts planning should start at least six months before your move.

IN THE BOX

Years ago my weekly jogging schedule down a narrow Hollywood Hills street often coincided with the jogging schedule of television star Ed Asner, of *The Mary Tyler Moore Show* fame. One day, as we stood recovering from a run, I gathered the nerve to ask the Emmy award-winning actor why he thought he had finally succeeded after so many years of trying. Between gasps of air he told me that the entertainment business was nothing more than a merry-go-round. "Everybody eventually gets their chance at the gold ring" he explained. "The secret is to stay on the merry-go-round long enough to get your shot at it!"

What Should I Do Before I Move?

Conduct a Personality Audit

Hundreds of new recruits to the acting entertainment industry arrive in Los Angeles on a daily basis to try their luck at the gold ring. What makes you different from them? Why do you think you will succeed when so many of them don't? You will need more than a "fire in your belly." Actors succeed in Hollywood by developing themselves into a marketable commodity. So, start by making a list of the personal attributes that will help you stand out from others: personality quirks, skills, talents, hobbies, special training, personal experiences, or accomplishments. Figure 1.1 provides a template to follow. Actor profiles utilized by talent agencies and electronic casting sites also provide checklists that specify the useful skill sets in everything from sports to technical skills. The more skills you have, the more marketable you will be. Evaluate your weaknesses as well. What will be the obstacles to your success, and how can you ameliorate them before making the move? If you are graphically inclined, design a logo for yourself as an exercise in developing your brand, that special quality that sets you a part from others.

Gather Your Resources

Your career move will require certain resources; a personal computer or laptop, a printer/scanner, a cell phone, and reliable transportation remain a necessity. A digital camera and/or video camera, along with a tripod and selfie-stick will be useful although they are not essential. Make a list of every friend, relative, acquaintance, or business contact you have in the Los Angeles area. Your local talent agents, casting directors, coaches, teachers, stage directors, or producers may also suggest contacts or friends in the business with whom you might connect. No contact is too brief or too insignificant to be explored. Gather as many names, addresses, telephone numbers, and email addresses as possible.

Join One of the Actor's Unions

Joining an actor's union is, admittedly, easier said than done. Actor's unions are closed organizations with restricted portals for membership. Success at joining actor's unions varies. Many actors in Los Angeles struggle for years before scoring a principal role and an invitation to join SAG-AFTRA, whereas others manage to solve the problem before ever leaving home. It is also true that film and television production is now more regional as many states offer tax incentives for production companies to film their projects locally rather than in Hollywood. Actors living near a major city may find opportunities for union casting which are less competitive than in Hollywood. But, if you find professional television and film work slim or nonexistent in your neck of the woods, you are likely to find that professional stage companies thrive in most regions. Equity's Membership Candidate Program permits actors and stage managers-in-training to credit theatrical work in an Equity theater towards eventual membership in Equity. After a year as a member of Actors Equity, or any of SAG-AFTRA's other sister unions (such as the American Guild of Musical Artists [AGMA] or the American Guild of Variety Artists [AGVA]), you qualify for membership in SAG-AFTRA.

Actor's Skills Checklist

Athletics	Weapons Training	Boating	Driving
☐ Extreme Sports	☐ Martial Arts	☐ Sailing	☐ Truck
☐ Competitive Sports	☐ Gun Training	☐ Kayaking	☐ Precision
☐ Snow & Water Sports	☐ Archery	☐ Skulling	☐ Motorcycle
☐ Track and Field	☐ Skeet	☐ Canoeing	☐ Cycling
☐ Skating	☐ Sword Play	☐ Fishing	☐ Gliding
Actor Training	☐ Kick Boxing	☐ Jet Skiing	☐ Snowmobile
☐ Improvisation	☐ Special Forces	☐ Scuba	☐ Super Cross
☐ Sketch Comedy	**Vocational**	☐ Windsurfing	☐ Stunt Driving
☐ Juggling	☐ Bartender	**Exercise**	**Aeronautics**
☐ Mime/Clowning	☐ Auctioneer	☐ Gymnastics	☐ Pilot
☐ Magic	☐ Chef	☐ Trampoline	☐ Balloonist
☐ Ventriloquism	☐ Waiter	☐ Mt. Climbing	☐ Sky Diving
☐ Voice	☐ Carpenter	☐ Aerobics	☐ Hang Gliding
☐ Impressions	☐ Audio/Video	☐ Weight Lifting	**Dialects**
☐ Musical Instrument	☐ Disc Jockey	☐ Trapeze	☐ Russian
☐ Pratfalls/Stilts	**Voice**	☐ Stunts	☐ Australian
Dance	☐ Country	☐ Yoga	☐ Cockney
☐ Clog	☐ Rap	**Equestrian**	☐ Italian
☐ Hip Hop	☐ Jazz	☐ Horseback	☐ Bronx
☐ Belly	☐ Musical Theater	☐ Bareback	☐ Southern
☐ Ballet	☐ R & B	☐ Rodeo	☐ Brooklyn
☐ Salsa	☐ Opera	☐ Roping	☐ Spanish
☐ Swing	☐ Pop	☐ English	☐ Middle Eastern
☐ Pole	**Language Fluency**	☐ Jumping	☐ Yiddish
☐ Flamenco	_____	☐ Dressage	☐ Texan
☐ Tap	_____	☐ Side Saddle	☐ Scottish

FIGURE 1.1 Actor's Skills Checklist

Do Some Research

To prepare for your journey, learn as much about the City of Angels as possible. Discover Los Angeles' website (LA Tourism, "Discover Los Angeles") offers comprehensive tourist information on all matters Los Angeles and offers the perfect starting point. The City of Los Angeles and the many independent municipalities that exist within the Greater Los Angeles area, all maintain websites that will furnish residents with useful information, including information on renter's rights. Online maps can provide geographic familiarity with 4,751 miles of Los Angeles County's various regions while real-time reports can be monitored on Sigalert's freeway traffic map. Public transportation routes and schedules can be found at the Los Angeles County Metropolitan Transportation Authority's website. Other websites, such as *LA City Beat* or *LA Weekly* afford windows into the regions' culture and life styles.

Prepare Two Contrasting Monologues

Anyone with any formal training in theater is likely to have two monologues honed and polished. Certainly every Hollywood actor should have theirs prepared at all times, even though they may not be requested very often. While professional theater directors still initially screen actors through prepared monologues, it is unlikely that anyone in film and television casting would ever ask to see them. Talent agents usually do ask to see a prepared scene before deciding whether or not to represent an actor, and so for them, an actor should commit two scenes to memory; a dramatic scene and a comedic one. These do not necessarily need to be from stage scripts. As this is the film and television industry, a cutting from a film or television script is permissible. Consult the Internet Movie Script Database (IMSDb) online for downloadable scripts. Work on your scenes with a coach until they are consistent, honest and present your talent.

Formulate a Business Plan

Business insiders caution that professional actors take, on average, five years to establish themselves in Hollywood and, thus, tempt failure if they are not able to sustain themselves while struggling to establish their career. Similar to any small businesses, you need a business plan, a strategy for establishing a physical workstation, a funding stream and access to the market. Banks require businesses to present an extensive plan, documenting goals, products, services, marketing analysis, organizational management, and finances before loaning them money. I recommend an actor draft their own five-year career action plan that delineates each year's objectives and action steps (see Figure 1.2). Like any other start-up company, you will need to take time and carefully consider your resources. This careful planning may mean the difference between success and failure! Your business plan should include the following:

A Funding Stream

A consistent and adequate source of income from a flexible form of employment represents the ideal. You should not be faced with choosing between attending an audition or going to your job, unless it really is a lousy job! Develop as many marketable skills as possible: clerical, technological, customer service—anything that one can rely on for a steady source of income.

```
                    Five-Year Career Action Plan Outline
I.    Year One
      A.    Objectives (List)
            1.    Action Steps
                  a.    Resources needed
                  b.    Obstacles
                  c.    References
                  d.    Backburners (solutions and reminders)
II.   Year Two (etc.)
      ─────────────────────────────────────────────────────

                              Example

I.    Year One
      A.    (Objective 1) Move to Los Angeles
            1.    (Action Step) Contact (friends, relatives, contacts)
                  a.    (Resources needed) Find telephone numbers,
                  b.    (Obstacles) Not sure where Uncle Roy lives,
                  c.    (Backburner) Remember to ask my cousin.
            2.    Arrange place to stay for two weeks
                  a.    Computer or laptop,
                  b.    Computer is broken—need to have fixed,
                  c.    Ask a friend if I can borrow his laptop.
            3.    Buy a car
                  a.    New or used,
                  b.    Not enough money,
                  c.    Need to sell stereo to help finance the car.
      B.    Find a permanent residence in Los Angeles
            1.    Decide which neighborhoods are best for your career
                  a.    Research online,
                  b.    Need to see for myself,
                  c.    Roommate Finders?
            2.    View in person
                  a.    Make list of housing needs,
                  b.    Draft monthly budget,
                  c.    Talk to neighbors.
            3.    Review and compare housing options
                  a.    Get advise from local friends,
                  b.    Start attending evenings and networking,
```

FIGURE 1.2 Five-Year Career Action Plan Outline

Location

Locate a temporary place to land when you arrive, such as a relative or friend's home, or as a last resort, a cheap hotel room. Having established a funding stream, you can find a suitable and affordable location to establish a home/office, but only then will you know how much you can actually afford to pay. Are you single or do you have a family? The average rent in Los Angeles is now over $1,900 a month (*Curbed Los Angeles,* "For Rent"). Housing will represent your biggest expense but should not cost more than a third of your monthly income.

Accessibility

Mastering the physical obstacles of transportation over approximately one hundred squares miles of urban landscape remains the most difficult challenge in Los Angeles. It was custom built for the automobile, but now that has become the city's nemesis. Savvy drivers know precisely where and when to travel to avoid gridlock. Others rely upon the puzzle of Metro buses, subways, and light rail that have become the Los Angeles public transportation system.

Save Lots of Money

Moving to Los Angeles will take considerable financial resources so count your pennies carefully before determining a plan of action. Los Angeles sucks the life out of a nest egg and can be either affordable or overwhelming in direct proportion to how complicated you make it. One sagacious truism to follow: the more possessions you bring, the more expensive it will be to live. The fewer needs you have, the more likely it is that you will live comfortably without compromising career goals. Thoreau advised, "Our life is frittered away by detail ... Simplicity, simplicity, simplicity!" (Thoreau, 173).

Develop an Employable Skill

If you have already lived the life of a starving artist in college or elsewhere, and learned at least one service profession such as server, chef, retail clerk, bartender, or office assistant, then you are eminently qualified for the actor's lifestyle in Los Angeles. Those jobs are always in demand. They may not pay as well as professional positions, but they do provide one very important feature— flexibility. If your work experience tends more toward the professional, seriously consider a brief stint of employment in any of the above-mentioned service jobs before making your move. Employment in these positions is plentiful but competitive, and employers will opt to hire someone with experience before considering a greenhorn.

Whatever work you pursue to accommodate your artistic bent, it must provide adjustable hours and few responsibilities, something that professional and managerial positions rarely do. So, if you have thus far lived a life of leisure and privilege, I strongly suggest that you gain some working-class skills quickly, unless you have the resources to finance your lifestyle indefinitely. Once established, you will find more lucrative alternatives through networking or entrepreneurship, but make certain you have at least one easily marketable skill before moving to Los Angeles.

Contact Relatives and Friends in Los Angeles

Securing a landing pad in Los Angeles helps immensely. It takes time to acclimatize to the city, find employment, and establish a career, as does finding a suitable long-term living space. Motels in Los Angeles are pricey, hostels less so. Apartments may require three months' rent in advance, equal to several thousand dollars. Craigslist has sublet listings as many residents are bi-coastal, bouncing between two locations, and they need to sublet a space while they are away, which is perfect for someone moving fresh to Los Angeles. If someone does offer temporary housing, think seriously about taking their offer. This can give you some breathing room while you become acclimatized to the city and secure employment. But remember that temporary housing means just that—temporary!

So, gather your resources while you can. If you have friends or relatives already living in the Los Angeles area, let them know your plans to move there. Some people will be helpful, others may not be. But always let them make the offer of assistance first. Otherwise, good intentions turn into a lost friendship or a distant relative. Still, moving, especially with limited resources, takes planning, and you will find any help will be much appreciated; especially things like meals, lodging, advice, and directions.

Finish Your Education

A BFA or an MFA degree in acting will not help in finding professional acting work in Los Angeles. Producers and casting directors will not care about your academic pedigree. But, the training you receive provides excellent preparation and discipline for a professional life. The more training and experience you obtain the more versatile and thus, more employable, you will be. So, complete those course requirements, finish those lab hours, and write those papers. And, while you are at it, take those juggling lessons, learn how to fence, explore martial arts classes, or get up on a horse and learn to ride. Success will, to some extent, depend upon your list of skills. There are still times when the actor who gets the part is the one who can juggle or rock climb, or just who fits the costume.

Have Photos Taken

How many hopeful actors spend money on photos, move to Los Angeles and find a talent agent who makes them spend more money on new photos? Should you save money and wait? No. An actor needs photos to land a talent agent. Have photos taken, but do not spend a lot of money on them. A talent agent will, most likely, request new photos. No matter how great a reputation the local photographer might have, Hollywood talent agents have a keener sense of what works and what Los Angeles casting directors are looking for. An actor must be packaged and marketed much like any other product. Once established with an agency, your old photos can be replaced by something more suitable to the current preferences of the industry.

IN THE BOX

When I moved to Los Angeles from Pittsburgh, I always planned it as a permanent move, regardless of how my career went. I could only bring what possessions my Chevy van could hold so I donated books to the local library and held a yard sale to liquidate furniture and other possessions. The rest of my belongings found refuge in my sister's basement until some future visit. Over the years, as I visited her, each time I left with suitcases stuffed with books and memorabilia. Fifteen years later I received five mysterious boxes from my sister. They contained my HO gauge train set, some old books, and assorted high school memorabilia. It was a walk down memory lane, but it made me remember how broke I was when I first arrived in Los Angeles, how many times I had to move, and how thankful I was that I had brought so little with me.

What Should I NOT Do When I Move?

Do Not Bring All of Your Worldly Possessions

Leaving possessions can be complicated or simple. Wives, husbands, and children cannot be discarded easily. Pets, large pieces of furniture, and four years of college books can. This would be the best time to clean your house. Sell, store, or give away anything you will not need. Pets force hard decisions. Cats and small dogs acclimatize to living in small spaces but they will limit your housing options. Most landlords will consider a small pet but rarely a big dog. Try to find ways to simplify your life, and then, depending on your accumulated possessions, plan to move in stages.

Stop and ask yourself, as Thoreau did, what are the necessities of your life? Thoreau identified "food, shelter, clothing and fuel" (Thoreau, 114). To that list I might add a dependable car, a fairly sophisticated computer, and an inflatable bed. Those items are all one really needs at first in Los Angeles. Everything else—furniture, electronics, and personal memorabilia—can follow once you are established.

Do Not Burn Bridges

Leaving behind friends and family does present an enormous challenge. We never know what seeds we sow today will reap an abundant harvest tomorrow. College cohorts, business colleagues, friendships and even family may help you find your destiny in the entertainment industry. Work begets work and that small-town stage director, college classmate, business associate, or next-door writing collaborator may someday succeed where you have failed, and drag you kicking and screaming with them to success. Always make a graceful exit from wherever your roots have been laid, but also consider that you may at any time return. Plan to have a back door, an escape hatch, a plan B, or a safety net.

Wherever you should land, Los Angeles or elsewhere, you will need to make many important decisions: permanent housing, flexible employment, survival strategies, not to mention establishing yourself as an actor with an agent and a union card. You will need to revisit your five-year plan from time to time as you progress or as your priorities change. The daily struggle to find the green shoots of success is enough to dampen the spirit of even the most dedicated artist. Wherever you can, make friends, all kinds of friends: friends at work, friends where you live, friends at cafes, and friends at auditions. They will help guide you through learning the ropes of living in Los Angeles as a working actor. They can answer questions about contracts, bookkeeping, audition scams, and lifestyles you never dreamed existed. They will help you find better housing, a better job, better parking, a better agent, and will keep you sane when things go wrong, as they inevitably will.

But most of all take care of yourself. The merry-go-round ride of living in Los Angeles, ages you. The healthier your lifestyle, the less likely you will need to change your headshot every year. Continue training as an actor, train both physically and mentally, by taking time for yourself and by enjoying the endless treasures of this eclectic city. The journey of a lifetime awaits you and you must be up to the task, or you may find yourself as did Rosalind Russell in *My Sister Eileen*, singing, "Oh, why oh, why oh, did I leave Ohio?"

ACTOR'S FORUM

When I first moved here, I lived in Long Beach. I had to go through some sketchy areas to get to work. My restaurant job was in West Hollywood, and I was interning at a manager's office. Long Beach was tough, and yet it was a pretty place because I had a lot of extra time to go to the beach every day and run. Whenever you're near the ocean, I would take advantage of it, but since then I've lived in Hollywood.

MICHAEL GABIANO

I've always been Hollywood centered. From the very get-go we arrived with a U-Haul with my stuff from Washington D.C., stayed overnight in a motel and had an apartment the next day on Hollywood Boulevard. Stayed there for a year, then moved to a little house in Hollywood and then up to Beachwood about six years later. It's a very central location for most voice casting, for voice-over work, for the studios. It's easy access to Paramount and the studios on Formosa Avenue. A lot of the voice studios are in Burbank. There's some in Hollywood, but it's a very central location and you can easily get to the places of work.

PETER LAVIN

Studio City is where I lived with my friend when I first got here because he was very close to Universal Studios. I lived on his couch for a month. At that time, there was the Los Angeles directory of apartments and stuff, but you had to pay $25 to get on the list. I signed up for several to try to find a place and still couldn't get an apartment. Somebody on the set said, "We have an apartment open up in Studio City," and I moved my stuff in. It was roach infested, and I moved out the next day. My girlfriend said, "I have this house. Just store your stuff in my garage and stay with me and then find another place and move." I never moved from where I live now (Highland Park) for the past seventeen years just outside of South Pasadena. It's away from the manic craziness and business of Hollywood. I like to keep business separate from my personal life, and as I live away from Hollywood, I have my own life. I have a room in a nice house that has a yard. We have the space where we're not piled on top of a bunch of actors. So, it really wasn't very hard for me. I didn't have to struggle like a bunch of my other friends had to do.

RICHARD DORTON

2 LIVING IN LOS ANGELES

Tip the world over on its side and everything loose will land in Los Angeles.

FRANK LLOYD WRIGHT

ACTOR'S RESOURCES

Wikipedia—Los Angeles County
(In-depth history, geography, transportation, and sites of interest)

Mapping L.A.
(Provides in-depth information and statistics for L.A. city neighborhoods)

Beachwood Canyon Neighborhood Association
(Beachwood Canyon news and community information)

LAPD Crime Mapping
(Provides real-time mapping of crime in Los Angeles neighborhoods)

Venice Neighborhood Council
(Reports on community activities and governance)

NoHo Arts District.com
(Provides community information for actors and other artists)

Larchmont Buzz
(News from Larchmont Village, Hancock Park, and the Greater Wilshire areas)

Laurel Canyon Association
(Sponsors community events and neighborhood watch groups)

Welcome to Los Angeles, all 4,083 smog-plagued miles of it! Served by five commercial airports, three harbors, a web of freeways, and a mix of heavy and light rail systems, it has a Gross Domestic Product (GDP) larger than Sweden, Norway, or Poland and remains a world leader in aerospace, clean technology, fashion, healthcare, tourism, and entertainment. Los Angeles is home to three of the world's leading research universities: Caltech, UCLA, and USC, and has 118 other colleges and universities. There are 841 museums and art galleries in Los Angeles, more per capita than any other city in the world (*Forbes online*, "Los Angeles, CA"). The annual rainfall averages 15.11 inches but, as the most recent drought demonstrated, years of "La Nina" (a drought of two inches or less per year) can quickly give way to "El Nino" (years of more than thirty inches) when hillsides move and freeways turn into concrete rivers. A balmy average temperature of 66 degrees can swell to 110 or fall to below freezing, all within a few days. (*Los Angeles Almanac*, "Weather"). This second largest US city finds itself also demographically the most diverse. Residents speak over 224 identifiable languages, the city emergency services respond to "more than 150 languages," and the Los Angeles Unified School District recognizes approximately 94 languages (Los Angeles Unified School District, *Fingertip Facts*). Los Angeles also hosts the largest populations of Armenians and Iranians, as well as other groups including Bulgarians, Ethiopians, Filipinos, Guatemalans, Salvadorans, Nicaraguans, Hungarians, Koreans, Mexicans, Pacific Islanders (such as Samoans), Russians, and Thais. And, with a population of over ten million, it tops the list of cities with the worst traffic in the United States, ranking tenth worldwide. Add a cost of living that hovers around 21.5 percent above the national average and you begin to see the challenges (*Forbes online*, "Los Angeles, CA").

Greater Los Angeles can be many things to many people. Ten million residents share a semitropical climate, virtually endless sunshine, and a penchant for quirkiness. They also share torrential rains, wildfires, mudslides, and earthquakes. Yes, earthquakes happen, mostly little 3.2 shakers that remind you that Mother Nature remains firmly in charge. After the Northridge Earthquake in 1994, long-time resident Bette Midler promptly packed up and moved to New York City. She could do that because she is

Bette Midler. A struggling actor cannot do so easily, so you had better make peace with the earth's occasional betrayals before settling into this geologically unsettled region.

Though somewhat confusing, the moniker of "Los Angeles" refers to both the county and the city, including the eighty-eight other municipalities that exist within its boundaries that collectively constitute this Southern California area, making for a patchwork of conflicting jurisdictions. Therefore, plan exactly where you want to live and work before making long-term decisions. The city of West Hollywood, for instance, has strict rent control regulations. But if you live one block in another direction you are in Los Angeles city jurisdiction with almost no regulation. It helps to learn a little about the county and the city that both bear the name Los Angeles.

What is the Difference Between Los Angeles County and the City of Los Angeles?

Los Angeles County has the distinction of being the most populous county in the United States—and the most fragmented. In addition to the City of Los Angeles, the county consists of many other incorporated cities, as well as odd unincorporated sections, some of them badlands, mountainous areas, or transportation right of ways. Governed by an elected five-member Board of Supervisors, the county assumes responsibility for implementing many of the state's requirements in the areas of transportation (LA Metro), justice (Los Angeles Superior Court), and public assistance (Department of Social Services), as well as providing a strategic health and safety redundancy in the form of the Sheriff's Department and the Fire Department. For instance, Los Angeles County/USC Medical Center, the nation's largest teaching hospital, provides accessible, affordable and culturally sensitive emergency, acute, HIV, and psychiatric care as well as many other public services. It cannot be stressed too much how important it is for a struggling actor to know about the public funded services and resources at his or her disposal. The time may come when welfare is better than no care, and the county's safety net can provide much needed temporary assistance.

The City of Los Angeles is governed by a mayor and a city council, which represents fifteen city districts. The city is served by the Los Angeles Board of Police Commissioners, the Los Angeles Fire Department, the Housing Authority of the City of Los Angeles, the Los Angeles Department of Transportation (LADOT), and the Los Angeles Public Library with streets patrolled by the Los Angeles Police Department (LAPD).

Los Angeles can be divided into eight regions: Downtown, Greater Hollywood, Mid-Wilshire, West Los Angeles, South Los Angeles, East Los Angeles, and the San Fernando Valley. The eighth, the Harbor District, located at the end of a long transportation corridor to the ocean, was created solely to give Los Angeles its own harbor and, while people do live there, its distance from the creative heart makes it unattractive for artists. The same is true for South Los Angeles and East Los Angeles. Downtown has become very artist friendly, but only if they have sufficient money. This leaves Greater Hollywood, Mid-Wilshire, West Los Angeles, and the San Fernando Valley, which actually constitutes three valleys, as reasonable locations to set up residence. Within these regions are hundreds of neighborhoods founded to escape the big government of Los Angeles and named after annexed farm towns or incorporated municipalities.

Where Should I Live in Los Angeles?

Within the eight districts the *Los Angeles Times* has identified 114 neighborhoods and nine autonomous cities, each with its own characteristics. (*Los Angeles Times*, "Mapping LA"). Successful actors have emerged from every corner of Los Angeles, but a few communities and neighborhoods offer the actor-friendly combination of affordable housing, a supportive environment, and proximity to the entertainment industry centers. The entertainment industry remains relatively close-knit, with its studios and offices located near four major transportation corridors, forming a kind of parallelogram or "entertainment industry zone." This is bordered by the

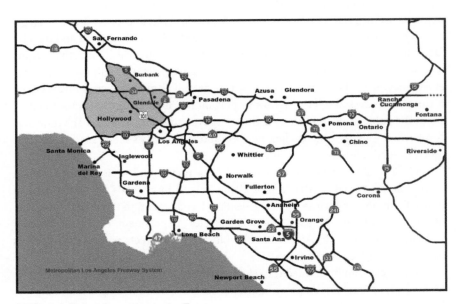

MAP 2.1 Entertainment Industry Zone

San Diego Freeway (405) to the west, the Golden State Freeway (5) to the east, the Ventura Freeway to the north (134), and the Santa Monica Freeway to the south as shown in Map 2.1.

Within this geometric quadrant are all the major studios and 90 percent of casting and talent agents, not to mention seemingly limitless support businesses. There are also many artist-friendly neighborhoods and communities that exist as either entertainment industry centers like Hollywood, Studio City, or Culver City, or that have a reputation for harboring and nurturing artists of all stripes. At its heart, Los Angeles is a collection of small towns populated by incomers from other small towns across America, each with their own dream. An actor need only find which "small town" fits his or her needs and for their lives to become sustainable. Here, organized topographically, are a few to consider. Those communities and neighborhoods are listed in Appendix A with supporting statistical data on demographics, crime, and rental costs. Map 2.2 is a map showing an overview of the geography of the city and Map 2.3 a map of the neighborhoods of Los Angeles.

MAP 2.2 Satellite Map of Los Angeles

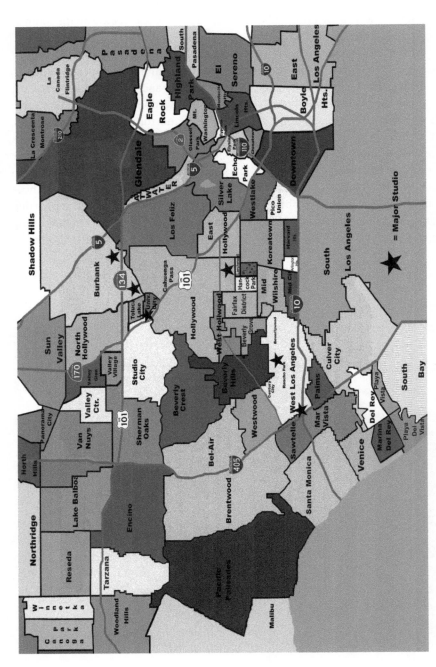

MAP 2.3 Los Angeles Neighborhoods

The Hills

The Santa Monica Mountains cover 250 square miles, rising out of the Pacific Ocean to a height of over 3,000 feet and dividing the City of Los Angeles in half, from the Pacific Palisades to Griffith Park. And while there are other hills in Los Angeles, such as the Whittier Hills and the Baldwin Hills, the Hollywood Hills section of these Santa Monica Mountains tends to be more central to the activity of the entertainment industry. At its eastern end sits Griffith Park, at 4,210 acres one of the largest urban parks in North America and home of the Greek Theater. Slightly west is the sprawling Universal City studio and theme park, Citywalk, the Amphitheater complex, and then the ever-popular Hollywood Bowl. From there to the Palisades topped by Mulholland Drive westward, cantilevered homes, mansions, chateaus, estates, and condominiums cling to the narrow hillsides upon both sides of the Hollywood Hills, in subdivisions that have names such as Mt. Olympus, Whitley Heights, Lookout Mountain Beverly Glen, Beverly Crest, and Bel-Air Estates. Nestled in their midst are small apartments, guesthouses, converted garages, and—within the constraints of the county safety code— anything imaginable for rent. Artists make popular roommates, housemates, or renters, making up over half of the inhabitants, especially if they can provide a needed service in return, such as gardening, housekeeping, or babysitting. Permanent residents tend to be well-educated, predominantly Caucasian, with few children, and while one finds violent crime rare in the hills, the same cannot be said about property crime.

The Canyons

Four long and winding canyon roads traverse the Hollywood Hills from north to south, connecting the San Fernando Valley with Greater Hollywood and the Los Angeles' urban sprawl, providing an alternative to the frequently congested freeways. These roads follow and branch off into deep canyons, where communities have evolved as distinct as the history they preserve. There are numerous artist communities such as Nichol's Canyon, Benedict Canyon, Franklin Canyon, and Mandeville Canyon where small grocery stores and cafes serve the distinct communities which have bulletin boards, neighborhood watch programs, and community supported websites with local news and local activities. Moving from east to west are the following canyons:

Cahuenga Boulevard parallels the Hollywood Freeway through the Cahuenga Pass from North Hollywood, emptying into the heart of Hollywood and providing major access to the Universal City complex. Much of "old Hollywood" still exists within the narrow streets that branch off this canyon thoroughfare, offering a myriad of bungalows, lofts, and apartments that have seen generations of struggling artists come and go.

Ever since folk songstress Joni Mitchell sang of "The Ladies of the Canyon" in the 1960s, Laurel Canyon has been synonymous with the music industry and with counterculture. Rock pioneers such as Frank Zappa, the Byrds, and Buffalo Springfield lived and played here, and their bohemian spirit still endures. But Laurel Canyon's history began much earlier with silent film star cowboy Tom Mix, golden-age heartthrob Errol Flynn, and legendary magician Harry Houdini. The canyon remains a major transit corridor between the San Fernando Valley and Hollywood. Savvy drivers often rely upon Cahuenga Boulevard as a quicker alternative.

Known principally for its ecological community and as the home of the TreePeople, an ecological non-profit organization, Coldwater Canyon lacks the distinctive historical mythos or aura of the other canyons, but what it lacks in personality, it gains in convenience. It provides a quick alternative connection between Sherman Oaks and Beverly Hills.

Still further west, Beverly Glen Boulevard connects Sherman Oaks with Beverly Hills, first wandering through the iconic neighborhoods of "old money," from Rancho Park north past Westwood and UCLA, then into Beverly Glen Canyon bordering Bel-Air, crossing Mulholland Boulevard and finally into Ventura Boulevard in Sherman Oaks. The summit of this canyon road has a long history of cafes and restaurants tied to the entertainment industry. Here are mostly upscale residential areas whose rental and sale prices are not for the faint of heart, but, where there is finds money, there are also often over financed homeowners in need of a renter to subsidize their mortgage.

Though not a connection to the San Fernando Valley, Beachwood Canyon's is known for a sign that advertised a real estate development in 1923. Beachwood Canyon was the "Hollywoodland," which that famous sign promoted. Only a stone gateway and guard tower remain, but much of old Hollywood survives, offering privacy within minutes of the studios. One can still take trail rides up to the Hollywood sign from Sunset Ranch or meet colorful industry folk in the quaint Beachwood Market, or the Beachwood Café located midway up the canyon road.

Living in the canyons remains very popular despite brush fires, mudslides, and earthquakes. Still, the simplest errand requires a thirty-minute drive, outdoor pets often fall prey to coyotes, and treacherous roads and scarce parking add to the inconvenience. But, spectacular views and exclusive addresses make it all worthwhile to those who can afford it. To the south lies the heart of Hollywood.

Greater Hollywood

Greater Hollywood is at the center of Los Angeles' central core known as the "Basin." The Hollywood of the Grauman's Chinese disappeared in 1973, replaced by tourist-trap lined streets of broken dreams, overrun by runaways, prostitutes, and drug addicts. Add a higher than average crime rate and Hollywood no longer looked so inviting. Enter Disney. The family-friendly entertainment goliath has done for Hollywood what it did for New York City's Times Square, by buying up decaying buildings and theaters and spearheading a redevelopment effort that has dramatically changed the Hollywood skyline. Hollywood remains the nominal center of the entertainment industry, a fact that has been acknowledged by the frequent major theatrical premieres at historic Hollywood theaters and the designation of the Dolby Theater, formerly the Kodak Theater, as the home of the Academy Awards. Most of the major studios have relocated to West Los Angeles or the San Fernando Valley, but a decidedly eastward shift has occurred. Both Netflix and Viacom have moved to Hollywood sites, joining Paramount, Sunset/Gower and Raleigh Studios, along with many casting and talent agents and other actor-related services.

Despite Disney's best efforts, the crime rate remains high, Hollywood Boulevard remains a quirky paean to Hollywood's mythology with a daily parade of the strange and the bizarre. Residents tend to be younger, single, and less affluent than older residents who have established roots because Hollywood is still the primary destination for actors new to Los Angeles. Rents remain relatively affordable, although what passes as a certified residence often boggles the mind. The Hollywood Freeway slices through its center, providing easy access north to the Valley or parts south or west through the Cahuenga Pass, all direct routes to major studios

West Hollywood, nicknamed WeHo by residents, claimed cityhood in 1984 after this sliver of unincorporated emergency transportation corridor attracted gay and lesbian businesses escaping institutionalized homophobia, as well as seniors seeking more affordable housing, and Russian Jews fleeing the dissolution of the Soviet Union. Though not known as a family-friendly city, with only 5.7 percent of residents under age eighteen, the city has seen a marked increase in families with children, both same-sex and traditional, amid gentrification. The typical West Hollywood resident remains primarily a single, gay male. The city's many famous clubs, bars, and restaurants on and around the Sunset Strip attract the rich and the famous and it employs legions of struggling actors. But, its popularity has led to gridlocked streets, increased crime, and hopeless parking options. It has also become a model of progressive innovations, embracing the needs of disabled residents, HIV sufferers, senior citizens, and renters. The city council has most recently battled gentrification by requiring all new development projects to include a certain percentage of affordable housing. The area is densely populated and renters far outnumber home owners, but rents tend to be on the high side especially toward the "West Side." Creative living arrangements exist and deals can still be found. West Hollywood's main deficit remains its lack of accessibility to major freeways, although the development of a "pink line" underground connection to the Los Angeles Metro is currently under study.

Continuing west, Beverly Hills, Bel-Air, Brentwood, and Pacific Palisades represent the consummate Los Angeles affluent lifestyle with the highest median household incomes in the city and a relatively low crime rate. Rentals are few and far between in these, mostly estate-lined, streets. Residents are also primarily Caucasian, older, and more educated. Given their reputation, one would automatically reject these communities as elitist and too expensive for a struggling actor. But, the rich need services such as nannies, pool men, chauffeurs, trainers, assistants, and gardeners, and may offer to provide housing in return. Any option that provides flexibility should be considered.

Moving westward to Interstate 5, the territorial barrier to the beach communities, lies Westwood, home to the University of California, Los Angeles (UCLA), the celebrated Geffen Playhouse, the second largest Mormon Temple in the United States, and Westwood Village, a planned commercial district. Very much a college town, Westwood enjoys a relatively low crime rate, most crimes being stolen bicycles. The population is predictably younger, more diverse, and more educated than surrounding neighborhoods. For some that may be a comfortable environment while for others, not so much. Whether a student or not, in Westwood one must be prepared to live with hopelessly crowded side streets, a parking nightmare and loud boisterous parties, all typical features of a vibrant college community. But, many of those students will also need roommates.

To the south, West Los Angeles, Rancho Park, and Beverlywood offer a "Westside" address, freeway access, and proximity to the entertainment industry centers without the frat party atmosphere. Residents are older, highly educated, and affluent. One finds rents surprisingly moderate in this area, considering its access to public transportation, the beaches, and the studios. Home to 20th Century Fox Studios and the Hillcrest Country Club, the area harbors no real business district although Beverlywood's Pico Boulevard (east/west) and Robertson Boulevard (north/south) have a well-developed mix of cultural and general retail businesses, not to mention quicker access to Interstate 10.

Los Feliz borders Hollywood on the northeast and extends north into the Valley, sandwiched between the Hollywood Freeway (Highway 101) and the Golden State Freeway (I–5). Pronounced Los Fee-lez, this frequently mispronounced neighborhood was the most chic and artsy neighborhood of Los Angeles in the 1920s. Once claimed as the birth place of Mickey Mouse, visitors more likely recognize it as the infamous site of the first of the many Manson murders, despite the fact that it has a relatively low crime rate. Older Spanish bungalows, duplexes, and apartments line the many major boulevards where some of Los Angeles' most expensive and architecturally unique homes exist. A diverse population, easy freeway access, quaint affordable housing, and a plethora of local restaurants, bars, clubs, theaters, (with various support industries that employ struggling artists) make it an ideal residential area for actors and artists.

Once a thriving farming community known as Prospect Park, East Hollywood lies to the southeast of Hollywood. It offers much lower rent prices and easy access to the Hollywood Freeway and the Metro subway, putting the downtown, the Valley and the Westside minutes away, but at a price; more than average violent crime, gang activity, traffic congestion, and a lot of neighborhood garbage. Lack of education and high population density contribute to the problems, with 97 percent of the population renting in this predominately foreign-born community. Cultural diversity is its strength, extending to areas known as Little Armenia and Thai Town with Ukrainian and Latino neighborhoods intermixed and an array of culinary opportunities for employment. This low-rent alternative to Hollywood has been the birthplace of many theater groups and productions in the past and has much history crawling out of its side streets.

Arrayed along the 1.5-mile stretch of Sunset Boulevard between Western Avenue and Hoover Street were the studios where D.W. Griffith shot many of his masterpieces, Charles Fox launched the precursor to *20th Century Fox* and the actor Charles Ray continued to build out what would later become the KCET studios.

GARNER, "Neighborhood Spotlight: East Hollywood,"
Los Angeles Times online

Moving east, Silver Lake also has a great deal of Hollywood history, as well as a manmade reservoir named, not after the water's color, but for a city bureaucrat, Herman Silver. His municipal namesake has become a culturally diverse artistic collective. For generations Silver Lake's residents had been primarily Hispanic/ Latino, until Silver Lake's LGBT community dramatically increased in the 1980s. This created a volatile situation for many years until all parties found resolute common ground in the form of a community music festival, the Sunset Junction Street Fair. Until its bankruptcy in 2012, this festival attracted visitors from all over the city and forged a diverse, groundbreaking community alliance that still thrives today. Crisscrossed by quaint municipal staircases for pedestrian access, Silver Lake's winding, hilly streets offer endless affordable residential options.

Further east, and one step from downtown and its interconnecting freeways, lies Echo Park and its quaint residential districts known as Angelino Heights, Elysian Heights, Filipinotown, and Victor Heights with its old Victorian mansions and cozy cottages. Echo Park's namesake park created in 1890 still has a lake with fountains, lotus beds, and pedal boats. Its residents, a mixture of Latino, Filipino, and Chinese immigrants, mingle with younger hipsters, working-class immigrants, and local artists, taking advantage of the lower priced real estate and rentals in this, one of the most densely populated neighborhoods in Los Angeles. Despite its proximity to downtown, its relatively low crime rate, easy access to four freeways, and a flourishing nightlife have reversed the area's past rough reputation for gangs and drugs and made it one of Los Angeles' best neighborhoods for actors.

South of Hollywood, Hancock Park, Larchmont, and Windsor Square each offer affordable rent and a family-friendly atmosphere despite their exclusive past. Windsor Square's older, well-educated population has increasingly become an

Asian enclave, mostly of Korean immigrants. Once a massive field of oil derricks, Hancock Park's stately homes and historic architecture built around the grounds of the Wilshire Country Club was once the Beverly Hills of old Hollywood, home to movie stars such as Mae West, Ava Gardner, and Clark Gable (Garner, "Neighborhood Spotlight: Hancock Park," *Los Angeles Times online*). Today Hancock Park has become home to a thriving community of Orthodox Jews, providing a quiet, clean and open neighborhood marred only by the thousands of commuters who use its east-west streets daily. City fathers created Larchmont to provide a business district for the upscale residents and celebrities of Hancock Park and Windsor Square. "It wasn't where all the moguls lived. This was the neighborhood for the costumers, stagehands, payroll accountants and continuity supervisors" (Garner, "Neighborhood Spotlight: Larchmont," *Los Angeles Times online*). Today its historic bungalow courts and apartments accommodate an increasingly younger, diverse but predominately Asian population that walk, skateboard, or bicycle to the trendy boutiques, fitness studios, and coffee shops in what has become known as Larchmont Village.

Moving west but south of West Hollywood, Beverly Grove, and the Fairfax District, offer an even trendier atmosphere but at higher prices. Fairfax became known as the center of Jewish life in the 1940s as Orthodox Jewish men in black *yarmulkes* on their way to *shul* walked the "Kosher Canyon," an avenue of kosher delis and bakeries, synagogues, and tailors. Today Canter's Deli must compete with trendy restaurants as the aging Jewish population and its businesses have moved to quieter places, like Hancock Park, leaving tattoo parlors, skate and streetwear shops, and a storied touristy past to become the "coolest street in Los Angeles" (Satran, "How Fairfax Became," *Los Angeles Times*). The Fairfax District is still home to CBS Television City, as well as the Pan Pacific Park, a farmer's market, and a trendy shopping mall, the Grove. Despite this odd confluence of skate culture and old-world Judaica, the population remains primarily Caucasian, single, well-educated, and professional and has higher rents than nearby neighborhoods, horrible traffic, and increasing crime rates.

Continuing south, Mid-Wilshire and Mid-City offer more diversity in population and housing with Park La Brea providing every option imaginable. Once developed as a shopping district, Mid-Wilshire's "Miracle Mile" has maintained its shopping vitality and historic traffic congestion. It has become a cultural center with the addition of several museums to Wilshire Boulevard's "Museum Row," including the La Brea Tar Pits, the Los Angeles County Museum of Art, and the Academy of Motion Picture Arts and Science. But, over 50,000 Angelinos of all ethnicities have found lower rents and a nexus of mass transit options in Mid-City, a quieter, family-friendly, suburban area stretching along Interstate 10 with corner stores and many neighborhood comedy clubs.

Five more neighborhoods make up a lower tier of neighborhoods in the Basin that follow the Interstate 10 east to downtown, offering actors a mixed bag of affordable housing, easy freeway access (albeit logistically miles from the entertainment industry centers), and the highest crime rate despite the LAPD's anti-crime efforts to clean up gang and drug dealing in this high-density area. Koreatown's access to the subway and the freeway system makes it an attractive option for all struggling actors. But, because of a higher than average poverty level, its high crime rate, and overcrowded schools, this area may not be a viable option for struggling actors with families.

The Beaches

A generation of moviegoers has worshiped the Los Angeles beach scene vicariously through a steady diet of beach, bikini, and surfing films, current and past. Despite a laid-back culture and the lure of fresh air and sunny beach days, a combination of distance from the entertainment industry centers and a high cost of living make the beach communities less viable alternatives for a struggling actor new to this city. Beach residents tend to be older, seeking a place where different cultures and socio-economic levels, for the most part, can get along.

Malibu Beach's $102,000 median income and reputation as a celebrity hideaway renders it an unlikely choice for a struggling actor, but, just to the south, lies the city of Santa Monica, with the crumbling bluffs of Palisades Park and the carnival at Santa Monica Pier a familiar backdrop for countless films and television shows. Today, a vibrant tourist economy and a booming pub and artisan culture have translated to a significant increase in lucrative and flexible jobs for actors, creating a substantial highly-educated artist community. Affordable housing was easier to find before the city's tough rent control law was overturned in 1999, but its progressive city governance has led to a responsive consumer-oriented city policy. The city also finds itself with a lenient homeless policy, rampant gentrification, and parking issues. Residents quickly learn that the infamous "Blue Bus" line connects to the LA Metro, offering the only viable alternative to the often-gridlocked Santa Monica Freeway that subdivides the city.

The Boardwalk defines the beach community of Venice, an oceanfront promenade known for street performers, tennis courts, basketball courts, a skate dancing plaza, numerous handball and volleyball courts, an outdoor gym renowned as "Muscle Beach," and hundreds of vendors selling tourist paraphernalia. Spiritualists, artists, performers, and musicians of all manner and method reside happily in this bohemian community with the exotic name. It has canals and gangs, unfortunately, making it somewhat dangerous after dark. Venice offers artists a safe haven, a free Family Clinic, eclectic artistic outlets (such as art galleries, nightclubs and trendy apparel shops), and affordable housing, depending upon its proximity to the ocean. But these are long distances from the business-end of Hollywood and narrow dense streets add to traffic congestion and delays. Property crime remains a constant issue in all the beach communities.

Marina del Rey, an unincorporated county development, exists for one reason and one reason only: the Marina, the world's largest manmade recreational harbor. Its pricey condos and apartments offer occasional housing opportunities for sub-rentals, but one will most likely find the Marina more a source of employment than housing with its many upscale restaurants and nightspots.

Playa del Rey, a bedroom community just south of the Culver City studios, has lost its surfing luster of the 1960s with the harsh realities of the last Los Angeles International Airport (LAX) expansion, but it still retains a small beach area. Sound abatement measures have not prevented the desertion of all but those who live farthest north towards Culver Boulevard, where less traffic, more affordable housing, convenient parking, a lower crime rate, and easy access to Culver City's studios has made this small beach community more alluring to actors desiring a beach lifestyle without the tourists.

Farther south lie Hermosa Beach, Redondo Beach, and Manhattan Beach, all charming beach communities, but too removed from Hollywood and the other entertainment industry centers to make a convenient base of operations. Those seeking more affordable options with less traffic and crime, while still near the beaches, may find solace inland. Just east of Santa Monica and Venice, Sawtelle and Palms' neighborhood residents tend to be younger, more middle-class, and educated, drawn to the area's easy access to public transport and to the beaches. Approximately 70 percent apartment houses, this once crime-ridden neighborhood has been more recently discovered by young professionals and college students with a very diverse population of Japanese, Middle Eastern, South Asian, and Brazilian immigrants.

Still further south, Culver City offers proximity to several major studios and four different freeways that crisscross this five square mile charter city. Unfortunately, it is also on the glide path to the LAX. The combination gives it arguably the worst traffic and most gridlocked freeways in the area, despite the Culver City station for the Expo Line light rail system. The city's highly diverse, albeit older, residents enjoy historically low rents, but also a higher crime rate. Along Washington Boulevard's wide street, Sony's Metro-Goldwyn-Mayer Studios (MGM) and Culver Studios still stand proudly, now the home of Amazon's entertainment arm, placing this charter city on a par with Studio City and Burbank as an entertainment-industry center.

The growth of Santa Monica and Venice over the years has given rise to Playa Vista, Del Vista, and Mar Vista, each a one-to-three-mile planned development of postwar, middle-class housing placed somewhat inland, with ocean views and easy freeway access. Together they form a barrier between the beach communities and the city's central core. Apart from Mar Vista, rents are second highest in the city, though the crime rate is relatively low. Many of these 1950s homes have been subdivided into duplexes and triplexes or torn down to build higher density townhouses, accommodating middle-class families, older, yet surprisingly quite diverse.

The Valley

Miles of strip malls, apartment complexes and high-priced housing subdivisions have replaced the acres of orange groves that once covered this expansive valley. Angelinos speak casually of "The Valley" often referring collectively to the San Fernando, San Gabriel, and Simi Valleys as one. They are not, as residents will remind you. Home to many major film, television, and recording studios such as CBS Studio Center, NBC Universal, ABC/Walt Disney, and Warner Bros. the Valley has also earned its nickname of "San Pornando," home to a multibillion-dollar pornography industry. Warmer than the Basin in the summer and colder in the winter, rents tend to be cheaper but jobs not as exotic or lucrative. Many people live in the Valley and work in the Basin, adding to rush-hour congestion on most connecting throughways, such as the Hollywood Freeway, Cahuenga Pass, and Laurel Canyon Boulevard.

Nestled against the Hollywood Hills on its north side, Studio City grew from the 1920s, Mack Sennett silent film studio, into a company town and an alternative Hollywood (Studio City Chamber, *About Studio City*). CBS Studio Center still produces a steady stream of television network programming, and Ventura Boulevard still offers a safe mom and pop atmosphere of hometown shops. Residents have historically been tolerant of diversity, less affected and predominately white. Ventura Boulevard parallels the Ventura Freeway, which connects Studio City to a vast web of freeways with easy access to the Hollywood area.

Moving progressively west, and nestled up against the north face of the Hollywood Hills, a series of upscale, family-friendly bedroom communities developed over the years. Studio City's success lured many of Hollywood's elite to relocate, seeking more privacy yet retaining proximity to Hollywood. Homeowners tend to be older, professional, very well-educated, and affluent, lured to the quieter, suburban atmosphere with a low crime rate, nearby recreational resources of Lake Balboa, and the Sepulveda Dam Recreational Area, and easy access to the freeway system. Unfortunately, that easy access has become a hopeless gridlock during an ever-lengthening rush-hour as no light rail system serves this area.

Sherman Oaks grew as a suburban alternative to Beverly Hills with Ventura Boulevard's high-fashion boutiques, trendy restaurants, and artist studios often parodied as the face of the 1980s mall culture. Ranch style houses, condos, and luxury apartments line the wider streets, where one finds affordable but relatively scarce rental situations, owing more to a higher percentage of single-family homes and condominium projects. But the financial pressures of the past years have forced many owners of these upscale homes to consider the rental of almost anything legal, from rooms to studio apartments, bungalows, pool houses, even communal arrangements. Better schools, better apartments and safer streets, though, also often mean higher rents.

If Sherman Oaks represents the Beverly Hills of the Valley, then Encino is its Bel-Air with large mansions and sprawling estates. Once the backlot for RKO Pictures, Encino now suffers from over-development despite its quiet, laid-back, suburban atmosphere with streets lined with apartments and condominium rentals, where a multitude of restaurants and watering holes offer limitless employment opportunities for actors.

Tarzana, Woodland Hills, Thousand Oaks, and Warner Ranch all represent historic developments, but their distance from the studios makes them less functional as a base of operations for any actor.

Directly north of Studio City sprawls Valley Glen, Valley Village, and North Hollywood, an eclectic mix of arts, religion, and strip malls. Struggling artists, Orthodox Jews, Buddhists, Ba'Hai, and Latino/Middle Eastern/Asian immigrants all coexist in this vast suburban stretch of apartments, strip malls, and entertainment-industry centered businesses with very affordable rents. Families with children will find a variety of high-quality public and private schools, and single parents will find considerable support services.

The NoHo Artists District represents North Hollywood's jewel, a once blighted area, now flourishing with art galleries, theater spaces, film screenings, music, dance, and the Academy of Television Arts & Sciences at its center. Coffee houses, clubs, cafes, and recording and post-production facilities have also followed. The Universal City/North Hollywood Chamber of Commerce boasts, "Anything that an artist, or arts-patron, of any genre could need is within our ever-expanding boundaries. We even have the Metro system for easy transportation" (Universal City, "Noho Arts District," 5). As the northern hub of the Red Line subway system, North Hollywood's station offers easy access to Universal City's studios and theme park, Hollywood, Mid-Wilshire, Downtown, and finally Union Station, the major transportation hub for Southern California. Finally, the multitude of apartment complexes that line the streets promise affordable housing options for most budgets. A very family-friendly neighborhood, North Hollywood has the highest percentage of children, a plus for some, but a minus for others.

As a neighborhood, the Hollywood Freeway separates Valley Glen from North Hollywood. Lacking much in character, its main claim to fame is the famous tourist attraction, the Great Wall of Los Angeles, a half-mile long mural, along the wall of the Tujunga Wash that depicts scenes from California's history as seen through the eyes of women and minorities.

Valley Village also separated from North Hollywood in 1985, when residents formed a homeowner's association to fight against the over-development with apartments that had turned the neighborhood into "stucco mountains," rife with crime and deterioration (Igler, "North Hollywood Growth," *Los Angeles Times*). Though crime rates have improved, gangs still rule its northern perimeter, and resident density continues to increase as apartment complexes continue to proliferate.

Deeper into the Valley and moving west, working-class neighborhoods such as Van Nuys, Reseda, Northridge all have their respective personalities but share many characteristics common to the San Fernando Valley's core: a large immigrant population, high population density, and significant gang issues. As such, median rents are among the lowest in the city, but the area offers few resources to benefit a struggling actor other than a variety of transport options.

To the east of Studio City and bordered by two studios, Warner Bros. and Universal, Toluka Lake once existed solely as a haven for film stars who wanted a short commute to the studios. A six-acre lake and a private golf club was also an attraction. Few stars inhabit this community now, but its tree-lined streets still offer reclusive, albeit pricey, neighborhoods. West Toluca Lake and Toluca Woods just to the north bordering North Hollywood, offer more reasonable rental rates. No real business district exists here, but Riverside Drive does boast a few restaurants and the Falcon Theater, now renamed the Gary Marshall Theater after its recently deceased founder. Within walking distance of five studios, one also finds cheaper rents here than farther northeast in the cities of Burbank and Glendale.

The aviation and entertainment industries, both searching for more wide-open spaces, developed Burbank in the 1930s. Lockheed Aircraft Company and the Warner brothers found inexpensive farmland here and Disney and Columbia studios soon followed. Lockheed is no longer here but it has left its legacy, the Burbank Airport, now renamed the Bob Hope Airport. But Warner and Disney still call Burbank home, now joined by the Burbank Studios, ABC, Cartoon-Network Studios, Nickelodeon Animation, Yahoo! and Clear Channel, and surrounded by many casting and talent agent offices as well as other actors' resources. As such, Burbank is happily referred to as the "Media Capital of the World" (City of Burbank, "History"). Rents are reasonable and residents find easy access to Hollywood with the Cahuenga Pass, one of the best-kept secrets in Los Angeles, where one can still drive from Burbank to Hollywood in less than thirty minutes.

The Verdugos

Moving eastward and north of downtown, the Verdugo Mountains separate the San Fernando Valley from the San Gabriel Valley, extending to the eastern perimeter of the city and south to Whittier. The communities in the San Gabriel Valley are inconvenient for the studios, but with the expansion of the Metrolink light rail system, actors have found more family-friendly options in the neighborhoods in and around the Verdugo Mountains with lower crime rates, lower population densities, reasonable rents, excellent school choices and a small-town middle-America mentality.

The tiny yet highly diverse community of Atwater Village serves as its gateway, following the eastern border of the studio zone, Interstate 5, along the Los Angeles

River. Its 1950s "Wonder Years" atmosphere appeals to many who left small towns where walking and biking were the norm, yet who want easy transportation access to downtown and Hollywood. Bungalows and small apartment complexes make up the bulk of affordable rentals, and residents prize the Los Angeles River's fishing, kayaking, and biking.

The city of Glendale represents the "American Dream" for its many foreign-born residents. Originally a white suburban enclave, Glendale evolved from its monolithic religious past to one now of ethnic and religious diversity. Still predominately white, ethnically Glendale leans heavily Armenian, who make up approximately one-third of the population (US Census Bureau, "2011–2015 American Community Survey"). Demographically, Glendale splits into two geographic areas, its southern half more densely populated and poorer for per capita income than its more affluent northern half. Home to three well respected theaters—The Alex Theater, A Noise Within, and Glendale Centre Theatre—Glendale's main attraction for actors lies in its equal proximity to Downtown, Hollywood, and the Valley while retaining a suburban environment that embraces many languages.

Named after a large rock formation and home to Occidental College, Eagle Rock's Colorado Boulevard retains the remnants of a bygone streetcar era with specialty eateries, coffeehouses, art galleries, and a Midwestern college-town atmosphere. Home to a growing Asian population and more than a dozen public and private schools, residents and neighborhood associations actively maintain Eagle Rock's homey character, despite the threat of gang violence from other nearby San Gabriel Valley communities.

With more than a dozen public, private, and charter schools within its boundaries, Highland Park has emerged as a go-to neighborhood for actors with families. As such, a highly diverse, creative, and younger hipster population has emerged, who, along with law enforcement agencies, have chased away the gang-banging element of the 1990s. This has created a mecca for artists with trendy shops, galleries, bars, and restaurants opening throughout the neighborhood. It has the lowest crime rate in the City of Los Angeles and currently some of the most affordable rents.

Finally, Pasadena has also retained its original charm. Its Old Town commercial district spans twenty-one blocks downtown, boasting upscale retail shops and a wide variety of restaurants, nightclubs, outdoor cafes, pubs, and comedy clubs that eagerly employ struggling actors. Home to the Pasadena City College, Fuller Theological Seminary, Art Center College of Design, the Pasadena Playhouse, the Norton Simon Museum, and the USC Pacific Asia Museum, the city also boasts a prestigious public school system. Rents and the crime rate remain higher than nearby neighborhoods, but the combination of art, culture, education, and city services make it one of Los Angeles' most livable communities.

Of course, one can find hundreds of other neighborhoods and communities in the Greater Los Angeles region, mostly less accessible to the core of the entertainment industry. But a free room might trump all other concerns unless its distance from work and the entertainment industry centers preclude having "a life." Whatever your priority, carefully consider the concerns of accessibility, affordability, and a support system. Closely research one's neighborhood preferences before signing a lease and committing what will seem like a life's savings to a future landlord.

ACTOR'S FORUM

When you move to any new city, you need some kind of job where you're going to work every day. It could be at a restaurant, it could be interning, but it's got to be something where you're making a little bit of money because if you think you're going to live on your savings, it will be gone in a few months. Even I faced that when I couldn't even get a restaurant job. About two months after moving here I had an interview for the Daily Grill, which was the difference between staying here a little longer and possibly picking up and going home because I basically had nothing left. I'm a people person, and I knew that the restaurant wasn't going to be a thing I hated. Any job you can get, find something you enjoy doing . . . When I was in Long Beach and I couldn't get anything, I would walk and look at the ocean. You just stop thinking about your problems, you absorb what surrounds you, and you realize how lucky you are that you're not homeless living on the street. It puts things in perspective. If you could tell every actor that; if you're having a bad day, just think of three things you're grateful for; and if you can't, then maybe rethink being in this business.

MICHAEL GABIANO

You have to have a way to pay the bills. You cannot be desperate because there is nothing as off-putting to anybody in the business as a hungry, desperate actor. Then anything you make from acting is a plus. It's a wonderful bonus and hopefully at some point you can transition to where it becomes more than a bonus but a larger and larger component. That cannot be the only way you're surviving because you can have a great job, you can make a film, a series, guest spots, whatever it is, and then not work again for months. You have to figure out a way to sustain yourself, and the more survival skills you have the better. I started off working advertising. Anything creative is going to be more fun for an actor-type. Waiting tables, that's not my preference. I've worked in advertising. I've worked in real estate. Anything that helps you develop skills and to work as part of a team, how to work well with others, how to take direction, or any job that calls upon those skills is going to be useful to your acting career.

PETER LAVIN

I was the manager of a store for ten years back East. I ran a costume store and dance wear where I learned how to fit tap shoes and ballroom shoes on people. I learned all my selling skills at a retail store. I learned from every small job that came through. I slept on my friend's couch for a month, I could at least contribute to some rent. I could buy my own food. You have to be prepared. You can't just come out here blindly. I have a nephew who wants to come out here, and I told him he could stay with me, but you have to get a job. I can't support somebody else. It's hard enough. You have to save money. You have to put a nice chunk of your paycheck away and that's the best advice I can give to people. I love technology, and I love my toys, but you have to put a chunk of money aside to survive because it's tough. . . . We've chosen a profession of 98 percent rejection. You have to be able to let that go. Go to your auditions and move on. Don't let it destroy you for the rest of the day. Don't dwell on it. We're lucky to have this as a job.

RICHARD DORTON

3 SURVIVING IN LOS ANGELES: EMPLOYMENT, HOUSING AND TRANSPORTATION

I do a lot of lectures on survival. I always say you can't change what happened, so have a little wallow, feel very sorry for yourself, and then get up and move forward. You can't change what happened.

JOAN RIVERS

ACTOR'S RESOURCES

Employment—Rental—Traffic—Information Sources

The Los Angeles Yellow Pages—Temporary Employment Agencies

California Department of Consumer Affairs—Boards/Bureaus
(Information for professional licensing)

Contractors State License Board
(Applicant information)

Guide to California Residential Tenants' and Landlord's Rights and Responsibilities

Los Angeles County Dept. of Consumer Affairs—County of Los Angeles
(Information for renters)

Housing—Los Angeles City
(Rent control, code enforcement, financial assistance)

Los Angeles City Department of Transportation—Live Traffic Information

Sigalert
(Real-time freeway traffic information)

Los Angeles County Metropolitan Transportation Authority
(Rail and bus lines, schedules, and fares)

Wherever you land in Los Angeles, it is not likely to be permanent. Friends or family will quickly grow weary of one's career quest and hotels eat up the nest egg. Many decisions await you, such as developing a dependable revenue stream, a permanent base of operations, and a transportation strategy.

How Should I Begin to Implement My Business Plan?

Sustainability should remain your primary goal. As housing and transportation costs will be determined by one's monthly income, or lack thereof, in some cases, employment, then, must be the priority, as your nest egg will not last long and bankruptcy has ended more than one promising career. Smart newcomers to Los Angeles formulate a budget and then stick to it. Rent should cost no more than one-third of your monthly income or you will risk financial default. Food can be inexpensive if you buy fresh and know where to shop. Utilities will nickel and dime you with gas, electric, water and trash. Add to that your cell phone and internet costs. Then consider career and health care expenditures. But until you actually have an income, budgeting is at best guesswork. Chart 3.1 illustrates the challenge.

EMPLOYMENT

Who Hires Struggling Actors in Los Angeles?

Finding a survival job in Los Angeles is easy. Keeping the job will be hard. Most employers want dependable, full-time employees available from nine to five,

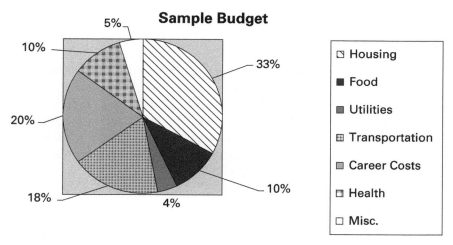

Sample Budget

5%
10%
33%
20%
18%
4%
10%

- ◩ Housing
- ◼ Food
- ▦ Utilities
- ▥ Transportation
- ▧ Career Costs
- ▤ Health
- ☐ Misc.

CHART 3.1 Professional Living Costs in Los Angeles

Monday through Friday. Actors, by the nature of their work, can never fulfill that requirement without abandoning their acting quest. But for what actors lack, they more than amply compensate for in areas of personality, teamwork, and skill. Here are a few businesses that by their nature hire struggling actors who need flexible hours.

Restaurants

Advantages

- Represent a surprisingly large sector of the Los Angeles economy, attracting epicureans of all cuisines and all pocketbooks from around the world.
- Provide flexible work hours.
- Tips can be lucrative depending upon the restaurant.

Disadvantages

- Restaurants come and go quickly in any trendy city and may not always provide a stable source of income.
- High-end restaurants, though lucrative, often include internal politics with kickbacks and percentages of tips expected to be paid to other employees.

Bars

Advantages

- No state laws regulate server training. The Department of Alcoholic Beverage Control (ABC) offers a voluntary training program for licensees, called LEAD (Licensee Education on Alcohol and Drugs). The program focuses training efforts toward new license applicants, licensees employed in high-crime areas, licensees who have violated ABC laws, as well as toward major special events and county fairs (California Department of Alcoholic Beverage Control, *LEAD*).

Disadvantages

- ABC laws hold bartenders personally liable, with substantial fines for serving an intoxicated person, as well as other violations (California Department of Alcoholic Beverage Control, "Frequently").

- The after-hours bar scene can easily harm a career for reasons too numerous to mention such as alcoholism, drug abuse, crime etc.

Hair Salons

Advantages

- The California Contractor's Licensing Board (CSLB) provides detailed information and study guides.

- The CSLB supports reciprocal out-of-state licensing and provides assistance for members of the military.

- Once licensed, the CSLB offers online licensing renewals, unless one has contravened their regulations (California Contractors State Licensing Board, "Applicants").

Disadvantages

- The California Barbering and Cosmetology Act closely regulates and licenses stylists, barbers, beauticians, cosmetologists, manicurists, and electrologists with strict requirements for health and safety.

- As with a variety of skilled vocations, substantial time and cost must be invested to either complete a course of instruction from a Board-approved school, or to complete an apprenticeship program from a Board-approved sponsor (California Department of Consumer Affairs, "Boards/Bureaus").

Temporary Employment Agencies

Advantages

- Los Angeles supports temporary employment services for professional and technical trades.

- Temporary agencies readily employ artists who have clerical business skills in all manner of office practices such as reception, data entry, and secretarial services. Generally, one must have proficiency in common software applications such as the Microsoft Office suite. Those proficient in more advanced programs and/or in web design and maintenance command higher rates (*Los Angeles Yellow Pages online*, "Temporary").

Disadvantages

- Temp. agencies generally pay only minimum wage, though some specialty skills can be negotiable.

- Some agencies prefer workers to make one or two-week commitments to an assignment, often to replace someone on a vacation.

Gyms

Advantages

- No licensing or certification for personal training is generally needed unless required by the gym, but certification of some kind can help your credibility.

- Provides a great place to network in the entertainment industry.

- Provides you with an opportunity to keep yourself in great shape.

Disadvantages

- Gyms hire personal trainers initially to train patrons, but pay them only minimum wage and then double them up as sales associates on straight commission.

Caterers

Advantages

- Always looking for workers with restaurant or bar experience but also hires those with no experience, especially when business is booming.

- This environment favors creativity, personality, and people skills.

Disadvantages

- Income depends upon tips to supplement the minimum wage.
- Hours work can depend on the season and the economy.

Talent Agencies/Casting Agencies—Internship/ Personal Assistant

Advantages

- Talent agents and casting directors often hire actors as personal assistants to help with the telephone and paperwork.
- Personal Assistants have access to casting breakdowns, are privy to insider advice, and can make important industry contacts.

Disadvantages

- Hours are not always flexible, and pay is minimal.
- Work is mundane, routine, and far from fulfilling.
- Celebrities' lives are not simple, personal assistants rarely have a life, and their acting careers often become afterthoughts.

Where Do I Look for Employment Notices?

Classified Advertisements

Los Angeles may be a metropolis of millions, but the monolithic *Los Angeles Times* still attempts to serve the needs of this massive market with multiple daily, regional, and online editions, all posting classified employment notices. As comprehensive as this approach may be, Los Angeles has many other community, cultural, and trade papers and magazines, all with online editions.

- *La Opinion*—Los Angeles based Spanish language daily.
- *Santa Monica Daily Press*—Santa Monica local news and community information.
- *Hollywood Reporter*—Greater Hollywood—Entertainment industry related jobs.
- *Variety*—Los Angeles—Entertainment industry related jobs.
- *Beverly Hills Weekly*—Beverly Hills weekly newspaper.

- *LA Weekly*—Los Angeles weekly alternative newspaper.
- *Santa Monica Mirror*—Santa Monica news, weather, traffic, classifieds.
- *Recycler*—Los Angeles classifieds.
- *Craigslist*—Offers a more comprehensive online service, but while advertisers encounter liability for fraudulent employment notices in the print media, online services offer no such protection to the naïve.

Employment Agencies

Most employment agencies, as opposed to temporary employment agencies, expect a long-term commitment from their clients and charge the employer that hires them a substantial fee. Be honest up-front. Remember, legitimate agencies do not charge a fee to find you employment, so do not waste your time unless the fee is for state licensing fees, fees for fingerprinting, or other legal governmentally mandated requirements.

Vocational Schools

Most vocational schools offer employment services for their graduates. Whatever the value of their training, an exam must be passed before being licensed. Schools may promise exam success, but be wary of any school that guarantees employment. This is not only a violation of the Federal Trade Commission Act, but it is an all too common scam.

Targeted Canvassing

Possibly the most effective way to find a job in Los Angeles is still the old-school method of selling yourself. Do some research and target the businesses in your vicinity that need your skill set. With resume in hand, knock on some doors. Ask for the owner/manager, and announce your desire to be employed there. Most will hand you an application to fill out which they will dutifully file for future needs, but timing is everything. Occasionally, but not always, your timely solicitation intersects with someone's immediate needs and you will find a job. Determination, confidence and chutzpah can go a long way.

Are There Jobs I Should Avoid?

At first, any job in Los Angeles will be a blessing until you get your head above water, after which experienced actors point to a few jobs you might prefer to avoid.

Jobs that pay straight commission rarely equate to even a minimum wage due to the large number of hours involved. Part-time jobs rarely offer benefits, so if health insurance is an issue, you may need to consider your options. Union jobs usually pay well and may offer substantial medical benefits, but usually lack the flexibility required by the serious working actor. Be wary of employers who wish to pay you under-the-table. Besides being cheated out of future Social Security benefits, you may risk complicity in illegal activity.

Managerial Positions

The concept of management and flexible working hours are incompatible. Higher pay generally means more responsibility and less flexibility. As a result, career goals can soon become secondary, and while many a career has been sacrificed at the altar of financial necessity, do not fool yourself over the reason why.

Telemarketing Jobs

Unless you need to improve your ability to handle rejection, avoid these jobs. They often pay only straight commission, so the amount of your income becomes a monthly gamble. While seductively offering flexible hours, employers may claim the product sells itself, when in truth, the only things moving out the door are former employees.

Drivers

Whether one drives a taxi, limousine, or a private vehicle, Los Angeles regulates commercial drivers closely. Licensing requires not only a medical test, involving standard drug testing at the applicant's expense, but also a written and physical driving test. Taxi drivers face long distances and high gasoline costs, making this also a daily gamble. Higher paying limousine drivers and private drivers live on call, they have little flexibility and must be licensed. Valet attendants face no examinations but still must be licensed (Los Angeles Police Department, "Valet Permits").

Entertainment Industry Production Related Jobs

What seemed like a match made in heaven has often sounded the death knell of an acting career and the excuse for a struggling actor to give up their acting quest. If you want to be a production assistant, then be a production assistant, but do not delude yourself that it will land you an acting gig.

What is Better, Employment or Entrepreneurship?

While employment presents a security blanket, an actor in possession of particular skills may want to consider pursuing entrepreneurship instead of employment. Owning your own business, though perhaps not the best idea initially, offers the most obvious advantage in flexibility of hours once you are established, and with smartphone and digital payment systems such as Square, anyone can be an entrepreneur almost anywhere. The disadvantages involve the financial start-up investment that may be required, the time needed to establish such a business, and the inevitable conflicts that turning a vocation into a business that will compete with your acting career will ultimately bring. Follow this simple guideline; a business of one is manageable with an acting career, a business with employees is not. Some vocations, though, do lend themselves to this limitation.

Stylists, Barbers, Beauticians, Cosmetologists

Salon owners often prefer to rent the extra chairs in their salon rather than hire employees to work them. But for this to be lucrative, you must bring with you an established clientele.

Personal/Sports Trainers

Though in great demand, personal and sports trainers must constantly market and advertise their services. Clients may come and go, but the gym owner will still charge a monthly fee for gym use. California requires no certification for physical trainers, but the sometimes-fierce competition among trainers will require the pursuit of some credible certification program. Those who teach Pilates, yoga, or offer boot-camp training and have certification do find themselves in great demand.

Massage Therapists

The abuse of this profession has led the City of Los Angeles to require practitioners to obtain certification and a permit from the California Massage Therapy Council (California Massage, "Requirements"). Massage therapy still thrives with an estimated 14,000 to 24,000 legitimate practitioners in California, most of whom work as independent contractors or unlicensed. Here again, obtaining certification does not hurt your credibility when you are building a loyal clientele.

Painters/Landscapers

California does regulate all practices in the construction industry. To work independently as a painter or landscaper requires a contractor's license as an independent practitioner. Undoubtedly many unlicensed painters and landscapers find work in Los Angeles but they risk significant liability for doing so. If you have significant experience in the past, passing the contractor's exam will still require some serious studying, but it will also provide a strong buffer from the financial liability one may encounter as an independent contractor.

Dog Walker

How many businesses can you run where your clients are so happy to see you they lick your face? Busy professionals have needs, and so do their pets. Early morning, late evening, and weekend hours easily accommodate auditions, and you can work either independently, using neighborhood flyers, or through a staffing service. You should, of course, love dogs, know basic obedience commands and be strong enough to handle any type of dog from the small and energetic, to the large and uncooperative.

Pet Sitting

If one does not mind sleeping in strange beds all over the city, this option can also provide flexibility either independently or through one of Los Angeles' many staffing services. Keep in mind, pet owners can have unrealistic expectations and not all pets will wag their tails for you.

Tutoring

Put your education to good use. You can post flyers on student union bulletin boards at colleges or universities locally or work through a staffing service.

Computer Services

Video editor, web writer, web search evaluator, technician, website designer: the list goes on. If you have technical computer skills, thousands of digital immigrants need your help, and freelancing can be very lucrative once you get the word out.

Script Reader

Film and television production companies, publishing houses, and agencies of all categories find themselves inundated with scripts and have little time to read them. So, they hire script readers to evaluate and prepare plot summaries called "coverage." Taking a class in this service can lead to as much work as you have free time and can generate anywhere from $50 to $500 of income per project.

HOUSING

Struggling actors find all manner of affordable, convenient, and supportive living spaces, in converted garages, wealthy estate pool houses, hillside cottages, rooms in attics and basements; and in traditional apartments and homes. New residents will encounter corporate real estate company managers, mom and pop apartment owners, naïve homeowners subsidizing a mortgage, or an individual or consortium of renters seeking a new roommate. Make certain you understand the ramifications of any financial relationship being discussed and its advantages and disadvantages. Once agreed upon and/or signed, any arrangement will be binding.

How Do I Rent an Apartment?

First and foremost, establish local residency and credit. Landlords rarely accept out-of-state checks. A cashier's check may have to suffice until you can establish a local bank account with your first paycheck and a Californian driver's license or ID Plan on making an appointment with your local California DMV to apply for one. Consult their website to find their locations and requirements.

Should I Rent, Lease, Sublet, or Live With a Roommate?

The answer to this question depends on your unique needs coupled with some pragmatic financial realities. Are you alone or with family? Do you have special needs? Do you have financial assets? First, carefully assess your anticipated monthly revenue flow. Housing should constitute no more than 33 percent of your monthly income. Then determine what you really need to sustain yourself in Los Angeles financially, physically, emotionally, and creatively. Do you need a five-room apartment, or just a guest-room in someone's house? What assets are at your disposal in case of financial setback? Do you have the help of a relative? Do you have the help of a friend? Do you have a vocation? Do you have a trust fund? Whatever the answers, be honest and set a realistic monthly budget. Rent in Los Angeles for a one-bedroom unit ranges from a modest $1,500 per month and for a two-bedroom unit twice that. Even a single room will cost at least $1,000 a month. How do you afford this? Struggling artists make sacrifices. Most live with roommates, often four to a two-bedroom apartment. Some share houses in artist communes. Still others find live-in jobs that provide housing. Pursue whatever financial relationship seems comfortable and affordable for the time being.

Rental

A written rental contract covers a full year and then continues on month-to-month. It permits the landlord to increase the rent after the initial year at any time upon a thirty-day notification. Tenants also may choose to end the agreement with a thirty-day notice. This may be prudent for the short term, but it provides no financial stability as rent may increase faster than your annual income.

Lease

This written agreement for fixed rent and fees over a fixed time period, which can be negotiated for more than a year, provides long-term financial stability, but, should moving become necessary, it leaves you financially liable for any remaining months, perhaps necessitating a sublease.

Sublet

Infinitely more complicated, this written agreement generally exists between a tenant with a lease who, for whatever reason, must live elsewhere, and someone in need of housing. The landlord also generally needs to approve and formalize this arrangement.

Roommates

Few single people live alone in Los Angeles due to the high cost of housing. Roommates cohabit in all possible arrangements from the arcane to the sublime. While generally only a match of financial necessity, roommates do need to at least enjoy each other's company. As such, the process needed to vet the living arrangements before making any agreements is crucial. Who pays whom, when, what amount, for what rights, and with what conditions? This may involve a formal or informal agreement, usually requiring a deposit, a set monthly payment toward the rent, and some arrangement over utilities, food, household needs, and so forth. Such an arrangement may range from two people in a small apartment to a dozen cohabiting in a large house. Often tenuous at best, roommate arrangements are predicated upon strangers living harmoniously. This is not always the outcome, and one roommate short on their monthly rent can bring down the entire house of cards (California Department of Consumer Affairs, "When you have decided . . .").

Where Do I Look for Housing Notices?

Classified Ads

The *Los Angeles Times* still dominates the classified advertising market, but you find mostly corporate real estate owners soliciting luxury rentals. Small apartment owners and homeowners can easily find cheaper advertising options, such as the smaller neighborhood papers.

Internet

The web brims with electronic real estate services. National services such as Zillow and Trulia are tailored more for real estate sales or to business clients relocating on a moving allowance. RentCafe provides the most comprehensive service, while many local services, such as RentGirl, provide a specialized service. Finally, Craigslist still reigns supreme as the most used site for finding rentals but with the usual disclaimer, "Reply at your own risk."

Bulletin Boards

Community bulletin boards in small grocery stores, community centers, and laundromats, especially in the canyons and other distinct neighborhoods, offer local listings.

Rental Services

For a membership or weekly fee, rental services offer access to their listings. In some cases, the "teaser" listings disappear immediately or never actually existed in the first place.

Roommate Services

A variety of services offer to match roommates of any age, gender, sexual orientation, or a combination thereof. The client pays a membership fee to access a photo/info database of other members seeking roommates. The rest requires chemistry and accommodation.

On-site Posting

Despite the web and digital technology, Los Angeles landlords still prefer to advertise a vacancy with the old-fashioned posted sign out front of the property, detailing the size of the unit, whether furnished or unfurnished, amenities, rental/lease rate, their pet policy, and a contact number. If you know the area you prefer to live in, ultimately driving up and down residential side streets and jotting down phone numbers to make appointments for viewing may be the most time effective and most successful means of finding an adequate apartment.

What Should I Look for When I Inspect the Unit?

Honesty! Landlords and managers seek honest, responsible clients as tenants and this is exactly what the tenant has the right to expect in return. Is the property and unit as advertised? The reality will tell you volumes about your future business relationship with this landlord. A "view of the ocean" can mean one must open an upstairs closet, stand on a chair, and strain out a tiny portal to catch a glimpse of a shoreline. Let experience be your teacher. After a handful of inspections, reality will intervene and certain essential concerns should rise to the surface, reinforcing the fact that the consumer needs to beware and ask a lot of questions.

General Physical Condition

California State law requires a unit must be "habitable," meaning with leak-free windows, doors, and ceilings. In addition, plumbing, gas, heating, and electricity must be in good working order; the building must be clean and sanitary; the grounds must be free of debris, filth, rubbish, garbage, and rodents; the stairs must be in good working order; and there must be working, permanent smoke detectors (California Department of Consumer Affairs, "Dealing with problems"). Check for any signs of damage and ask lots of questions.

Paint

Has the unit been newly painted? Many jurisdictions require the painting of all units prior to new occupancy regardless of the length of a previous occupancy.

Carpet

Most jurisdictions require carpet replacement every seven to ten years with generally no requirement to replace them prior to a new rental. But, if you ask about the carpet, a landlord must provide an answer. At the very least, carpets must be steam cleaned prior to a new rental.

Utilities

Check that the utilities work! Check who pays: the client, or the landlord? Are there additional charges? Ask how much utilities usually average per month and inquire about future planned increases. In some cases, the landlord supplies the gas and/or water communally with each tenant paying their portion.

Appliances

Gas or electric? Who pays? Are there additional charges? Do the existing appliances come with the unit? Landlords may charge extra for providing a refrigerator.

Bathroom Fixtures

By law, toilets must work! Look for tell-tale sign of leaks, mineral deposits, and discolorations. Nothing creates a vacancy faster than a dysfunctional bathroom.

Parking

Is there any parking on the street or elsewhere, or will you have to wake up at 5:45 a.m. each morning to move your car from a 6:00 a.m. restricted parking space? On-site, secured parking may cost extra, but, depending upon the neighborhood, may be well worth the extra cost.

Laundry

Most large apartment complexes will provide coin-operated laundry facilities, and their cleanliness and functionality are often a warning of what you might expect about the facility in general. If these are not provided, locate a neighborhood laundromat. If you are a waiter, bartender, nurse, or a service professional of some type, remember you may someday, as with life, live or die by a drying cycle or in search of one clean shirt.

Amenities

Landlords often promise pools, hot tubs, saunas, and fitness centers. Conduct a close physical inspection to see if these actually work (County of Los Angeles: Consumer and Business Affairs, "Your home before . . .").

Finally, before making application for a unit, walk around and talk to the existing tenants. Most will be more than happy to share their experiences regarding the management, good or bad.

What Application Fees May I Be Charged to Rent/Lease an Apartment?

Depending upon the jurisdiction, landlords may charge the following application fees:

Credit Check Fee

A landlord may charge up to $49 to conduct a credit check on each adult on the application.

A copy of the report must be provided if requested, nominally to prove the landlord did not just pocket the fee. Consequently, a landlord cannot reject an application or charge a higher rental rate for bad credit, often a pretext for discrimination, unless this is evident on the credit report (County of Los Angeles: Consumer and Business Affairs, "Your Home").

Holding Deposit

Usually nonrefundable and equal to one month's rent, this deposit removes the unit from the market pending results of a credit check. Make certain you receive a receipt that spells out how the deposit will be applied once you are approved. (County of Los Angeles: Consumer and Business Affairs, "Your Home").

Application Fee

This covers the clerical costs of processing an application.

Are There Additional Fees I Can Be Charged if I am Approved?

Most landlords use standard rental/lease forms, but read yours carefully. All charges, fees, and incremental increases must be delineated. California law, and most municipal jurisdictions, allow for a variety of additional charges and fees under the city's Rent Stabilization Ordinance.

Security Deposit

In addition to the first month's rent, a security deposit can be required, ranging from a nominal fee to twice the monthly rental fee. Security deposits may include a key and/or pet deposit, can be raised upon a thirty-day notice, and can be applied as cleaning fees when you move out. But, Californian law requires the remaining deposit be refunded (County of Los Angeles: Consumer and Business Affairs, "Moving out of your rental").

Late Payment Fee

Most jurisdictions allow a landlord to charge a late fee of less than 5 percent of the rental fee three to five days after the due date (County of Los Angeles Consumer and Business Affairs, "Living").

Pet Fee

Landlords generally tolerate cats more than dogs. Often the "no pets" requirement really means "no dogs." But, regardless of this, a landlord has the right to charge up to a $100 per pet deposit as a security against damage.

Registration Fee

Many jurisdictions require landlords to pay a yearly registration fee currently $12.25 which is recoverable from the tenant (Housing and Community Investment Department of Los Angeles, "Property Owners").

Systemic Code Enforcement Program (SCEP) Fee

The Los Angeles Housing Authority requires all landlords to pay an annual regulatory fee of $3.61 which may be charged to the tenant (Housing and Community Investment Department of Los Angeles, "What is Covered").

Utility Fee

If utility costs are included in the agreement, a one percent increase may be charged annually to cover the cost of their eventual increase (Housing and Community Investment Department of Los Angeles, "What is Covered").

All in all, the initial cost of rental/lease may equal as much as three times the monthly rental fee, which can require the tenant to lay down thousands of dollars, just for the right to move into a space smaller than your mother's bathroom and nowhere nearly as sweet smelling. Some landlords count on tenants having little rental savvy. The solution? Get some. In whatever neighborhood one decides to settle, whether it may be Los Angeles County, city or other, inquire as to what rights tenants have.

What Are My Renter's Rights?

The rights of renters vary greatly between Los Angeles County, city, and other municipalities, such as West Hollywood and Santa Monica, as does the degree of enforcement. Most landlords play by the rules, but discrimination exists, sometimes with impunity. Whatever the community, research what rights renters have there. Basic California renter's rights are as follows:

- Landlords are restricted from inquiring about race, ethnicity, national origin, religion, sexual orientation, marital status, age, disability, or family status (having children living with you under age eighteen).
- Limits exist on the amount of security deposit required.
- Limits exist on the landlord's right to enter the unit.
- Tenants are entitled to a refund of their security deposit within thirty days of vacating the unit, or must be provided with a written explanation of what charges have been applied.
- Tenants have the right to sue the landlord for violations of the law or the rental agreement.
- Tenants have the right to repair serious defects, such as broken appliances and deduct said costs from the monthly rental fee, if the landlord does not act within a specified period of time.
- Under certain circumstances, tenants have the right to withhold rent.
- Rights under warranty of habitability (unit is habitable with all appliances and utilities working properly).
- Tenants are granted protection against retaliatory eviction.
  (California Tenant Law, "What are your rights")

In addition, some jurisdictions have enacted rent control ordinances that limit when rents may be increased, the payment of accrued interest on security deposits, and limitations regarding eviction. Prospective tenants may need to contact the responsible municipal agency in their jurisdiction to understand their rights under their respective rent control ordinances (County of Los Angeles, Consumer and Business Affairs, "Living").

Knowing your rights puts you on an equal footing with the landlord when negotiating an agreement. Many landlords make demands that violate local ordinances. Renters have recourse, but usually only after having suffered consequences.

TRANSPORTATION

Do I Really Need a Car in Los Angeles?

Los Angeles has a surprisingly effective public transportation system, but side streets and winding canyon roads fall outside of its system, making a car mandatory for an actor. As such, the third tier of a business plan should involve transportation. Having established a revenue stream and a base of operations, sustainability requires learning the appropriate transportation means that connect your home, job, and career. Within the entertainment industry zone, specific transportation corridors do exist, both freeway and side street, utilizing both public and private modes of transportation.

What Are Transportation Corridors?

Los Angeles has many streets and boulevards that, for whatever reason, have evolved into major transportation corridors between certain points. Canyon roads such as Laurel Canyon, Coldwater Canyon, and Cahuenga Boulevards connect the San Fernando Valley with the Basin. Fountain Boulevard connects Silver Lake with West Hollywood. Wilshire Boulevard crosses mid-city, connecting the Westside to Downtown. Wherever one settles, these corridors provide a fast connection at various times of the day in order to get through the sometimes unpredictable traffic flow of Los Angeles. While auditions and callbacks generally occur at studios and casting offices, location shooting can occur anywhere. Always check the Sigalert website for real-time traffic reports before setting out on a freeway jaunt.

An actor also needs to be as familiar with the city streets as a taxi driver. A side-street route, though longer than the freeway, may make the difference between making, or missing, an important audition. Smartphones and GPS systems provide the best solution, but buying a Thomas Guide map book can help you to plan your route.

What Is With the Freeway Names?

Los Angeles' love affair with the automobile has resulted in an extensive system of freeways, connecting all the disparate parts of this great city as illustrated by Map 2.1. In addition to their designated number, freeways may also have more than one name, which can be confusing. Angelinos generally refer to a freeway by its number: the "5" or the "101"; in addition, depending upon the direction, the 10 Freeway may be the Santa Monica Freeway (west) or the San Bernardino Freeway (east); the Golden State Freeway northbound becomes the Santa Ana Freeway southbound. Most people find it easier to just to call it the "5".

What Are My Public Transportation Options?

Take your pick: light rail, train, subway, bus. The Los Angeles County Metropolitan Transportation Authority, better known as LA Metro, has desperately attempted to keep up with unrestrained growth and to provide public transportation options from sea to mountain and valley. You still need an automobile to function in Los Angeles, but public transportation provides a real alternative to get most anywhere, if one has the time.

Metro Rail

Three light rail lines, one subway, and one shuttle service, each differentiated by a color, connect sixty-two stations that incorporate Downtown (Civic Center), Union Station (Amtrak), North Hollywood, Universal City, and the Los Angeles Airport (LAX) with more lines and extensions being added each year.

Metro Link

Regional heavy rail systems that run through Los Angeles connect to this local rail system, providing a commuter service to and from more distant suburbs.

Metro Bus

LA Metro provides four kinds of bus service and maintains 191 mostly CNG-powered bus lines along 15,967 stops on almost all major boulevards of Los Angeles County. Orange buses designate a local service; red buses are express. Additional bus services include Transitway and Busway services on specific freeway routes. The system, though admittedly complex, certifies almost 35 million riders per month and intuitively aids the rider (Los Angeles Metropolitan

Transportation Authority, "Facts at a Glance"). Bus stops display route numbers; LA Metro publishes weekly schedules, easily accessible online; and Los Angeles bus drivers, to their credit, are known for their gracious manners. Don't be afraid to ask questions, such as, "What is the best way for me to get . . . ?"

Public Transportation vs Private Vehicle?

Owning an automobile in Los Angeles often gives one a false sense of security. Casting directors do not like to hear the words, "My car broke down," talent agents and employers even less so. A savvy newcomer should note LA Metro bus routes and stops to and from various key places, such as work, home, classes, and casting, as well as train options, regardless of the current state of their vehicle. Distances magnified by traffic congestion may take hours longer by automobile than by public transportation. The cost of gasoline is another factor in public transportation's favor with fare structures for college, senior, and disabled patrons (Los Angeles Metropolitan Transportation Authority, "Fare Structure"). Though affordable and comprehensive, public transportation cannot serve every need, and the busy actor still must primarily depend upon a personal vehicle or do a great deal of walking.

Is Parking a Problem?

Like most big cities, parking in Los Angeles can be a problem unless you do not mind walking a few blocks. Casting agents, by necessity, locate near to available parking, both on-street and off-street. Parking garages, valets, and meters all cost money. But usually within a few blocks you can find free on-street parking. Watch the signs carefully, though, as most parking, metered or otherwise, comes with restrictions, permit requirements, and limitations. Most apartments include an assigned parking space, but if you are relegated to street parking, be wary of street signs for street cleaning or permit only parking. One missed sign can earn you a very expensive ticket.

Surviving in Los Angeles is really a matter of common sense and using the resources at your disposal. Learning the ins and outs of this city takes time, research, experimentation, networking with others, and trial and error—a lot of error! So, make friends, ask questions, and seek out advice.

ACTOR'S FORUM

You are a business. As a very dear friend of mine always tells me, they don't call it show fun, it's called show business. Whether you are an agent, or a union representative, or a casting director, it is a business. So, to say that they're just an employee, well, yeah, you are when you're working for a specific network. You're an employee for that time, but you're not just an employee when you have another person, your agent or manager, negotiating a contract with you because most people just go "hire me," and you have a job. . . . You have to love this business. The only reason that I'm still doing it is because I love it. I get absolute joy out of doing it. If I didn't, I would have given it up a long time ago because it's not easy. It's not as hard as people say. It's also not as easy as people think it might be when people are just starting out and think it's going to happen overnight. And it could happen. You could land here and book that huge job. But that job could end.

MICHAEL GABIANO

I think it is hard to break into voice-over, but I think there are opportunities there, if you have something specific to offer. I think like anything about acting, it's not that you have to have a gimmick, but that you have something specific that is useful, something that you do well, or is within a range of something that you do well, that can open doors for you. With voice-over, don't try and be every voice. Often when they shoot it in a far-flung location, they're not going to bring in smaller characters to loop their own lines. So, often they just replace the voice entirely. So, if you have the facility to sync your voice to someone else's lip movements. It's a skill, but it's also an entre for actors without a lot of credits. Once you get known for being able to do it, the loop actors are a kind of closed shop, but they'll recommend you for another gig. Someone will say, "Oh, we're doing this. Do you know a young Irishman? Well, I know someone who can do a Scottish accent, I'll see if they can do an Irish accent."

PETER LAVIN

Motion capture production companies or the game companies aren't hiring me. They're hiring the motion capture studio, and the studio is hiring me. Real time is the new thing where they can drop the animated character on your skeleton so you can see how it moves. The technology is moving so fast. You couldn't do it where you could watch somebody's face move in real time. You could see the body move, but they've now perfected that. One company has this game called "Hell Blade," and they've scanned the actor's body and face. They're filming her now with a high-res camera, and her animated character is talking, too. But, they have spent thousands of dollars on her before she's acted one line for the preparation for building her character. But the money that goes into motion capture. You don't see it until you find out a game costs $200 million, so you have to be really good at your craft. That's why I tell my students that you have to be really good for me to spend $10,000 on you before you even open your mouth.

RICHARD DORTON

4 THE BUSINESS OF HOLLYWOOD

It's somehow symbolic of Hollywood that Tara was just a façade, with no rooms inside.

DAVID O. SELZNICK

ACTOR'S RESOURCES

Support Groups	Publications	Advocacy Organizations
Meetup.com —Actor's Helping Actors —The Actor's Place	*Daily Actor* www.dailyactor.com	Alliance for Women in Media http://allwomeninmedia.org
Facebook —The Actors Network	*Hollywood Reporter* hollywoodreporter.com	GLAAD www.glaad.org
National Arts and Disability Center University of California, Los Angeles 11075 Santa Monica Boulevard #200 Los Angeles, CA 90025 (310) 825–5054	*Variety* Variety.com	Media Action Network for Asian Americans http://manaa.org

Deadline Hollywood http://deadline.com	Coalition of Asian Pacifics in Entertainment
LA.com www.la.com	http://capeusa.org
Backstage www.backstage.com	National Association of Latino Independent Producers www.nalip.org

What Is Meant By the "Media and Entertainment Industry"?

Part mythology, part backdrop, Hollywood may have earned its reputation as an empty façade, but behind its veneer of overindulgence and moral turpitude beats the heart of a $1.9 trillion market that produces and distributes film, television, music, radio, books, and video games worldwide, generating a $13.4 billion trade surplus (SelectUSA, Media and Entertainment, 5). Led by a handful of multinational conglomerates, the media, and entertainment sector of the United States economy posted record growth in 2017, most notably in streaming services and international ticket sales, thanks, in part, to a growing Asian market. As it continues to transition from a physical marketplace to a digital economy, studio consolidation, consumer cord-cutting, piracy, copyright infringement claims, and uncertainly over new technologies such as virtual reality continue to roil the industry (United States Department of Commerce, "2017 Top Markets," 1).

Technology remains the television industry's own worst enemy. LED, LCD, OLED, 4k, 5k: No sooner has the newest television technology been perfected than Las Vegas' Consumer Electronics Show has rolled out something grander. Ask anyone who owns a 3D television. Film is no exception. New HDR formats require new production equipment, new transmission modes, new infrastructure, and new production costs that moviegoers pay in increased ticket prices. In 2016, the average ticket price was $8.65, almost two dollars higher than 2007, averaging a 3 percent increase year after year, far ahead of the United States economy's annual inflation rate (Motion Picture Association of America, *Theatrical Market*, 12). As box office receipts falter, theater owners turn to gimmicks, such as 3D projection and recliner seats, which in turn increases costs, and eventually, ticket prices.

In fact, the world today would seem divided between digital natives and digital immigrants. As a digital immigrant, I hold fast to old ways of doing and grudgingly cede control to the future. For the digital native, life is to be reinvented to their specifications. No one can overestimate the effect of cord-cutting now that over 22 million United States adults, mostly the eighteen to forty-nine demographic, have canceled their cable or satellite television service as of 2017. Such seismic shifts in consumer decision-making ripples through this industry as opportunity creates competition, which in turn drives corporate decision-making that effects the working lives of thousands of professionals.

In recent years Los Angeles has struggled to retain its position as the center of that universe, as the continued exodus of production companies to cities like Atlanta, Austin, or New Orleans in states that offer tax incentives and lower labor costs, threatened to collapse Hollywood's complex support system of studios, technical services, and suppliers. But, in what has been termed the second "golden age of television," Los Angeles has enjoyed a resurgence with a 92 percent sound stage occupancy rate in 2017, amid the filming of 173 out of a record-setting 487 scripted series. This number will only increase as a generation of millennials, who view television as an appliance and not a delivery system, cut cords in favor of streaming video services that compete with broadcast and cable networks. This is good news for actors, as well as the 6,600 California businesses and the 212,000 employees that service this industry (*FilmLA Inc.*, "Hollywood at Heart"). Despite these rosy statistics, making a film in Hollywood is still a gamble at best, and to be a player in this complex multilayered marketplace, one must first understand its operating system and identify the real players in this high-stakes media poker game.

Who Are the Players?

Major Studios

The Golden Age of Hollywood in the 1930s saw eight major studios dominate filmmaking and control all aspects of production, distribution, and exhibition. Today this same beleaguered studio system has been reduced to five with Disney's acquisition of Twentieth Century Fox. Joined by Warner Bros., Sony Pictures, Viacom's Paramount, and Comcast's NBCUniversal, these venerable studios still churn out box office blockbusters and the occasional fizzle that in 2017 collectively represented over 60 percent of the worldwide gross ticket sales (McClintock, "Box Office"). Their tentpole franchises usually top the list of the most profitable films, despite domestic box office revenue slipping each year, as more and more movie goers opt for the couch over the theater seat. Despite their profitability, these major studios still only released collectively a total of ninety-two out of 738 domestic films. But to be sure, whether through direct production, rental, distribution, sales, and/or financial partnership agreements, the major studios in Hollywood have their fingers in the vast majority of domestic film and television projects and influence their content and marketing in many ways behind the scenes.

Independent Filmmakers

The bulk of film releases comes from independent filmmakers, referred to as "indies," that are either privately held production companies or limited liability companies set up for a specific production. The larger independent companies such as Lionsgate, STX Entertainment, the Weinstein Company, DreamWorks, MGM, and CBS Films, known as the "mini-majors," form partnerships and distribution agreements with the major studios, but produce their own projects and reap their own profits. Thousands of other smaller production companies produce critically-acclaimed independent films yearly, but often lack the funds for a national release. But while independent film companies may produce more critically-acclaimed projects, the major studios still control the business process. Technology is not cheap. These studios own the facilities and the technical resources that the film industry has come to expect, as well as the distribution network needed to provide more media products at a lower cost and at higher profit margins. Independent film companies, lacking these facilities and technical resources, must rent them from the studios, devouring a giant chunk of their production budget and gross profits in the process. Still, many experimental films and innovations have emerged from these shadows, and will continue to as technology and distribution advances toward digital methods.

Streaming Up-Starts

When Netflix transitioned from a mail-order business to a video streaming service, few recognized it as the game-changer it became. Its subscription-based, streaming, video-on-demand (SVoD) business model was soon copied by Amazon and Hulu, but not until Netflix premiered *House of Cards* did Hollywood understand the depth of its revolution. Armed now with over 17 million subscribers and obligations for $15.7 billion in original content, Netflix continues to upend the television industry by prioritizing diversity in casting as cable-cutting millennials find less and less reasons to patronize broadcast or cable television (La Monica, "Netflix plans").

With Netflix leading the way, Amazon Prime has played catchup, but a planned move into the historic Culver Studios in Culver City follows its own considerable $4.5 billion investment in original programming. Hulu, originally formed by a consortium of studios to monetize their deep vaults of old television series, and now owned primarily by Disney after the Fox acquisition, has its own original programming ambitions with an initial $2.5 billion investment. Even Apple has joined the game with a modest $1 billion stake in its own subscription service.

Telecom Greybeards

Before there was HBO, or Netflix, or Facebook, there was ABC, NBC, and CBS. Now joined by Fox and the CW, these venerable pillars of American broadcast television have long been losing market share to direct-to-consumer streaming services. Recent studies indicate that cord-cutting has slowed down but will continue with reports that 22 million US adults had canceled their cable or satellite television service by the end of 2017 (Spangler, "Cord-Cutting Explodes"). Not to be undone, broadcast and cable companies recognize their future survival also depends upon SVoD. Disney, owner of ABC Television, has already announced its plans for several SVoD services, CBS has already launched CBS Access, and Comcast, owner of NBC Universal, plans to compete directly with Netflix in the coming years.

Social Media Wannabes

A certain inevitability surrounded social media's foray into streaming original content since YouTube for years has championed monetized "channels" for content providers, so its investment in its own original content and subscription service was predictable. Even Facebook's rumored $1 billion original content commitment follows a pattern of leveraging its two billion users by socializing an event on its advertisement-supported website, making the announcement of its new "Watch" tab a logical next step. But then Twitter's announcement of its own agreement with the NFL to live stream future football games and other live events, setting itself up to compete directly with broadcast and cable outlets that have far more resources, begs the question, "Have these social media stakeholders come too late to the party?"

Snapchat provided the answer to that question when it announced its partnership with Comcast's NBC Universal to produce original content through utilizing their website and Universal's studio. Now over a billion loyal users have embraced YouTube's streaming subscription platform, Red, settling that uncertainty. And, with its acquisition of Oculus, Facebook has signaled its own intentions. The release of its Oculus Go virtual reality headpiece has thrust Facebook into a territory for which there exists no viable commercial application . . . yet.

China?

China's interest in Hollywood is no secret. Opening the second largest world cinema market to United States domestic films has substantially increased Hollywood's profits and rescued more than one budget-buster from box office obscurity. But, China's interest extends into multi-billion-dollar on-again, off-again, investments in production companies and production partnerships, setting off alarm bells in the United States government who questions its intentions. Beyond its secrecy, China fears Hollywood's cultural influence and United States filmmakers fear China's power to transform or diminish future financial trends. At present, its role in this game remains a big question mark as no one can say for certain how much they bring to the table, and for how long they will remain in the game.

Hollywood has decidedly embraced the digital economy, and as it grows, so, to, will Hollywood's finances, and so will the number of players at the table. The year 2017 ended with over a hundred streaming services available to the consumer, divided between subscription-based and advertisement-supported models. Many of the Hollywood players are committed storytellers; others are only in it for the money. Some will survive; many will not. A merger here, a buyout there, a scandal, a firing, or corporate reshuffling; soon productions are rescheduled, canceled, or put on hold. Generally, only one individual in a production company has the power to greenlight a project, but once begun, each new twist and turn in the Hollywood corporate ecosystem puts hundreds of actors, and thousands of technicians, on notice or out of work. Nothing is for certain. Nothing is long term. Even the production process itself follows a treacherous path of focus groups, screenings, ratings and budget meetings, and an actor, rarely invited to the bargaining table, remains hostage to the business of Hollywood and its high-stakes game of buying and selling dreams.

What Is the Product Being Bought and Sold?

While Hollywood may market actors as the product being bought and sold, in truth, all of us in the creative arts exist to service a story. Those stories involve specific characters that are too often portrayed as types: cops, lawyers, younger leading metrosexuals, funny fat family men, female fantasies, and action heroes. Casting directors are often criticized for casting stereotypes of what they think young middle-American audiences think those characters look and act like. Actors exist to humanize that story. We provide a face, a voice and a physical presence to an audience as a portrait of life in which, hopefully, we all see ourselves reflected. That has not always been the case.

How Well Do Minority Actors Do in Hollywood?

In 1962, picketers from an organization called Hollywood Race Relations Group protested the lack of inclusion in Hollywood films at the Academy Awards, carrying signs that read, "All Negroes Want a Break." Ironically, the same year *West Side Story,* featuring Natalie Wood as a Puerto Rican Maria, won as Best Picture. Over fifty years later in 2016, Latina actress Eve Longoria led a Brown Ribbon Campaign to bring attention to the lack of Latino representation in the entertainment industry amid a viral #OscarsSoWhite tweetstorm. For decades, the entertainment industry has weathered criticism, especially from within, for its lack of inclusion of minorities in film and television. Despite these very public protests, data from the most recent casting studies indicates that little has changed overall (Chart 4.2) as

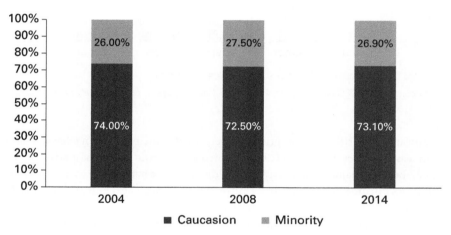

CHART 4.1 Percent of TV and Theatrical Roles
Source: 2004 SAG Casting Report; 2008 SAG Casting Report, 2017 Hollywood Diversity Report, and Inequality in 700 Popular Films.

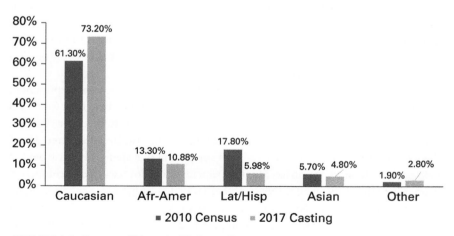

CHART 4.2 Percent of Theatrical Roles to Population
Source: 2017 Hollywood Diversity Report and 2010 U.S. Census Report.

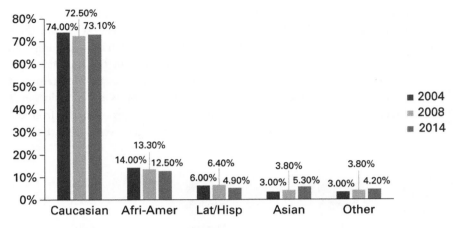

CHART 4.3 Share of TV and Theatrical Roles by Ethnicity

Source: 2004 SAG Casting Report; 2008 SAG Casting Report, and Inequality in 700 Popular Films.

minority actors still only comprise 26.9 percent of principal roles in television and film casting, a net increase of 0.9 percent from 2004. And when comparing the 73 to 27 percent majority–minority casting divide to the actual 61.3 to 38.7 percent statistics documented by the 2010 United States Census, the depth of the disparity at 11 percent becomes clear (see Chart 4.3).

Casting data from three different studies between 2004 and 2014, shown in Chart 4.4, illustrate that while opportunities for Asian actors have improved incrementally, they are still underrepresented, African-American and Latino/ Hispanic actors have actually lost visibility. Again, comparing this casting data to their actual percentage in the population in Chart 4.3 suggests that while all minorities are underrepresented, Hispanic/Latino actors have the greatest challenge with only approximately 6 percent visibility compared to representing 17.8 percent of the population and 20 percent of all domestic ticket sales (Motion Picture Association of America, *Theatrical Market*, 14).

Further analysis suggests that while minorities continue to be underrepresented in film, television provides at least one bright spot for minority actors. Chart 4.5 indicates that broadcast television provides the most opportunities for African-Americans actors. Nielsen data has repeatedly demonstrated the strength of African-American television viewership, a correlation that stems directly from the fact that broadcast television has a higher percentage of shows with casts comprised primarily with actors of color (Nielsen, "For Us By Us"). On the other hand, digital television provides a greater opportunity for Hispanic/Latino actors who represent 10 percent of the speaking roles compared to 3 percent of film roles. One explanation would stem from the digital revolution and its effect on streaming television. The seemingly overnight explosion of new scripted television series has

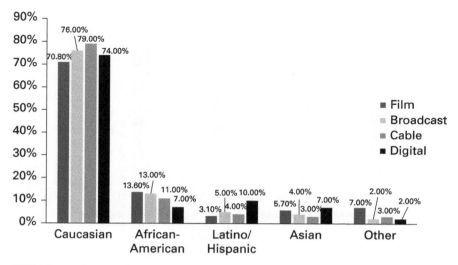

CHART 4.4 Share of Roles in 2016–2017 Scripted Projects by Race
Source: Inequality in 900 Popular Films and 2017 Hollywood Diversity Report.

driven producers to look beyond mainstream storytelling and storytellers to fill the space, providing opportunities for minority writers and directors to tell minority stories with minority actors.

Is There a Gender Disparity in Casting?

Similarly, despite the high-profile complaints and promises of inclusion by Hollywood executives, women remain underrepresented in all mediums as Chart 4.6 illustrates. With only 31.4 percent of the principal roles in film despite comprising over 50 percent of the population, women rarely drive the action of a film and rarely drive the production either. Women remain underrepresented in all areas of production, encompassing only 4.2 percent of directors, 13.2 percent of writers, and 20.7 percent of producers (Smith, Choueiti, and Pieper, *Inequality in 900*, 1–3). Despite those dreary statistics, this represents an improvement, incremental at best, over past years (which saw far greater gender disparity).

The past few years have also seen incremental gains for women in television casting, once again primarily in the realm of digital television. In truth, streaming services, such as Netflix's *Orange is the New Black* and Amazon's *Transparent,* have followed up on their promises to make diversity a top priority of their programming strategy. To some extent so have some cable networks, with, for example, Lena Dunham's *Girls.* Again, the phenomenal growth in scripted television programming has provided opportunities for women who now represent 20.9 percent of show

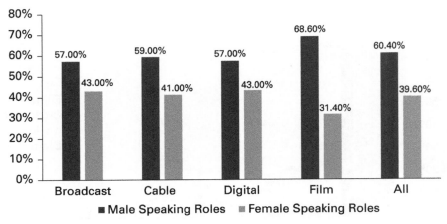

CHART 4.5 Percent of Speaking Roles by Gender
Source: Inequality in 900 Popular Films and 2017 Hollywood Diversity Report.

creators for cable television and 20.4 percent for all streaming services (Buncie, *2017 Hollywood Diversity*, 29). Indeed, the incremental success of female writers and directors has opened some doors that have remained closed for film projects, but evidence still abounds that the playing field is anything but even. The Equal Employment Opportunity Commission has investigated the major studios for allegations of discriminatory hiring practices against female directors and has moved into a settlement phase, suggesting that evidence of discrimination was found.

Is There Bias Towards Disabled Actors?

Inclusion would seem a double-edged issue for actors with disabilities according to several recent studies. While disabled individuals comprise 20 percent of the population, only 2 percent of the characters on broadcast, cable and streaming television portray disabilities. In addition, when portrayed in film and television, 95 percent of the roles portraying disabled individuals were performed by able-bodied performers (Woodburn and Kopić, *Ruderman White Paper*, 1). A similar study of film portrayals produced comparable results and conclusions (Smith, Choueiti, and Pieper, *Inequality in 900*, 2).

Apparently, disabled actors must struggle to overcome more than just their disability. Industry insiders point to financing pressures to cast name actors. Others suggest bias and lack of empathy. In their defense, all three actors' unions have convened committees and launched a major disability rights campaign to increase the visibility and equal employment opportunities for actors. In addition, the Casting Society of America now organizes workshops for industry professionals (SAG-AFTRA Foundation, "Casting Access").

Is There Bias Against the LGBT Community?

LGBT actors have thrived in Hollywood over the decades primarily by staying in the closet. But Hollywood is a small town and your gender or sexual orientation rarely remains a secret for long. The question remains whether to promote your uniqueness or not. Out LGBT actors have consistently complained that it is a no-win situation in which they are passed over for heterosexual roles yet rarely cast in LGBT roles. Transgender actors especially face this situation in that while transgender roles are few and far between, transgender actors are rarely cast in them, producers usually opting for a name actor such as an Eddie Redmayne or a Jeffrey Tambor. LGBT visibility in the media, especially in television programming, has been an ongoing process of education and incremental progress for decades. Not unlike women in Hollywood, LGBT actors tend to thrive in an environment in which LGBT producers, directors, and writers focus on telling their own stories.

The most recent studies by the Gay and Lesbian Alliance Against Defamation (GLAAD) reported significant increases in LGBTQ characters in broadcast, cable, streaming services during the 2016–17 season (*Where We Are*, 4), whereas film demonstrated some incremental progress (*Studio Responsibility*, 4). This may be good news for the LGBT community, but LGBT actors, like their heterosexual counterparts, understand that the issue is not about what you are, but about what you can play. For them, the issue remains discrimination and the work environment.

SAG-AFTRA's most recent study of 5,700 members suggests less positive outcomes for LGBT actors in the workplace. Consider the following results:

1   One in eight non-LGBT actors witnessed discrimination against LGBT actors, including anti-gay comments from crew, directors, and producers.

2   Over half of LGB performers heard directors and producers make anti-gay comments about actors on-set.

3   One-fifth of LG performers experienced casting directors making comments about their sexual orientation that made them uncomfortable.

4   Nine percent of LG respondents reported being turned down for a role because of their sexual orientation.

5   Twenty percent of gay men and 13 percent of women have experienced discrimination.

6   LGBT actors are less likely than their heterosexual counterparts to have an agent.

(Badgett and Herman, *Sexual Orientation*, 7–9).

Every LGBT actor must make his or her own decision regarding coming out or pursuing a gender nonconforming identity in the industry. The reality provides some sobering statistics for LGBT actors, indicating that while the public may be more accepting of their visibility in the media, the industry is not. Industry insiders have speculated that much of the anecdotal evidence suggests the discrimination comes mainly from casting, directing, and producing professionals who, for whatever reason, remain in the closet. LGBT actors should know that in the state of California, discrimination over sexual orientation is illegal. Of course, proving it may be another matter, and pursuing such a course of action could affect your career. Still, LGBT actors should take solace in that 72 percent of respondents in the same SAG-AFTRA study relate that coming out had "no effect on their careers and many would encourage other LGBT performers to come out" (Badget and Herman, *Sexual Orientation*, 9).

Can Senior Actors Still Find Work in Hollywood?

No one would dispute the fact that the youth market drives Hollywood's dream machine, but it is also indisputable that age discrimination exists in Hollywood, especially towards female actors. Senior women have, for years, decried the lack of roles for women over forty and recent casting studies illustrate this point. Comparing the twenty-five Best Picture-nominated films, out of 1,256 speaking characters, only 11 percent were classified as aged sixty or older despite United States Census data documenting them as 18.5 percent of the population (Smith, Choueiti, and Peiper, *Over Sixty*, 6). When comparing senior characters, by gender over three previous years (Chart 4.7), the disparity between senior men and women grows wider, once again, despite the attention given to the issue by the press. When broken down by ethnicity or LGBT status, the disparity between white and minority senior actors only increases, presenting the conclusion that the majority of seniors portrayed onscreen are white and straight. Perhaps this is not that surprising when one understands that much of what is written is written by twenty-year-olds for twenty-year-olds, with older actors nearly invisible in television casting and relegated to pharmaceutical commercials. Ageism, like sexism and racism are against the law, but proving anything is difficult in Hollywood where casting decisions are made subjectively. Any senior actor contemplating launching a career must be aware that the odds are stacked against him, and especially against her.

What is the simple lesson to be learned from all this statistical data? If one is a young, straight, able-bodied, Caucasian male actor in Hollywood, limitless opportunities await. For all others, the challenge will be just getting in the door.

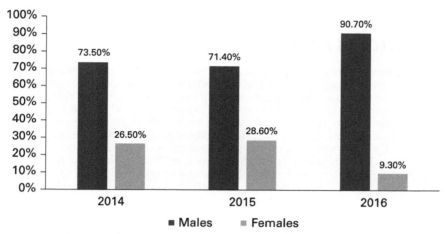

CHART 4.6 Senior Characters by Gender and Year
Source: Smith, Choueiti and Pieper, *Over Sixty, Underestimated.*

But, the success of streaming television services should serve as an example and a lesson for the next generation of actors. Minority, female, and LGBT writers, directors, and producers tend to tell their own stories. The more they succeed in Hollywood, the more minority, female, and LGBT actors will be hired, and those who have the talent to persevere will find a great deal of support among the rank and file working actors. The recent success of superhero films from the Marvel and DC Comics universes, such as *Wonder Woman* and *Black Panther,* underscore that fact and suggest that changes are afoot in the film industry as well.

ACTOR'S FORUM

The marketing of yourself is almost a 100 percent your responsibility. You get a really great headshot and people know exactly who you are. Or you can get a glamour shot that doesn't look anything like you. You are like Frosted Flakes, you are a product. Am I going to take a picture with a Polaroid and put it on the box of Frosted Flakes, or am I going to find the best photographer to make me look good and sell me? Also, you could send emails back in 2004, and you'd get back responses of, "Please don't send me an email about your show. I live in Sheboygan Illinois." Here you just put it out on Facebook, on Twitter, on Instagram, on YouTube. So, anyone who goes, "How does he look on-camera?" can click and see. It's invaluable. If you were going to be on "Grey's Anatomy" tomorrow, you do a little blurb, and you instantly can post it in all of these social media sites. So, anyone you know can see it. It's the speed of light. Everything happens in a click.

MICHAEL GABIANO

I think you've got to market yourself and prep yourself like a business. I see how people now are developing brands, developing careers, and that, I think, is fantastic. I have what's called a "commercial demo reel" which is obviously used for more than commercials. You show a wide range of abilities. For that you should do some classes. Learn the kind of techniques that will be useful to you, and then find a good demo producer. It's an upfront cost, but you can use it for a long time. The other demo reel is an "animation demo." If you're going to be a voice actor, you have to do animation. You need to watch a lot of animation and see what kind of voices are they using, what kind of characters are current. For example, I just did a new animation reel. I've done an animation reel about ten years ago. Those animated shows were gone. You've got to keep current with what kind of material is getting produced, what kind of voices are they looking for? Those are your two biggest marketing tools.

PETER LAVIN

I market myself on Facebook, Twitter and Instagram. Newer technology is wonderful. Social media is huge. You also have to have a reel. And, I'm still an actor. I still have a regular headshot just like everybody else, but I also put together a comp card of my motion capture stuff in the suit. I created marketing for me by doing whatever it took. I made stuff up for comp cards like people used to make. One of the trends in Hollywood for a while was making odd shape sized business cards or comp cards so that when you put them in a pile, yours was a little bit bigger than anyone else's. Yours was horizontal, everyone else was vertical or something like that. I jumped on my computer and started working Photoshop right away when it came out. You have to know technology. And YouTube has helped us a lot. People will play the video game within the first twenty-four hours after its released and post it on YouTube. I can go and find my scenes, rip them and put that into my reel. What I like to teach now in my classes is how to put together your reel, a movement reel, because if you do hard cores stunts, if you're a rock climber, if you do weapons, you can now create your own specialty reel of that stuff.

RICHARD DORTON

5 MARKETING YOUR CAREER

To market, to market, to buy a fat pig,
Home again, home again, dancing a jig;
To market, to market, to buy a fat hog;
Home again, home again, jiggety-jog;
To market, to market, to buy a plum bun,
Home again, home again, market is done.

MOTHER GOOSE

ACTORS' RESOURCES

"Forums"—*Backstage.com*
(Discussion and advice for *actors* and performers new to the industry)

Social Media Guide for Actors—Brian Medavoy
(Manager, Producer, Hollywood Navigator)

Los Angeles Acting Blog—David August

"Headshot Printing in Los Angeles"—*Yelp*

"Podcasting Legal Guide"—*Creative Commons*

"How to Make/Create Your Own Website: The Beginner's A-Z Guide"—*thesitewizard.com*

"YouTube Space—Los Angeles Unlock"—*YouTube.com*

Is Hollywood a meat market? Hollywood remains its own worst enemy and this image still rings true, although admittedly it is a bit simplistic. Without a doubt, actors both young and old, represent commodities, physical or otherwise, worshiped here on the altars of youth and sexual gratification. Any novice in this industry must confront that reality. Many fall victim to its expectations. The smart ones focus on developing that which makes them unique or different from the rest. Any marketing analysis begins by identifying that special quality and then communicating it to potential customers. Now is the time to revisit the logo you created, identify what qualities you wish to emphasize, and begin developing your personal brand as a professional actor.

What Marketing Materials Do I Need?

Twenty years ago, an actor needed only a black and white headshot and a resume to launch a career. Today the digital and corporeal worlds have collided with digital media now the primary marketing tool for actors with your headshot, resume, reel, personal website, or social media sites. Your marketing materials should be as professional as your work as an actor. The headshot and resume still remain an actor's primary calling card, but in order to compete in this marketplace, the actor must also create a variety of specialized professional marketing materials such as business cards, photocards, an actor's reel, and these days, a website, and social media accounts.

Headshots

The entertainment industry now relies upon electronic casting for most projects. Yet an actor still needs hardcopy headshots and resumes. Why? Some people occasionally need a photo to hold and physically handle, display, categorize, compare, or discard. Many casting directors still direct actors to bring a hardcopy headshot and a resume to auditions, especially for stage projects which still primarily depend upon them for casting.

What Makes a Good Headshot?

An actor's headshot functions as a business card. Casting directors spend on average only a second or two scrutinizing each of the thousands of photos that cross their desk for each project. Imagine looking at a thousand faces a day? Most will remain a blur, but certain faces may stand out. Why? a smile? a look in the eyes? a body? An actor's headshot must convey more than a body beautiful. An actor needs to create a persona. True, it may be enhanced by wardrobe, makeup, or a spectacular setting, but the photo must catch the casting director's eye within that two-second window. An actor must, therefore, have good professional photos to compete in today's global marketplace, not amateur snapshots by well-meaning friends or loved ones.

An actor must also have confidence in that headshot's ability to produce bookings. Finding the right photographer takes a systematic search. Even the best headshot eventually gets old. Casting directors expect actors to look like their headshot. Nothing will end an audition more quickly than an actor who arrives ten years older, twenty pounds heavier, and twice as bald as advertised. New photos will need to be taken every five to ten years. Each time evolves into a born-again experience. Hope springs eternal. If the last headshot did not produce work, maybe this one will!

How Do I Find a Good Photographer?

Los Angeles teems with hundreds of professional photographers who specialize in theatrical and modeling photos. These photographers have an almost symbiotic relationship with actors. They advertise in every industry resource from the trade papers to electronic casting services. But, selecting the proper photographer involves dynamics not unlike choosing a good dentist. Selecting one randomly is never a good idea unless it is an emergency. Photographers practice in vastly different styles, with different equipment and price schedules, as well as with different personalities. Feeling comfortable with the photographer should be an actor's primary consideration. A good photo shoot requires an actor to reveal an inner self and risk looking ridiculous in the process. An actor should pursue several steps before selecting a photographer.

Ask Talent Agents and Managers

If you have an agent or manager, schedule a meeting to discuss their headshot preferences before moving forward. Word of mouth also remains the best recommendation. When first representing an actor, a talent agent or manager may request new photos and may recommend a photographer or even arrange a discount. But be cautious! Agents and managers have also been known to recommend a photographer in exchange for a commission or kickback from the photographer, despite its illegality. On the other hand, some talent agents and managers do have contacts with well-known photographers. Check them out carefully. It might be a bargain or just a photographer struggling to keep a studio open.

Check Out Other Actors' Headshots

Other actors provide the best source of referrals. When at auditions, workshops, readings, and so forth, make friends, ask questions and purposely look at other actors' headshots, especially those of a similar age and category. Look for a style that catches the eye. Ask questions about the photographer and collect a name and telephone number. Actors usually give a more "real world" recommendation than a website or advertisement.

Consult Websites

Most electronic casting websites have advertisements or resource lists of photographers. These same photographers may link to their websites to display samples of their work. Once armed with a name, post a query on one of many online actor's forums, chat rooms, or discussion boards. Other actors will respond, sharing their experiences, positive or negative, and warn about unprofessional, unethical, or unsavory photographers. Women especially should exercise caution. Unfortunately, the entertainment industry draws its share of predators masquerading as professional photographers.

Check Out Photoduplicating Shops

Most photoduplicating services, to impress potential customers, plaster their entry walls with the headshots of their more successful clients. It may or may not impress, but it does provide a great comparative source of poses, styles, or looks employed by gainfully employed actors. Styles do change. Once again, scan for a photo that stands out, then look for the photographer's name, often printed somewhere in small print on the bottom corner of the photo.

Interview Selected Photographers

Insiders recommend that an actor interview up to eight different photographers before making a decision. Those consultations offer each the opportunity to ask questions and to meet. Look for "chemistry," a symbiotic energy, something that suggests that this person can capture and eternalize one special moment of time. Interview the photographer, but also closely scrutinize his or her portfolio. Are the photos clear or muddy? Is the background obtrusive? Do the poses look stiff and posed? Does the photo draw your interest? What is happening in the eyes?

Ask Questions

The photographer will make a series of recommendations regarding wardrobe, hair or makeup, photo location, shooting style. Listen to the photographer suggestions but make certain the following questions are answered to your satisfaction.

- *How long has the photographer been shooting headshots?* Everyone must begin somewhere, including photographers, but if paying top dollar, you want a photographer who has a track record of professional theatrical headshot work, not weddings, proms, or Bar Mitzvahs. On the other hand, if strapped for cash, seek out a beginning professional photographer who desires to build a portfolio book. Check out Craigslist or contact photography schools to find photographers willing to shoot for free in exchange for the use of your photos.

- *What is the photographer's style?* Styles change with the times and the market. A headshot in New York will look somewhat different than one for the Los Angeles market. Some photographers specialize in traditional poses and some prefer more creative sessions. Some prefer outdoor shoots while others remain studio bound. Some specialize in particular types of actors, such as children, fashion models, or character actors. And, some photographers prefer actors to improvise and move around while others stick to poses. Once again this all depends upon what you prefer.

- *How much will it cost and what is included in the headshot package?* A headshot session of several hours can cost anywhere from $200 to $2,000, depending upon the photographer. First establish the fee and what it includes. Photographers generally charge an hourly rate for studio time. This usually includes approximately seventy shots, proofs and perhaps two or three 8 x 10 prints, rarely more, so beware the "packaged deal" pitch. Conventional wisdom also might suggest that the more expensive the photographer the better the photo, but such is not always the case.

- *Digital or 35mm photographs?* Digital cameras have reached professional quality, but understandably some old-school actors, reluctant to switch, believe 35mm remain the superior format. A digital camera allows the actor to see the photos immediately while a 35mm does not unless the photographer also shoots a Polaroid first. Either way an actor still needs both a digital file and a hardcopy photo. Digital photos lend themselves to Photoshopping to eliminate imperfections and distractions, but with a good digital scan of a hardcopy photo, one can do the same. With either format, the photographer generally shoots a set number of exposures for a set fee and provides contact prints or digital prints on a disk. But these do not always display sufficient detail. You will want to choose half a dozen or more exposures for enlargement in order to have a satisfactory selection. Once chosen, the photographer will provide final hardcopy prints and/or a disk of the digital photo files, usually in a high-resolution format.

- *Studio lighting or natural light?* Photographers live or die by their lighting technique. Some have elaborate studios with complex lighting equipment, and others provide only the basics. Still others prefer to work outdoors, dueling with Mother Nature over sunlight angles and shadows. Outdoor photos lack the smoothness and subtlety of indoor photos, but they offer a variety of backgrounds that suggest role-playing.

- *How long is the photo session and how many wardrobe changes are allowed?* Wardrobe requires a series of individual decisions based upon the persona the actor wishes to portray. Photographers may suggest three, four, or even more wardrobe changes. Just remember, your fee pays for the photographer's time. The more time you spend changing clothes, the less time you will spend in front of the camera. In addition, glamour shots require an extensive wardrobe and makeup. Fantasies need to be costumed elaborately and can cost serious money for professional makeup and hair design. On the other hand, photography inspires improvisation. Take a close look at your wardrobe, check out local thrift and value stores, find something that looks good, and go with it. Always remember that wardrobe selection, whether formal or informal, cultural or generic, hip or professional, sexy or wholesome, should reflect positively upon the product, namely you. The photographer will provide suggestions for style and color. Set the number of wardrobe changes and types of clothes you will wear.

- *What is the turnaround time?* Time is money for an actor who cannot compete for roles without an adequate digital headshot to submit. Asking this question will establish a timeline to which an actor can hold a photographer accountable.

- *Who keeps the negatives or digital files?* Generally, a photographer keeps the fruits of their labor and charges the actor for each individual negative or digital file, but on occasion, if asked, the photographer may provide the raw product for a set fee, thus allowing the actor to change photos in the future without having to track down the photographer.

How Do I Prepare for the Photo Shoot?

Once you have chosen a photographer, agreed upon a fee, services, and a specific time and place, the work has just begun. Whether you are male or female, laundering, grooming, and gathering clothes remain imperative. Keep in mind that the photo should feature you, not your accessories.

Wardrobe

Set the wardrobe. If possible, let the photographer preview the selections. If not, bring a variety of choices and trust the photographer's suggestions. In general, avoid white, green, yellow, or orange, as well as loud patterns, busy prints or logos. Find a color that compliments your skin tone. Inspect the clothes and try them on in advance. Just because something fitted two months ago does not mean it fits today. Clean, press, and organize each item into the filming order. Make them transportable in garment bags, easily loaded and unloaded.

Grooming

Whoever you are, male or female, young or old, make definite decisions about your hair color, style, and length. An actor must commit to those decisions. Having a beard for a headshot means appearing at an audition with the same beard. The same is true for hair color, general length, and style. Gather grooming and makeup paraphernalia for the shoot. Some photographers offer makeup and hair technicians to assist. Either way, bring rescue tools: hair dryer, curler, gel, spray, and hairpins.

Makeup

Men should bring face powder. Photographers often play music during the shoot to set a mood and encourage the actor to move or dance. Under the hot lights, an actor's makeup can quickly be ruined by perspiration. Powder periodically applied removes the sheen from a sweaty face. On the other hand, a spray water bottle may be used to create a hot and sweaty appearance. Any veteran stage actor knows how to use an eyebrow pencil to correct any imperfect eyebrow features, and a mascara brush instantly masks gray in a beard or mustache.

If affordable, have makeup professionally applied just prior to the photo shoot. And if it is not affordable, seek out an aspiring makeup artist who needs practice. Make a deal! Or, bring a friend to keep the chaos organized.

Jewelry

Not a necessity, but if you must, choose conservatively, remembering less is more. Avoid piercings of any kind, and keep tattoos covered.

Props

Once again not a necessity, but some actors find holding a book, a pair of glasses, or some other item suggests a particular persona.

What Should I Expect During the Photo Shoot?

You have the right to expect professionalism. The photographer has the right to expect the same. If at any time the situation turns uncomfortable, speak up. Keep yourself hydrated, and bring a snack to keep yourself energized. A good photographer should create a comfortable atmosphere. Some burn incense, set mood lighting, play music, or jabber about the morning news. Many actors bring their own music to set a mood. Photographers usually offer a selection as well. The rest depends upon the camera and the subject with the assistance of some verbal and non-verbal communication. The photographer should follow your lead, but if you feel awkward in front of the camera, the photographer may suggest poses and looks. But remember, the photo should focus on the personality in your eyes. Tilting your head down and looking up often increases intensity. At this point the personalities of the photographer and the actor should engage and the result, hopefully, emerges as artistically and aesthetically satisfying.

How Do I Choose a Headshot?

The photographer should provide contact sheets of proofs, small exposure-sized prints that show little detail but when viewed with a magnifying glass provide enough clarity to enable you to choose the shots to have enlarged to 8 × 10s. The final choice will ultimately be subjective and may not even be yours to make. Talent agents or managers generally want input and may preempt the actor's choice based upon their expertise. A commercial agent will most likely want a different photo than a theatrical agent. But if given the choice, consider the following questions:

To Smile or Not to Smile?

Thirty years ago, a nonsmiling photo suggested an actor had bad teeth. Today it reads as dramatic, but not comedic. Actors still need to appear more neutral, mysterious or downright seductive. Versatile actors may need to choose two different headshots—a commercial and a theatrical headshot. This gets pricey, but it solves the conundrum.

Body Shot or Close-Up?

Most photographers will shoot both body shots and close-ups unless the actor directs otherwise. But remember, casting directors see your headshot as an electronic thumbnail picture. Close-ups will read better than three-quarter shots. The final choice may depend upon ultimately what the actor wishes to sell: a body, or a face, or both?

Where Do I Have Headshots Printed?

Photo reproduction services flourish in Los Angeles for obvious reasons. One needs only a digital file on disk or a hardcopy 8 x 10 photo to have bulk headshot reproductions processed. Most offer approximately the same services and charge similar fees.

Sizes

Customers can select bulk reproductions of 8 x 10 headshots, 4 × 6 or 5 × 7 postcards, business cards, or a zed or composite card for fashion models which displays three or four different high-fashion poses.

Quantity

Order in groups of one hundred. Reproduction services usually offer package deals.

Formats

Portrait, landscape, bordered or borderless? Color printing, now cheaper than in the past, has become the industry standard, though black and while photos still offer a more stylized alternative that some actors prefer for dramatic impact.

Finishes

Gloss finishes are prone to fingerprints. Pearl finishes provide a kind of luster but tend to look manufactured. A matte finish weathers better but is cheaper—and may look cheaper.

Text

Have your professional name, your talent agent's name and logo, and your union affiliations imprinted at the bottom of the photo.

RESUME

What Should I Put on My Resume?

A resume always accompanies a headshot, sized to 8 x 10 inches, either printed directly upon the back of the headshot or on an attached sheet. As with any professional, the resume represents one's professional accomplishments, training and special skills, and it may drop a name or two along the way. But, beginning actors may only have college credits.

What if I Have No Professional Credits?

Everyone begins a career at the beginning. Beginning professional actors should list those college and community theater productions, but, when possible, mask their amateur status by eliminating the words "community" and "college" from the listing. Needless to say, replace these credits at the earliest opportunity. A resume is always a work in progress and needs updating each time more experience or training has been earned, always eliminating lesser credits in favor of those with more weight.

How Should I Organize My Resume?

Just as in other professions, the entertainment industry has a resume standard. Hollywood insiders recognize a newcomer's resume in one of two ways: it may lack organization or it may not be stapled to the back of the headshot's upper left hand corner. The latter reflects laziness to the casting director. For the professional standard, try the template shown in Figure 5.1.

Nameplate

The top three inches of the resume forms the nameplate and should contain some essential information.

Name (or a stage name)
The union requires a unique name for membership. Check with SAG-AFTRA first. Even if you are not a union member now, you will be in the future, so best not to build a career around a name that will eventually have to be changed.

Union affiliation(s) and status
List membership in any of the unions, including SAG-AFTRA eligible, but do not lie. College honor societies do not count.

Height/weight
Be honest here as well; casting directors expect an actor to appear for an audition as advertised, not ten pounds heavier or two inches shorter.

Hair and eye color

Age range
List the age ranges you can comfortably play.

Vocal range (if any)
List this attribute only if you wish to advertise this talent.

Credits

Divide your resume credits into genres, such as film, television, web series or internet, music video, new media, and stage, generally in that order. Understandably in a film town such as Hollywood, stage ranks lowest even though at first it might include the bulk of one's credits. Many of our great actors have emerged from a stage background. But like you, they came to Hollywood to do film and television.

Television
Arrange these credits in three columns with your best projects first: (1) the project title, (2) billing of the role (Guest Star, Recurring, Co-Star, or otherwise), and (3) the network or production company. Place in parenthesis the name of any celebrity name connected to the project as a director, producer, writer, or actor.

Film
Also arrange in three columns: (1) the project title and the writer's name, (2) billing (Lead, Supporting, Featured, or Extra), and (3) the production company. Once again, list the director, producer or actors if noteworthy. Student, educational and industrial films count as well.

Web series or internet
Follow the same format.

Commercials
A commercials agent will most likely prefer you state only "Commercials provided upon request," on your resume. Why? Commercials represent a complicated system of residuals, holdovers, and conflicts. Commercial agents prefer to submit and field any concerns before they turn into a legal complication.

Music videos
Once again arrange in three columns: (1) the performer and song title, (2) the role played, and (3) the production company and director, if possible. Film directors, new and experienced, often direct music videos to showcase their talent.

Stage
Arrange in three columns: (1) play title, (2) venue and/or theater company, and (3) the role performed.

Training

List college degrees or actor training, whether voice, martial arts, or whatever, and the teachers with whom you studied.

Related Skills

List sports, stage skills, dialects, language proficiencies, or any other extraordinary skill.

What Should I NOT Put on My Resume?

Never provide personal and private information on a resume, such as a home address, a telephone number, a Social Security number, marital status, date of birth,

John Doe	SAG-AFTRA/AEA
Ht: 5'10" Wt: 195 Voice: Baritone Hair: Black / Eyes: Hazel	No Name Talent Agency Contact: Joan Doe (xxx) xxx-xxxx nonametalentagent@yahoo.com

Television   http://www.sag.org/iactor/JohnDoe

Who's Your Daddy?	Principal	Fox Television
Untold Stories from the ER	Principal	TLC-TV / GRB
Entertainment		
Seventh Heaven	Day Player	Wamer Bros TV
Detroit Central	Principal	TKS Productions
Mike Hammer	Featured	CBS - Dir: Xxx Xxxxx

Film

Whiskey Neat	Supporting	Lane City Films (Dir.
Le Petomane (Film Festival Winner)	Day Player	Hero Films
The Method (writer: Xxxx Xxxxx)	Featured	NYC Light & Noise
Americathon	Day Player	Lorimar Films
That Damned Thing	Principal	Lovecraft Film
Productions		

(Commercials provided upon request)

Internet

Your Webisode	Principal	A New
Production Co.		

Music Video

Nelly – *N' Day Say*	Roman Gladiator	HSI Prods.
The Click Five – *Just the Girl*	School Teacher	DNA, Inc.

Stage

The Producers	Roger DeBris
Your Local College	
As You Like It	Duke Frederick
King Richard III	Cardinal Bourchier
Macbeth	Macduff
Hollywood Shakespeare Company	

Related Skills: Horseback Riding – Snow & Water Skiing – Stage Pratfalls & Combat
Accents: British/Australian/German/Southern/Russian/Scottish/Irish/Italian/Yiddish

Training: BA/Theatre – Your University Cold Reading – Xxxxx Xxxxxxxxx Voice –
Xxxxxx Xxxxx Stage Combat Training – Xxxxxxx Xxxxxxx Xxxxxxx

FIGURE 5.1 Sample Resume

or even an exact age. Cultivate a sense of mystery. If represented, use your agent's phone number or a number used exclusively for professional work, not your personal number. The same goes for your email address. Avoid curriculum vitae or corporate styled subheadings, such as "Career Objectives" and "Salary Requirements." Technical or directing credits should be kept to a separate resume specific to that purpose.

Do All Actors Lie or Exaggerate On their Resume?

Actors do pad their resume; dropping a name, listing a canceled production, elevating a role, or even switching productions and venues. But, true working actors do not need to lie. They have the credits. Novice actors without serious credits need to fill that void, but they take a risk when inventing roles for themselves. Consider this example supplied by Academy Award-winning actor Michael Caine.

> I wrote down as part of my experience that I had played George in *George and Margaret*. I was summoned to an audition, and when I walked into the theater the first thing the producer said to me was, "It says here that you played George in *George and Margaret*?" "So, I did," I replied. "You are a bloody liar all right," roared the producer, "or you would know that the plot of that play centers on the fact that the entire cast spends the whole duration of the play waiting for George and Margaret to turn up, and they never do!"
>
> **CAINE**, *What's It All About*, 88

Inside Hollywood beats a small-town heart. Padding a resume can eventually lead to an embarrassment. Casting directors recognize past projects, especially if they cast them. Better to list high school, college, or community theater credits, dress them up a bit, and then systematically replace them with each new credit even if only a student film or nonunion project. Eventually, you will accumulate enough union credits to replace them all.

How Should I Format and Reproduce My Resume?

Since a resume attaches to the back of an 8 × 10 headshot, format your resume to exactly fit an 8 × 10 rectangle even though printed on standard 8.5 × 11 paper. Simply trim to fit. Not doing so will appear unprofessional. Xerox copies will suffice, but always treat a resume as a work in progress. Update it conscientiously as a Word file and then print copies as needed. Some even print directly on the back of the headshot, saving paper, staples, and time.

Photo Postcards

Occasionally actors may wish to send announcements regarding an upcoming television role, stage appearance, or film release, especially to casting directors who have previously auditioned them. Most casting directors, but not all, appreciate receiving updates on an actor's work, if they are known to them, as do some producers, directors, and other actors. Working actors often mail out photo postcards, which photo reproduction services can print at a bulk rate with a headshot on one side and the announcement on the other. Add the cost of postage and labels and the expense can mount, but as in all advertising, the residual effect over time may lead to more auditions and more work.

Photo Business Cards

Hollywood's small-town ethos means busy actors will find ample opportunity to network or make important contacts. Though not a necessity, some actors find it convenient to carry business cards with their headshot, but business-minded actors usually keep a headshot or two in their car.

Actor's Reel

Every actor, whether dramatic, comedic, stunt, motion capture, or voice-over needs an actor's demo reel. The term *actor's reel,* now a misnomer, initially referred to the actual metal reel on which actors long ago spliced clips of their best scenes to show to producers and casting directors to demonstrate the range of their work. The digital age has transformed that metal reel into a DVD or a digital file. Today's digital actor's reels can be easily reproduced, uploaded, and transported. Casting directors often request them in their breakdowns. The actor's dilemma lies in collecting those clips.

How So I Get Clips of My Work?

Nonunion projects often specify "deferred pay" and lure actors with the promise of "copy, credit, and meals." But, securing that "copy" can be problematic. Student film makers graduate and move on. Some projects are filmed on a whim and a prayer. Production companies come and go, move, or warehouse a project. They ultimately have no real requirement to provide talent with a copy of any finished product. All too often an actor must beg, steal, borrow, or buy their copy in order to secure documentation of their work. Always record any television project when it airs. Film projects will eventually appear as DVDs or downloads, but not for some time. Music videos can generally be downloaded online. Student films or industrial/

educational projects may be more difficult. Videotape must first be transferred to a digital file. Commercials, though, do offer a challenge as actors rarely have advance knowledge of a commercial's airing. Actors must contact the production company personally to obtain a copy of the commercial, often for a fee. All these clips should then be edited down to a three-minute showcase of your talents.

What If I Have No Clips?

Actors starting out who may not have any footage to use must create their own. With the help of some actor friends, simply film three short scenes and edit them into two- to three-minute montages using any of the media editing software programs available. Do not worry about plot, continuity, or narration. Scenes should focus on your acting ability alone. Avoid gratuitous violence or sexual content. Remember to add a few seconds of your headshot, name, website, and contact information at the beginning. If you lack the technical expertise to accomplish any of this, a professional videography or editing service can help.

PERSONAL WEBSITE

The twenty-first century has already seen cyberspace create virtual explorers of us all, pioneering new domains and establishing new digital communities, while homesteading with personal websites or "spaces." Like any other small business, actors need a personal website in which they can display their promotional materials easily and cheaply to prospective clients, and linked to digital resumes and social media sites. Some production companies actually provide links on their film website for each cast member's personal website where all forms of self-promotion are possible, easily changed, updated, or deleted if need be, providing a twenty-four-hour, 365-days-a-year product showroom. Personal websites should be simple and straightforward.

How Do I Establish a Personal Website?

Actors have a variety of options beyond Facebook and YouTube. First one must register a domain name, preferably your professional name. Many online services register domains. Once registered, you will need an account with a web host before you can begin designing your personal space.

1   Most electronic casting services offer a personalized web page as an incentive for membership. Options are usually limited unless one pays additional fees.

2   Several online services such as GoDaddy or WordPress allow the client to "build their own" website, giving the user a variety of options and tools from which to choose, but often requiring maintenance fees on the service's server.

3   For the most individualistic, a website designer can not only customize your website but also maintain it, though additional fees will apply for any updating.

4   Web creation software such as Dreamweaver is a powerful tool to build, maintain and update your own website', but generally these require some tutoring to learn how to use them.

A personal website should be simple and straightforward. Utilizing Google Analytics provides important data on your website users. Whether you wish to use a service or build your own, if you build it, they will come.

SOCIAL MEDIA

For an actor, social media as a marketing tool has become obligatory from all quarters. Talent agents want actors who have an online "presence." Casting directors care more about the number of "likes" or "followers," as a reflection of your casting marketability. Producers just want you to publicize their project. The social media analytics company MVPindex, publishes a weekly Top Actors chart that ranks the most popular actors on Facebook, Instagram, Twitter, YouTube and Google Plus, based on a blend of social engagement on the platforms along with weekly additions of followers/subscribers.

What Social Media Sites Should I Use for My Career?

For a beginning actor, social media represents a place to build a professional brand first by joining social media sites of trade publications, electronic casting sites, casting directors, showrunners, and other industry forums that will keep you informed and begin to establish name recognition and industry relationships. Follow the actors, musicians, directors, and producers that you admire. Opportunities for auditions and industry events may be announced. Solicit advice and help. Posting your own content then begins to personalize your brand. Keep your online profiles consistent, using the same headshot and bio, and then link them. Prioritize quality over quantity, and keep it authentic, remembering that the internet is forever and postings should be planned, strategic, and interesting. Only show what you want the public to see and target your demographics if possible. Give them a story, a journey, an insider's view, a peek behind the curtain, and ask yourself intermittently, "Why should someone follow me?"

IMDb (Internet Movie Database)

Any actor who has worked a union project will find themselves already listed in this comprehensive database of film and television projects with their own short biography and a full filmography. Now owned by Amazon, IMDb's popularity grew as a free service to look up the profiles of Hollywood contacts in order to determine their credibility. IMDb Pro, a paid subscription service, now allows an actor to add their professional contact information as well as a full resume. Without the paid subscription, actors can only make correction requests to their own profile. Some controversy still surrounds the website's policy to post an actor's age. California passed legislation to force the website to remove an actor's age upon request, but it has been enjoined by a federal court and still awaits final adjudication.

YouTube

Most actors post their reel to YouTube. But, unless you have a license for your film clips, you may receive a "takedown notice." The Digital Millennium Copyright Act that Congress passed in 1998 allows a website host to take down your clip if it receives notice that it contains copyrighted material. Unfortunately, being paid to act in a piece does not give you a license to use it publicly. But, you can post it privately and provide others the password. Perhaps more importantly for an actor, YouTube provides a space or "channel" to post your own original content. More than one actor, notably Lena Dunham, has found success by first becoming a YouTube "star" (someone who creates original programming that builds a dedicated online following supported by the number of likes and followers). Whether an original idea or just recreating famous film scenes, a YouTube channel can be monetized and may represent a substantial monthly income for those with an established following. Most recently, YouTube Space LA opened a 41,000-square foot production facility in Playa Vista with state-of-the-art production resources, advanced workshops, and classes for qualified creators. (Check out their online orientation, *Unlock the Space*.) In addition, Amazon Video Direct and Vimeo provide another self-service platform where anyone can upload an original video and make money.

Facebook

Most actors probably already have a Facebook page. If so, create a new one exclusively for your professional career to keep your casual, social life separate from your professional life. You can join any of the many actors' groups that populate this site.

You can create a fan page by uploading your reel, your headshots, your resume, a link to your website, and other social media accounts. Upload the YouTube videos you create or broadcast live interactive streaming video. Share news and professional updates to incite conversations with friends, fans, and family that others will share or repost, thus increasing your number of followers. Post sparsely, though, as followers may soon become annoyed with constant emails announcing your new post.

Twitter

This communications medium has disrupted governments, fed revolutions, and eviscerated personalities. For an actor, Twitter serves more humble purpose, by providing communication with other members of the industry and your fan base allowing 280 characters per post. Joining Twitter feeds for trade publications, electronic casting sites, and other industry forums will keep you informed. Actors post links to projects, changes to their life, and comments related to their career, usually strategically linked to the project's own marketing campaign as they gain followers to their feed.

Instagram

This picture posting app provides an obvious venue for publicity pics of all kinds, professional or otherwise, but if publicizing a project, make certain you have permission before you run afoul of your employer for posting confidential information or photos. When posting, use hashtags to encourage responses and avoid long or intrusive captions. Savvy actors have discovered Instagram as a tool to connect with established professional photographers for future headshots or website photos.

LinkedIn

Though not really a "social media" site for actors, LinkedIn provides actors with connections to other professionals such as writers, directors, technical professionals, and professional-specific forums that can provide advice and help with their career. Here, you can create your own actor's group on any specific current topic.

What Social Media Etiquette Should I Maintain?

Consider one's professional standard of etiquette on social media part of your personal brand. Perception trumps intent, and more than one actor has sullied an otherwise vibrant image by projecting a negative, combative, or argumentative persona. Building a brand takes considerable time and mere seconds to sully. Hollywood influencers stress the following:

- Manage your image. Keep it positive, and do not post anything you would not want to see on the front page of your newspaper.

- Never post when angry or inebriated, remembering that the internet is forever and even an actor can be fired for lewd or disrespectful content.

- Build followers by connecting with friends, family, and colleagues in your network and following other industry professionals. Then retweet, reply, react, and follow.

- Do not just post about yourself. Social media means engagement by soliciting questions, comments, posting interesting information, or commenting on other posts.

- Always remember that it is not you they "like" but the persona you project.

What Other Computer Software, Extensions, or Apps Will I Find Useful?

Speed Dial

This Google Chrome extension organizes all your social media websites on a single tab page for quick access.

LastPass

This password manager securely saves all your usernames and passwords, automatically logs into your sites, and syncs your passwords for quick access.

Google Analytics

This web analytics service tracks and reports website traffic and statistics related to reads, links, and reposts.

Buffer

This social media management app allows the user to write posts in advance, and then schedules each individual release, tracks the performance of the content, and manages all your accounts in one place.

Photoshop

Adobe's powerful image manipulator has become the graphic standard for raster graphic editing, but its hefty price tag makes it impractical for the humbler promotional needs of most actors. Adobe has recently rolled out a cheaper subscription service for those with simpler needs.

Paint.net

This free open source alternative to Photoshop provides a more powerful interface than Microsoft Paint but is not as complex as Photoshop.

Shutterstock

Offers royalty free images for licensing use in promotional materials.

Final Cut

This series of non-linear video editing software programs has become popular among independent filmmakers and offers a range of tools for editing film clips.

ScreenFlow

This screen casting and video editing software for the OS X operating system can capture and edit the audio and video from your iPhone quickly and professionally.

Lightworks

For actors on a budget, this award-winning program ranks highest among the many open source alternatives to Final Cut.

KnowEm

Automatically checks user names, domain names and trademarks to determine their availability across a wide selection of social media networks.

Basecamp

Most production companies use this project management software tool to organize and communicate information such as shooting locations, times and personnel for film projects.

MyHeadshots

Use this program to edit headshots for mobile devices.

ACTOR'S FORUM

It's really important that you get access to an online directory called the Call Sheet. Everybody who's legit, from casting directors to agents and managers, is usually in that book. *Backstage* publishes it, and I recommend that for any actor. Get to know people. If you know people socially who are working out here, get them on the phone and ask, "Do they know any agents looking for new actors to represent?" Ask questions. Don't be afraid. Do you know how many people fail because they're afraid to ask questions? Remember you're a product. Yes, we are individuals; yes, we want to think that we're unique. When I first moved here they said, "I'll sell you as a young Kevin Kline type." They put you in a box, and I found it important that you know who you are and what you can do and then be willing to go outside your comfort zone with what you can do and what you think you can do . . . I actually had a manager before I had an agent. Before I moved here, I exchanged emails with an actor who had moved here about a year before I did, and he said, "Hey, I'm interning in a casting office, and across the hall there's a manager who I intern for whatever time I have, and she can always use a hand. And in turn, she'll put you in her submissions." So, I met with her, and we hit it off instantly. She's a good friend to this day, and one of the women who worked in the casting office where I interned all these years later is now my theatrical agent.

MICHAEL GABIANO

Most actors don't just rely on their agent but also try to get breakdowns themselves. But for them, they look at age and cultural identity which are things voice-over actors don't have to worry about. There's a lot of good voice-over actors. I'm with an agency called SBV Talent, which is a very good voice-over agency. They also have a theatrical on-camera division, but this is a stand-alone voice-over division. There's a really good one called DPN Talent which used to be ICM. It was the voice-over component of ICM and then spun off into its own agency. So, there's a number of these voice-over agents. To get started, you don't necessarily need to have an agent, but obviously, if you wish to have any sort of career, you need an agent because the jobs are being disseminated to them. They set up the auditions. Sometimes you'll go into the agency to record it, but more often than not, you're expected to record it at home.

PETER LAVIN

In Hollywood, you have your managers, and you have your agents. I have both. I have an agent that works better for me for TV and film stuff. My manager works better for me on voice-over and motion capture. Because I've been in the world for so long and everybody knows me as the mocap man, I can call the studios up. I had agents call me and ask how to run a motion capture audition because they've never done it. They come to me. I think you could have an agent that does TV and film as long as you prep your agent with the right material. I've seen actors who have never done motion capture walk onto a set and are just horrible, and they're making a ton more money than I am because they either have a name or they have a really good agent who has tried to capitalize on it from the very beginning.

RICHARD DORTON

6 TALENT AGENTS AND PERSONAL MANAGERS

Being a star is an agent's dream, not an actor's

ROBERT DUVALL

ACTOR'S RESOURCES

Association of Talent Agents (ATA)
http://www.agentassociation.com
Website provides list of members and information on relevant California licensing and laws pertaining to talent agents.

SAG-AFTRA online
https://www.sagaftra.org/
Website provides:
- list of SAG-AFTRA franchised agents,
- Young Performer's Handbook,
- Personal Manager Code of Ethics and Conduct.
  (voluntary agreement between an actor and a personal manager)

Talent Manager's Association (TMA)
https://www.talentmanagers.org/
Website provides a Code of Ethics.

SAG-AFTRA Foundation
https://sagaftra.foundation/
Streamed or archived workshops, panel discussions, and interviews.

Why Do I Need a Talent Agent?

Most entertainment industry histories ascribe the emergence of the talent agent to the breakdown of the studio system in the 1950s, when actors became free agents and turned to attorneys to negotiate their contracts. But those histories ignore the contributions of William Morris, the German emigrant who in 1898 opened his vaudeville booking agency in New York. He represented clients such as W.C. Fields, Will Rodgers, and Al Jolson. Morris, recognized the potential of the "talkies," opened a satellite office in Los Angeles in 1927, and eventually became Hollywood's first super-agent. The Hollywood "studio system" had not taken root yet, and the more decentralized environment of the 1920s and 1930s created fertile ground for small time talent agents from vaudeville (Heyt, "Hidden Talent"). As the studios grew in power, actors were offered studio contracts, side-stepping agents who eventually became absorbed into the studio system as "scouts." The eventual collapse of that power structure once again presented agents with an opportunity.

Today, the William Morris Endeavor Agency still tops the list of Hollywood's mega-agencies that package multimillion-dollar deals involving actors, directors, and writers. Films and television have cemented in the minds of Americans the image of the Hollywood talent agent as a wheeling-dealing, ego-driven, type-A, control-freak who hobnobs with Hollywood moguls and makes or breaks an actor's career. While some agents may fit that stereotype to one degree or another, it falls far from the reality. Mega-agencies aside, most talent agents are mom and pop operations, who run small offices, tied to a world of electronic casting via the web, telephones, emails, and fax machines, with an ever-changing contract environment and little time for the so-called Hollywood social scene. They often rely upon actors as volunteers just to deal with the sheer volume of telephone calls, mail, headshots, and casting notices they process. But, without an agent, an actor stands little chance of building a career.

What Does a Talent Agent Do for an Actor?

The primary role of a talent agent is to procure employment for the talent under his or her representation through marketing, promotion, and submissions to casting directors and other industry contacts. They do so while networking with personal managers, following up with auditions, negotiating the best contract possible, processing those contracts, and advising their clients on the legal complexities of union regulations and production company requests. In their spare time, an agent may attend workshops and theater productions or showcases, always on the lookout for new, talented, fresh, faces to represent. For their efforts, an agent receives a union-capped 10 percent commission rate on their client's commissionable income as per Rule 16 (g) of the Screen Actors Guild Codified Agency Regulations (SAG-AFTRA, "1991").

Part den mother/father, part business partner, and part mentor, a talent agent provides a buffer, a filter, or liaison for the actor; acts as an advocate who markets, promotes, and even packages the actor's talents; and then serves as a mediator during contract negotiations. Some negotiations proceed smoothly; others not so much. An actor may choose to stay in the background, providing distance and deniability, or not. If successful, the agent then processes the contracts and shepherds the actor through its documentation. In fact, many bookings do not issue contracts until after the shoot. A good agent will secure a deal memo of some type, providing a guarantee as to the final terms of compensation.

The unions also provide sometimes complicated and legalistic contract guidelines to safeguard actors' rights. Talent agents must understand the complexities of these union requirements, and then when requests exceed contract terms, they intervene if warranted. When issues do arise on the set, the agent will act as an advocate. The agent protects and defends the actor for one important reason: the more the actor makes, the more the agent makes. But, an agent is not licensed to be an attorney, although many successful agents have degrees in entertainment law. On matters of contract law, an agent should refer the actor to an entertainment law attorney for counseling, if only to avoid any question of a conflict of interest.

IN THE BOX

As I sat talking to my talent agent, her ubiquitous phone rang, and as she answered I overheard a brief conversation in which an actor working on a film set had called to complain that he had been required to perform an action sequence that clearly fell within the realm of stunt work, despite the fact that he had not been hired for this. My agent instructed the actor to sit quietly and do nothing until she called back. She then dialed the number of the production company in question, identified herself as the actor's talent representative and asked to speak to the production manager. The conversation proceeded civilly but pointedly. The actor had been hired as a day player and had now been required to perform stunt work, which entitled him to an additional day's pay. The production manager's reply was noncommittal and hedging, at which time my agent pulled out the SAG-AFTRA Basic Codified Agreement and read him the specific requirement to which the production company was a signatory. They then quickly reached agreement on the additional compensation, at which time my agent called the actor on the set and instructed him to go back to work. The entire conversation took less than three minutes. My agent apologized to me and calmly continued our conversation. Less than inconvenienced, though, I had witnessed firsthand why an actor needs a knowledgeable talent agent to represent his or her interests in this competitive business.

Must an Actor Have a Talent Agent to Submit?

An actor may self-submit for any project. But, union signatory producers use talent agents as a screening process to separate professional actors from the wannabees. Producers submit their breakdowns exclusively to licensed agents who immediately submit appropriate clients. Unrepresented actors must learn of pending union projects from the trades or word of mouth, often long after completion of primary casting. For the most part, internet casting services post mostly nonunion projects that pay little or nothing. Union projects occasionally appear, but only because the casting director needs to trawl a broader ocean. Most television and commercial casting occurs quickly. But whether for the sake of credibility or to facilitate the process, an actor commonly needs a licensed agent to submit them in time to a SAG-AFTRA signatory project.

What is the Difference Between a Talent Agent and a Personal Manager?

A personal manager provides an actor with a variety of services once provided by a talent agent, such as career advice, promotion through industry contacts, networking, and mentoring. The agent of yore no longer exists in this more technological market. Managers offer a more objective and personal approach to career building. To that end, they normally represent fewer clients. Their personal contacts and experience inside the industry may provide them an insider's advantage with insight and access to offices that agents cannot reach. But, managers have their limitations and differences.

- Unlike agents, managers are not licensed or bonded by the state of California. As such, while managers may build relationships in the entertainment industry, they may not solicit employment or enter into contractual negotiations on behalf of an actor. That, only a licensed and bonded agent may do (California Department of Industrial Relations, "Laws").

- SAG-AFTRA caps talent agent commission rates at 10 percent. No such restriction exists for managers who can charge as much as a 25 percent commission rate.

- The Talent Agencies Act of 1978 (TAA) prohibits talent agencies from any investment in production companies. Managers are not prohibited from doing so, and often enter into investment deals with the very productions employing their clients, opening the door to a variety of opportunities and potential conflicts of interest (Zelenski, "Talent Agents," 983–984).

How Do I Know a Manager or Management Company is Legitimate?

Many actors succeed without the services of a personal manager. Others have found them indispensable. An actor must decide for themselves whether the benefit to their career offsets the added cost of a manager. If considering such a relationship, actors should research a potential manager or management company as they would any other professional service to make an informed decision as to the depth of the manager's experience in Hollywood, the number of clients the manager represents, his or her office support system, and how much effort will be directed to the actor's career. The Los Angeles Better Business Bureau, the Association of Talent Agents (ATA), and the California Division of Labor Standard Enforcement all offer the actor assistance by providing information on incidents of complaint, current violations, and prosecutions. Often just a message on an actors' forum such as *Backstage.com* yields sufficient positive or negative feedback. In addition, SAG-AFTRA also suggests the following criteria for a personal manager contract:

- affiliation with SAG-AFTRA,

- signatory to SAG-AFTRA's Personal Manager Code of Ethics and Conduct which sets basic protections for the actor (SAG-AFTRA, *Personal Manager Code*),

- no advance fees required for representation,

- a firm timeline for the disbursement of the actor's funds,

- no requirement for the actor to contract with third-party businesses, such as photographers or acting teachers,

- a dispute resolution clause that avoids costly court fees,

- delineates the working relationship with an agent,

- caps commissions at 10 to 15 percent, and

- contains no self-renewing provisions.

Are There Different Kinds of Talent Agents?

Talent agents for actors in Hollywood fall into two categories: theatrical (film, television, stage) and commercial. An agent may specialize in one, or the other, or both, or offer to represent an actor in one, or the other, or both. Some actors may prefer to engage an agent to represent them in one, or the other, preferring to have two agents hustling their talent. Some talent agents may require dual representation as a condition to signing an actor. Some may handle only voice-over actors or stunt actors. Still others represent only children, teenagers, or models. An agency may also have a literary department that handles writers or agents that specialize in representing directors. The largest agencies, such as William Morris, Creative Artists (CAA), United Talent (UTA), and International Creative Management (ICM), employ a small army of agents, exclusively representing only star players and covering every base of the creative process. This range of clients provides them with the ability to package a project in-house from soup to nuts: the writers, the directors, and the actors. At the other end of the spectrum stand the mom and pop agencies that, in order to make ends meet, must represent all categories of actors.

How Do You Become a Talent Agent?

A talent agent in the state of California must be both licensed and bonded. A prospective agent must make written application to the California Labor Commission, providing full disclosure of the name and address of all owners, business partners or corporate entities; their financial interests; prior employment history; the address where business will be conducted; and two sets of fingerprints and affidavits from two reputable residents testifying to the applicant's "good moral character." Finally, the applicant must post a surety bond of $50,000, placed in a trust account. This protects the actor against the potential of fraud since agents often process an actor's salary and withhold taxes as well as their commissions before disbursing the remainder.

Upon receipt, the commission conducts an investigation into the character of the applicant and the proposed business premises, reserving the right to refuse licensing if an artist's "health, safety, or welfare" could be jeopardized by the location. As a condition of licensing, the applicant must agree to:

- file a schedule of fees to be charged and collected in the conduct of their business;
- file all contracts with the Labor Commission;
- disburse all funds due an artist within thirty days;
- abide by state Dispute Resolution Rules; and
- agree to never divide fees with the actor's employer.

Additional conditions apply when seeking employment for minors (California Department of Industrial Relations, "Laws Relating").

What is Meant By a Union Franchised Talent Agent?

Historically, the role of a talent agent has provided a lucrative environment for questionable business practices, such as requiring fees for photographs or other services as a condition of representation, promoting bait and switch scams, or receiving kickbacks from photographers. In 1978, California lawmakers enacted the TAA to prevent such abuses. In addition, SAG-AFTRA franchises talent agencies, requiring them to sign a union franchise agreement that among other things:

- requires them to maintain a California business license,
- caps their commissions at 10 percent of an actor's income above scale (minimum wage), excluding reimbursements or late penalties,
- prohibits ownership by production companies or investment in productions as a conflict of interest and a breach of agent independence, and
- establishes the fiduciary responsibilities of the agent to act in the best interests of the actor at all times.

(Shope, "The Final Cut," 128)

The agency must also undergo a union inspection to confirm (1) it consists of at least two rooms, a reception area and office, or has a built-in room divider, (2) located in a commercial office building space used for business purposes and not for residential use, (3) with the agency name clearly posted on the building's directory, open and available during reasonable business operating hours, and (4) does not employ individuals or exist in a location that would endanger the health and safety of the actor (SAG-AFTRA, "16 (g) Instructions").

Are All Talent Agents SAG-AFTRA Franchised?

For over sixty years, the union has effectively enforced its standards by requiring that no union talent could legitimately conduct business with a talent agent, who had not agreed to the above references requirements and limitations set out in the 1939 master franchise agreement negotiated between the union and the agents' trade union, the ATA. This agreement expired in 2002, and during negotiations ATA proposed amending Rule 16 (g) to relax the rules governing ownership of an agency and allow investment in or part ownership by production companies. SAG conducted a referendum of its members, who overwhelmingly rejected the proposal, effectively rendering the 1939 agreement and Rule 16 (g) null and void. Anticipating this eventuality, ATA had already drafted their own general services contract (GSA) that incorporated these changes that had been preapproved by the California Labor Commissioner. This set up a conflict with SAG, forcing actors to choose between their agent and their union. Dozens of dissident talent agencies led by William Morris and other industry leaders surrendered their SAG franchises, and formed a new guild, the National Association of Talent Representatives (NATR).

Today, talent agencies have no legal obligation to abide by Rule 16 (g), though many continue to do so through their franchise agreement. SAG-AFTRA has since temporarily suspended enforcement against agencies that have surrendered their franchise in order to not disrupt ongoing talent agent/actor relationships. But, these agencies may require the actor to sign a GSA (see Appendix C) which has significant deviations from the union approved agreement (see Appendix C) and may not be used for AFTRA related work.

What is the Difference Between a SAG-AFTRA Agency Contract and a GSA?

Both the SAG-AFTRA contract and the GSA have approval from the Labor Commissioner, but the GSA is written much more broadly and binds the artist more comprehensively. The union strongly encourages its members to resist signing a GSA without first bringing it to the union for approval, and/or negotiating terms more beneficial to the artist. For instance, an actor may carve out some types of employment or certain pre-existing projects from the agreement, or depending upon the actor's track record, negotiate better commission terms. In general, the following differences may be noted:

Commission Rates

SAG-AFTRA caps a talent agent's commission at 10 percent above scale across the board on all applicable income. For the moment talent agencies using the GSA have limited their commission also to 10 percent, but unlike New York which caps commissions at 10 percent, California allows commissions to exceed 20 percent.

Commissionable Income

SAG-AFTRA sets a minimum wage (scale) for all actors in all television projects. Commissions may only be paid on amounts over and above this minimum wage, and the union restricts commissions on many other residual payments. A GSA considers all of the actor's earned income commissionable, including all travel and living expenses, as well as reimbursements for travel and mileage, even though this may have been paid upfront from previously commissionable earned income.

Check Authorization

An actor usually signs an authorization form that permits his or her wages to be sent directly to a talent agent, who checks on its accuracy and inclusion of issues, such as missing meal penalties, turnaround fees, overtime, and other deal points. The agent then deducts the applicable commission and disburses the remaining funds to the artist within thirty days. When an actor needs funds immediately, this arrangement may be revoked by the actor at any time under a SAG-AFTRA contract. Under a GSA, these check authorizations remain irrevocable.

Scope of Representation

SAG-AFTRA has always supported an actor's right to have different agents for commercial and theatrical representation, as well as different agents in different local jurisdictions and different agents for other fields, such as writing, directing, or music performance. The union limits an agency's representation to a fifty-mile radius, except in Los Angeles, which extends its jurisdiction throughout the state of California. This limit allows an actor to have different agents in different cities. A GSA revokes this limitation and stipulates worldwide exclusive representation for all entertainment fields.

Term of Contract

SAG-AFTRA restricts initial contracts with a talent agent to a one-year term as a reasonable exit door for an artist/agent relationship. In addition, artists may break a contract if the agent has not procured employment within any four-month period. Most current GSAs maintain the same conditions, but state law allows up to seven years, and more successful actors may find themselves retroactively contracted for longer terms.

Fiduciary Responsibilities

Nowhere in the GSA appears the word "fiduciary." As such, the actor's interests could become secondary to the agent if it benefited the agency's ownership interests or production investments. Information about perspective roles or auditions could be withheld from the actor, false or misleading advice given, or outright deception might occur. A SAG-AFTRA contract prohibits this behavior, and if it did occur, the union would represent the actor in a breach of fiduciary duty claim. Under a GSA, an actor still has the right to bring such a claim as state law still protects actor's fiduciary rights under the TAA, but the union cannot assist in these matters and actors may not be aware that their best interests are not being pursued (Shope, "The Final Cut," 139–141).

Conflict Resolution

In the event of a conflict, SAG-AFTRA provides binding arbitration for the dispute, but agencies using the GSA submit its members' conflicts to the California Labor Commission for declaration, where the actor may find themselves in an inferior bargaining position. The union has no legal standing in such instances (SAG-AFTRA, *Your Relationship*).

Why Would an Actor Sign a GSA?

The GSA clearly attempts to redefine the artist/agent relationship. Agencies affiliated with ATA and NATR, such as the William Morris Agency, CAA, and ICM, have surrendered their SAG franchises and now require actors to sign the GSA. Together these top agencies represent the A-list celebrities that earn them large commissions and can arguably make or break an actor's career. These agencies gambled on actors deciding that a bad contract was better than finding new representation. Smaller agencies use the GSA when they sign actors just starting in the business who believe it is the only way to obtain representation (Shope, "The Final Cut," 141). Ironically, the TAA still attempts to preserve the traditional actor/

agent relationship but even it has been under attack, as a consortium of personal managers have, so far unsuccessfully, challenged its restrictions in court. But, assuming one is not an A-lister, new actors to Hollywood should have little trouble finding a SAG-AFTRA franchised agent that will sign them.

How Do I Find a Licensed Talent Agent?

An actor does not find a talent agent, the talent agent finds the actor, and arguably the best agent is not the one you solicit, but the one that seeks you out. Most agents represent a stable of clients, perhaps a dozen in each age, gender, and ethnic category. If an opening occurs, a talent agent may solicit actors for representation. They may respond to an actor's direct solicitation for representation or attend showcases and workshops looking for interesting faces. In the old days, the 1980s, talent agents explored Hollywood's considerable talent showcases, such as "comedy houses" or "music rooms". Today's agents can preview an actor's reel in the privacy of a den, but one must first get their attention. Veteran actors recommend the following three strategies:

The Drop

Potentially the most effective approach, but also the most expensive, is when an actor mails a headshot, resume, and possibly an actor's reel to every talent agent in Los Angeles that meets their criteria. Care should be taken to separate out agents who represent only children or other categories out of your expertise. SAG-AFTRA's online portal provides a list of franchised talent agencies and those affiliated with ATA and NATR. The online casting service, NowCasting, provides online label-formatted downloads of current names and addresses of all legitimate licensed California talent agents. Bookstores and magazine kiosks also sell complete packets of preprinted labels, though their accuracy is hard to verify. Next, photos and resumes must be assembled into labeled 9 × 12 envelopes with a well written cover letter requesting a meeting, and then "dropped" into the mail. The odds favor a 10 percent response rate. Telephone follow-up calls are an acceptable practice.

Showcase

Audition for a good theater company, showroom, or comedy venue, and when performing, send invitations to those talent agents with whom you have become acquainted. The role should be substantial, not the second spear holder in *Julius Caesar*. If interested, a talent agent will make contact and offer to observe a performance. Proper etiquette means offering complimentary tickets, usually for two. Expect the agent to come backstage after the performance. If the agent does not do this, consider it a bad sign. You will know quickly whether the talent agent has any interest. He or she may proffer a business card and request a phone call to set up an appointment. The rest will be up to the actor.

Referral

Actors have little to offer other actors, other than experiential advice, but the act of referral represents one exception. An actor may ethically recommend another actor to their talent agent. But, always be mindful of their integrity, as they do so with great discretion.

What Should I Expect When I Meet with a Talent Agent?

Expect to be evaluated, appraised, assessed, and universally assayed on various scales pertaining to potential productivity. A talent agent must believe that you will make them money. The enthusiasm with which the agent represents the actor directly relates to the degree to which the agent perceives the actor to be a "hot property." Prior to the meeting, have your headshot, resume, social media and/or website set up and ready to be studied. Most mentors advise actors to just be themselves during the meeting, admittedly a simplistic piece of advice. Actors must be everything and anything. True, authenticity counts, but so do professionalism, poise, and confidence, the polish that convinces an agent that you can hold your own in a casting director's office. The agent may ask questions about training, experience, resume credits, and personal interests. They look for versatility. The agent will also ask to see a memorized monologue, perhaps two contrasting pieces, which, anyone graduating from a college theater arts program should have prepared long ago. But, be prepared to perform in a busy office full of interruptions and phones ringing.

After a face-to-face meeting, potentially several, if the actor meets the agent's criteria, he or she will be offered a contract for representation for a period of one year with a four-month probationary period. If the agent does not procure employment within that period, the actor or the agent may cancel the contract.

How Do Talent Agents and Personal Managers Work Together?

Talent agents and personal managers work together in this industry every day. A manager carefully scrutinizes the daily breakdowns and requests submissions to the agent on behalf of the actor. A manager coordinates promotional materials based on the agent's needs, pursues personal contacts and shares this information with the agent. Daily communication between these two team members optimizes an actor's visibility. This all occurs to the benefit of the actor, but conflicts can arise:

Double Submissions

Without careful coordination, the double submission of the actor for the same role occurs, a pet peeve of casting directors who often receive hundreds of submissions per day.

Inequity in Commission

Talent agents are often reluctant to cooperate with personal managers who sometimes demand a higher commission rate than the 10 percent mandated talent by SAG-AFTRA. They cite their business license as the primary authority of employment, and truly, an actor can ill afford to lose a talent agent.

Stepping on Toes

While a personal manager can provide an essential service to an actor's team by making follow-up calls after auditions, forming initial contacts, or acting as a liaison on behalf of the actor, the talent agent must set the ground rules to avoid miscommunications and territorial blunders. Giving mixed signals can quickly end a casting discussion.

What Scams Should I Watch Out For?

Most talent agency scams in Hollywood involve money and the exploitation of young naïve actors or their parents, using a familiar pitch. You or your child has "raw talent." With the right "package" he or she could be a "star." The "package" frequently involves a headshot session with a "top photographer," acting lessons with a "top acting teacher," a "guarantee" of a meeting with "top casting directors," and representation by their talent company for the hundreds of auditions they will set up. The cost of this "package" usually runs into the thousands of dollars. What makes this scam legal is that the talent agency usually follows through with photographs, acting lessons, and a casting audition, all of which one could have accomplished for considerably less money than paid, and, of course, will be rendered useless when the talent agency disappears or fails to produce any auditions.

These scam artists often advertise in mass media for some variation of a "talent search" or "casting search," usually for some type of Hollywood talent showcase, promising hundreds of Hollywood casting directors will be in attendance. Here are some warning signs.

1 **Talent scouts who will make you or your child a "star."** You have been "selected," implying credibility where none exists. You may have innocently participated in a talent contest. They may promise immediate work, extoll the benefits of their representation, guarantee work, or a refund, or promise large salaries, but only if you act now (Federal Trade Commission, *Look Out for Modeling Scams*).

2 **Personal managers who promise employment**. Only licensed talent agents in the state of California may solicit theatrical employment for an actor. Personal managers may advise and network for the actor, but may not enter into contractual negotiations.

3 **Talent agents who charge advance fees for services or required classes.** Whether called "registration," "consultation," or "administrative" fees, a scam by any other name would smell the same. Legitimate talent agents earn their income strictly through commissions, not from fees for photographs and career counseling. Those who charge "advance fees" are not a talent agency but a service, neither licensed, nor SAG-AFTRA franchised. State law allows the actor ten days after signing such a contract to cancel. Extra casting services prove the exception as they may charge an administrative fee for processing your information into their database because they actually do extra casting for real production companies.

4 **Acting schools that promise employment**. Legitimate modeling and acting schools earn income by charging fees for instruction just as talent agents charge a commission—but neither should be doing both. This is where the conflict of interest lies (Los Angeles Better Business Bureau, "Los Angeles Modeling").

5 **Anyone who prefers to work without a contract**. Though legal, verbal agreements often end in conflict, are heavily litigated, and are expensive to the loser.

6 **Any acting/modeling contract requiring the performer to "pay-to-play."** An actor may need better photos or a class in acting technique, but other than providing a referral, an agent may not require an actor to purchase those services from a specific source without violating California state law. In the past, too many unscrupulous agents padded their income by receiving kickbacks from the photographer or acting teacher to whom they referred the actor.

Be aware that these scam agencies often use names similar to well-known legitimate talent agencies, drop the names of celebrity clients or studios such as

Disney, and dangle the glittery promise of fame and success with flattery and ego massages. Their offices look legitimate with a lobby filled with photos of famous actors and a waiting room filled with gullible wanabees. But in the end, the high-pressure sales pitch comes for "screen tests" or a "photo book," and the demand for money upfront. If you find yourself in one of these situations, stop, take a deep breath, and remember that you came to Hollywood to be paid to act, not the other way around.

All in all, talent agents and personal managers have a symbiotic relationship with actors and provide a very important service. There are celebrity stories rife with examples of corrupt and fraudulent agents and managers, but most are hard-working and sincere in their enthusiasm towards their clients. Finding ones that are honest, straightforward, and effective can be a challenge, but once you are under representation, doors will begin to open and your legitimacy will increase. Success may still not be assured, but you will finally be a true player in the industry.

ACTOR'S FORUM

I had done some nonunion film work on the East Coast but was mostly an Equity actor. I really wanted to join SAG, but at one point in 2004, the fee was astronomical for me. I did not have that kind of money. Around 2005/2006 SAG announced that they were doubling the initiation fee from $600 to $1,200 to join. I said, "I better do this." So, I scraped up the cash as I belong to a sister union. I went down to Wilshire and filled out the paperwork. Within a month I got a call to audition for an industrial film which paid a nice amount of money for a SAG industrial film, and it was literally across the street. I literally went out my front door, waited at the crosswalk, and walked into my audition. I booked that immediately, and that was my first SAG job. So, my initiation fee, which was about to double, had paid for itself.

MICHAEL GABIANO

They're working hard to negotiate vocal stress protections. I don't believe they're really there yet. I think you just have to protect yourself. A lot of the voice-over work that I do is film, television, and ADR. For every piece of film and TV show they only really record the principals. All the other voices need to be recreated. That's a lot of union work for a lot of actors. Having the facility for accents, facility for different ages, facility for improv, will allow you to break into group ADR and voice-replacement. It was a lucky break that I booked a commercial. It was a four-day shoot. It paid well; it ran well. And that's how I got into the union. . . . The contracts obviously are crucial, especially to voice-over actors, because once you've laid it down, they can try to cheat and reuse the material in different projects. So for example, you're working on a movie that has battle sequences, and you're creating the sounds of those battle sequences, the human sounds of those battle sequences. Well, there's a lot of movies with battle sequences. You don't want them to be able to use that material on something else without compensating you. The union is very good at protecting the rights of you as an artist and your work not being used without compensation.

PETER LAVIN

I got into the union back East when I was in DC before I came here. Because of all the movies that came to town, I earned my stripes by getting my vouchers and getting to do extra work and doing government films. All of those government agencies do corporate films and do commercials and stuff, so I earned my SAG card pretty easily and then moved here. It's really hard here. Extras are treated. . . . the rate is so bad. There are thousands of actors here. Prepping to come here what do you need? You need a union card. . . . The mocap studios hire union and nonunion, so when you have thousands of new actors everyday who want to break in to the business, I will get undercut so fast. People will work for $300 a day, and that just hurts us all.

RICHARD DORTON

7 THE UNIONS

I remember being amazed that actors had a union. I thought only coal miners had unions, or guys that worked in automobile plants. That's an indication of how naïve I was.

PETER FALK, Murray, *AV Club*

ACTOR'S RESOURCES

The Performing Arts "Sister" Unions

Screen Actors Guild (SAG/AFTRA)

National Headquarters

5757 Wilshire Blvd.

Los Angeles, CA 90036–3600

(323) 954–1600 (main switchboard)

(323) 549–6648 For Deaf Performers Only: TTY/TTD

(800) SAG–0767 (outside Los Angeles)

Actor's Equity Association (AEA)

The Western Region
LOS ANGELES
5757 Wilshire Boulevard,
Suite One
Los Angeles, California 90036
(323) 634–1750

National Headquarters
NEW YORK
165 West 46th Street

New York, NY 10036
(212) 869–8530

American Guild of Variety Artists (AGVA)

National Office
184 Fifth Ave., 6th Fl.
New York, New York 10010
(212) 675–1003

West Coast Office:
11712 Moorpark Street, Suite 110
Studio City, CA 91604
(818) 508–9984

(212) 633–0097 Fax   (818) 508–3029 Fax
agva@agvausa.org   agvawest@earthlink.net
agvany@aol.com

American Guild of Musical Artists (AGMA)
National Office
1430 Broadway, 14th Floor
New York, NY 10018
Phone: (212) 265.3687
Fax: (212) 262.9088

Hollywood's "Golden Age" of film had its casualties. Film legend Lillian Gish suffered frostbite during the filming of *Way Down East* (1920); Buster Keaton broke his neck during the railroad water-tank scene in *Sherlock Jr.* (1928); while filming *Frankenstein* (1931), Boris Karloff worked for twenty-five hours straight in his heavy costume and makeup. Then, producers could tell actors who to marry, when they could get pregnant, what professional names they must use, and even what morals and political opinions they could hold. History has well documented the studio antics of the 1950s and 1960s involving alcohol and pharmaceuticals (Hutchinson, "The silent-era"). In the early years of silent movie making, actors worked without a net, often required to do their own stunts at minimal wages in sometimes harsh conditions and long hours with fame one's only security blanket. Because of those abuses Boris Karloff used his fame as a founding member and avid recruiter for the Screen Actors Guild in 1933.

One can hardly comprehend a film and television industry in which unions did not exist. In a truly free market, given the rules of supply and demand, actors would without a doubt be paying to perform without regard to personal safety or privacy rights. Why—because it is a business. The union stands as a buffer to those impulses, and nothing provides professional validation more than union membership. But in most working trades, professional status means only joining one union. If pursuing a career as an electrician, one joins the International Brotherhood of Electrical Workers; a miner, the United Mine Workers of America, and so on. Prior to 2012, actors needed to join not one, but three separate unions to pursue an acting career and four if also a variety artist, creating a tangle of jurisdiction, contracts, dues and residuals. The merger of the Screen Actors Guild (SAG) and the American Federation of Television and Radio Artists (AFTRA) has greatly benefited actors with increased negotiating power, one contract structure and one set of semiannual dues to pay.

A Brief History

As the financial optimism of the 1880s gave way to the working-class angst of the 1890s, the turn of the century saw the birth of the worker's union movement. Amid these frequent "rebellions," several attempts to form a stage actors' union failed, until on May 26, 1913, 112 performers gathered at the Pabst Grand Circle Hotel to adopt the Actors Equity's (AEA) Constitution and elect its first president, comedian Francis Wilson (Actors Equity Association, "About Equity"). Their strike ended the iron-fisted dominance of the Theatrical Syndicate, a consortium of producers whose monopoly over contracts and bookings controlled wages below free market levels often with subhuman and unsafe work conditions.

Equity served the acting profession well through the Golden Age of Broadway in the 1920s as well in its continued growth during the 1930s and 1940s. But as the film industry evolved, AEA's attempts to organize film actors met stiff opposition by Hollywood mega mogul Louis B. Mayer, head of Metro Goldwin Mayer (MGM).

Rather than bow to the demands of disgruntled artists in his employ, Mayer formed the International Academy of Motion Pictures Arts and Sciences, not to honor excellence in filmmaking as it exists today, but as "a thinly disguised studio pressure group to keep further unionization at bay" (Holden, *Behind the Oscar,* 89). Mayer pitched the Academy as an organization that would mutually benefit the various working groups of the film industry, a kind of "League of Nations for the motion picture industry," as Mary Pickford called it (89). Its charter empowered the Academy to set fair wage and working condition guidelines. But Mayer controlled the Academy from the beginning, using his own studio attorneys to draft the organization's bylaws and then pressuring MGM actors and technicians to join. His plan worked for a while, dividing dissident actors, some convinced that the Academy had their best interests at heart—until 1933 (133).

At the outset of the Great Depression, the Academy responded to Roosevelt's call for industrial self-regulation by mandating a 50 percent pay cut for all film industry employees—everyone, that is, except studio executives. Even MGM actors bolted from the Academy in response (Holden, *Behind the Oscar,* 114–115). That year saw the birth of both the Writers Guild of America (WGA) and the Screen Actors Guild. Over the years, actors benefited with increased wages, benefits, and safer working conditions, while film companies struggled to maintain control over their actors. But Congress and the Courts dealt the fatal blows to the old studio system with antitrust legislation, finally liberating contract players to become independent players.

In the 1950s, television created an entire new business. Immediately, actors formed two temporary guilds to set fair work standards for this new medium. In 1952, the Television Authority and the American Federation of Radio Artists merged to form the AFTRA to represent actors in both electronic mediums. But film actors already had SAG to represent them. Eventually the two organizations agreed to split jurisdiction based on the format utilized to record the actor. If the television program was "filmed," SAG has jurisdiction; if the television program was "taped," AFTRA had jurisdiction.

What Led to the Merger Between SAG and AFTRA?

This split structure remained intact over many years despite conflicts over contract negotiations, jurisdiction, and the obvious aggravation to actors caught in the middle. Several attempts to merge the two guilds failed over the years due to issues involving pension, health benefits, and membership rules. In the meantime, the digital revolution had transformed the media market with new platforms, such as video-on-demand (VOD), under which the unions had no jurisdiction, making the then current SAG and AFTRA contracts moot. During the 2008 contract negotiations with the Alliance of Motion Picture and Television Producers (AMPTP), SAG took a hard line on the issue of profit participation for VOD while AFTRA did not, which allowed AMPTP to play one union against the other. AFTRA prevailed while SAG's negotiations stalled and new television projects shifted to AFTRA. As a result, SAG's discontented rank and file membership voted in new leadership in 2009 with a mandate to seriously pursue a merger that would eliminate the overlapping jurisdiction, provide greater negotiating leverage and establish a stable structure for health and pension benefits. After seventy-five years of intra and interunion battles, SAG and AFTRA merged in 2012 after ratification by the rank and file (Handel, "The SAG-AFTRA Merger").

What Have Been the Results of this Merger?

Merging the two memberships had been the main obstacle to merging the two unions. As a union shop in which one must be offered a principal role before attaining membership, SAG had been ambivalent about absorbing AFTRA's open-shop membership in which anyone could join at any time. The solution had been to essentially declare AFTRA members who had not worked yet under a principal contract "SAG eligible," a designation that allowed them to compete for union roles with the requirement that they join the union upon acceptance of a second union job. The newly ratified contract negotiated in 2017 provides the clearest indication of how the resulting expansion of the membership led to increased negotiation leverage with the producer's guild, which produced the following improvements to past contracts:

- an increase in minimum wage rates as well as significant improvements in the timely payments of residuals to performers for exhibition of their performances on streaming platforms like Netflix and Amazon;
- increased contributions to actor's health and pension benefit funds;
- increases overtime wages for background players; and
- improved travel provisions among other issues.

In addition, the merger of the two union's health plans allows SAG-AFTRA members to qualify more easily for eligibility for coverage in a single health plan. The merger also solves the problem of overlapping jurisdiction with the union, now the sole bargaining unit for actors, voice-over artists, radio personalities, recording artists, broadcast journalists, announcers, dancers, disc jockeys, news writers, news editors, program hosts, puppeteers, and stunt performers.

What Are the Issues Still Before the Union?

Despite the above-mentioned benefits, significant issues must still be addressed by the union's leadership.

Pensions

Discussions continue as to the best way to merge the SAG Pension Fund and the AFTRA Retirement Fund without affecting member's benefits;

Right-to-Work Legislation

Legislation in "right-to-work" states, such as North Carolina, Florida, Louisiana, Texas allows actors to benefit from union wages and benefits without joining the union. Union lobbying efforts continue in Washington DC and statehouses nationwide to emphasize the benefits of union membership.

Direct Deposit

Union leadership has announced a multiyear agreement with Exactuals LLC, a third-party payment processing company, to facilitate the delivery of residuals via direct deposit sometime in the near future.

Set Safety

Recent high-profile stunt accidents and deaths have placed a new emphasis on safety on-set. Discussions continue regarding the role of stunt coordinators and safety concerns for voice-over and performance capture actors.

Digital Theft

Residuals, estimated by the union as 43 percent of the average actor's income, pays the bills for many performers. The union continues to lobby Congress to address the issue of online piracy by increasing penalties and shutting down websites that traffic in illegal sales or streaming of stolen movies and television shows.

Spanish Broadcasting System (SBS)

After the National Labor Relations Board in Los Angeles issued a formal complaint of unfair labor practice charges against SBS, negotiations continue for a fair contract for their unionized employees (SAG-AFTRA, "Keeps the Pressure," 11).

Video Game Strike

The eleven-month strike of voice actors against the video game industry ended with a tentative agreement that secures a "bonus" compensation for video game voice actors and has been reviewed by the national board and ratified by the rank and file.

Are There Other Unions I Should Join?

While SAG-AFTRA remains the sole union with jurisdiction over film and television acting, actors often support themselves through membership in the sister unions.

Actor's Equity Association (AEA)

Stage work in Hollywood provides both experienced stage actors and those with no experience the opportunity to showcase themselves, hone their craft, and subsidize their income. A variety of contracts cover different venues and environments, such as the Hollywood Area Theatre agreement for theaters of 500 seats or less and the Los Angeles Transitional 99-Seat Theatre Code, which replaces the old Equity-Waiver Plan for Los Angeles County.

American Guild of Variety Artists (AGVA)

Several generations of Hollywood actors have subsidized their income by performing as characters at Disneyland, Knotts Berry Farm and Universal Studios. Likewise, cruise ships leaving Los Angeles' harbors carry casts of singing and dancing actors on musical revues. These performers—as well as circus performers, skaters, comedians, stand-up comics, cabaret and club artists, and variety show stage managers—now work under this AFL-CIO affiliated labor union with negotiated salaries and conditions, such as rehearsal and performance hours; overtime provisions; safe and sanitary work conditions; travel stipulations; vacation and sick pay; publicity and promotion; audition procedures; and general work rules.

American Guild of Musical Artists (AGMA)

The performing artists employed by choral, operatic, and ballet companies fall under the jurisdiction of this labor union that has advanced their rights by setting minimum wages and work standards, such as reasonable rehearsal periods and adequate rest.

Regardless of which unions you join, each has a substantial initiation fee and semiannual dues as well as taking a slice from your working wages. Nonpayment of dues will result in suspension of membership rights until it is paid in full. The first question a talent agent will ask when notifying an actor of a union booking will be, "Are your union dues paid up in full?" If they are not fully paid by the end of the day, that booking can be revoked.

What Does a Union Do For an Actor?

One can only imagine what exploitation would ensue in an unregulated marketplace, but current sexual harassment allegations provide a disquieting window into the possibilities. While union membership provides no guarantee of work, the doors it opens will guarantee mandatory work standards and standardized wages. Over the past ninety years, actors' unions have won important victories, establishing:

- minimum pay scales and residual compensation rates,
- health and pension credits earned toward participation in a benefit plan to which union signatory producers must contribute,
- nonexploitive work hours and safety conscious work conditions, and
- specific steps regarding hazardous conditions, overtime, nudity, privacy, and method of payment.

IN THE BOX

I had been cast as a one-line day player on a television series. The production assistant had been very clear in his email. My call time at the location site was 6:00 a.m. I would meet a shuttle bus in a parking lot that would transport me to the film site. I arrived that morning promptly at 6:00 a.m. along with a dozen other sleepy actors and waited patiently for a bus that never arrived. An hour later, one actor contacted a studio assistant via cell phone who informed us that the shoot was really scheduled for 6:00 p.m. This created a problem for me, as I was already committed to a stage performance that night. I regretfully called my agent and explained I needed to turn down the role.

Later the production assistant called to apologize for his error. He explained, with great regret, that despite his having made the mistake and while I had shown up at the assigned time and place and had turned down other work for the day, the studio wouldn't be paying me for the missed job. He assured me instead that he'd "keep me in mind for future roles." I politely thanked him, hung up, and called the SAG hotline. I gave them the details, forwarded the PA's email and received a check two weeks later. That production assistant no longer works for the studio, but they have since called again for an audition.

As a result, actors now participate in the financial success of their work, receive fairer compensation for dangerous or extreme work conditions, negotiate their own projects through their talent agents and expect a fair and equitable word environment. In addition, the union also provides considerable tools for career assistance, such as:

- a New Media department that exclusively administers both the New Media and Interactive Media contracts,

- a low-budget Short Film Agreement that allows groups of actors to produce their own independent projects,

- a Contact Center that offers live-support for member's questions regarding membership, residuals, and contracts,

- a conservatory that offers a variety of workshops taught by industry professionals,

- the SAG-AFTRA Foundation's Casting Access program that sponsors "legal" workshops with prominent casting directors in cities nationwide or online through the Foundation's online portal,

- Life-Raft, another Foundation program that offers seminars to educate actors on issues such as set etiquette, taxes, talent agents, and commercials,

- iActor that provides members with a free online casting directory,

- the Actors Fund that provides services for affordable housing, sideline work, health insurance, social services, and emergency grants, and

- *Tools for Young Performers*, a handbook with detailed orientation and legal information for parents.

How Do I Join SAG-AFTRA?

Until 1947, unions were mostly closed shops, requiring union membership in order to be hired. In that year, Congress passed the Labor Management Relations Act of 1947, better known as Taft–Hartley, prohibiting, among other things, the closed union shop ("Radio Artists," *Los Angeles Times*, 10). This law required a portal, an opening in which an employer might hire an individual despite their nonunion status. The individual would still be expected to join the union after thirty days to continue working under union membership thereafter and could be required to pass a proficiency test or pay an initiation fee. The producer must also pay a penalty, but no longer could labor unions restrict their own membership. Beginning actors must look for this portal.

The industry favors its own and for nonunion actors, attaining union membership can be daunting. You must first be offered a contract as a principal player in a union signatory project before union membership can be obtained. How do you do this when breakdowns, auditions, and casting directors all favor union members? Several ways exist thanks to Taft and Hartley.

Be in the Right Place at the Right Time

Sometimes the actor who gets the role is still the one that fits the costume, or has a unique skill, or who is an odd size, or resembles someone famous, or just has a quirky persona. Rarely does anyone achieve their first SAG-AFTRA contract on talent alone. Physical appearance plays an important role. Television and commercials thrive on fresh new faces. Breakdowns often specify size, coloring, ethnicity, skills, and odd physical characteristics. Sometimes casting directors need to match faces and body types over several age categories to approximate familial relationships. And, of course, young, beautiful bodies, male and female, still get noticed, as do very unusual character faces of all ages. Casting directors receive thousands of pictures from nonunion actors, and while they generally only consider union actors, commercial casting directors often cast nonunion actors with unusual looks and skills. Either way, if you have the look or skills a casting director seeks, a contract could be offered and the production company will be required to fill out a Taft–Hartley report to the union (see Appendix C). At this point you are considered SAG eligible, which means you do not have to join the union unless you wish to keep working in union projects, for which you have thirty days to decide.

Work as a Background Extra

Atmosphere or background casting still represents an actor's best chance of attaining union status. Actors, both union and nonunion, simply register with a handful of agencies specializing in atmosphere casting such as Central Casting (see Appendix B). Production companies contract with these extra casting agencies to provide the needed background actors for each day of shooting. Under a union contract, the producer must hire a set number of union extras; the rest may be nonunion. Scripts often contain one-line roles not crucial to the plot but for which the cost of casting is prohibitive. Some producers or directors prefer to cast these roles on the set from the pool of extras. Still other directors prefer the creative flexibility of improvisation and may invent new speaking characters on the fly. Either way, if chosen to speak a line on-camera, any small meaningless phrase, whether it makes it into the film or ends up on the cutting room floor, you should immediately inform your on-set representative. You will be upgraded to principal status, paid accordingly, and provided a Taft–Hartley report as SAG-eligible that, along with your pay stub, you may use to apply for union membership.

The Voucher Game

SAG-AFTRA provides still another portal for background actors through a voucher system. As the union requires producers to hire a certain number of union members before they are permitted to hire nonunion actors at a cheaper rate, if a union actor fails to show, a nonunion actor's status may be "bumped up" to union status and paid accordingly. That actor receives a voucher for each workday when this occurs. After obtaining three vouchers, the nonunion actor becomes SAG eligible. Unfortunately, accumulating those three vouchers requires lightning to strike the same location three times. Meanwhile, unscrupulous casting directors, and producers exploit nonunion actors' eagerness with fake vouchers, bait and switch tactics, and a financial con game (SAG-AFTRA, "Voucher Scam").

IN THE BOX

One of my former students moved to Hollywood, registered with a nonunion extra casting agency and soon found himself working as a permanent extra on a weekly network sitcom. The daily pay was meager but the production assistant in charge of extra casting had made him a promise: hang in for three years and be rewarded with the three vouchers, the number needed for SAG membership. Three years was a long commitment but the promise of union membership seemed fair and worthwhile. The next year, sagging ratings forced a reassignment of the production crew. The production assistant had moved on and the new production assistant knew nothing about this arrangement. The actor was screwed. The lesson: always, always, always get it in writing. If they can't put it in writing, then you'll know exactly what that promise is worth.

Become a Producer

The union's New Media department and contract structure encourages actors to become entrepreneurial by producing their own projects and hiring themselves as actors, thus becoming SAG-AFTRA eligible in the process. This only works if the actors in question have a head for business and can successfully find the low-budget financing needed. Anecdotal evidence suggests that many actors are taking advantage of this option, with web series such as *Misanthropicon, Diary of a Wedding Planner, Secret Millionaires,* and *Crowded House* all produced by actors who, along with others, have used this option to become SAG-AFTRA eligible themselves.

Be a Special Case

The National Board of the union created this designation as a way to encourage recruitment by conferring union status on individuals who can advance the union's organizing efforts among groups not already covered by the union's jurisdiction. If you fancy yourself an activist, this may then be your ticket into the union.

Use the Casting Couch

No one seriously suggests this as an effective or professional approach and it often backfires. Hollywood crawls with opportunists who make promises they cannot keep. Anyone can print business cards promoting themselves as a producer or casting associate, claim to have a project in development, or know someone who knows someone. The casting couch very much exists, a fact that most actors must confront at some point in their career. If someone offers to make you a star, in return for "special favors," ask them to put their promises on paper. How one responds to such an offer is a personal decision, but remember to know your talent and its worth.

Use the Stage Door

Membership of one of the other "sister" unions opens the door to the others. Those who are members of ACTRA (Alliance of Canadian Cinema, Television and Radio Artists), AEA, AGMA, or AGVA for a period of one year, and have worked at least once as a principal under that union's jurisdiction, may join SAG-AFTRA under the terms of reciprocity. AEA membership, though, especially those with established stage careers, provides the best side-door entrance to SAG-AFTRA membership. In addition to internships, Equity requires producers to set aside time for nonunion actors for auditions, and though one must still be offered a union contract before obtaining an AEA card, after one year of membership in AEA, an actor may join SAG-AFTRA or vice versa.

Do I Have to Join SAG-AFTRA?

Whether you have been upgraded to a principal role, gathered three vouchers, produced your own self-starring web series or slept your way to a principal role, you have become SAG eligible, meaning you have thirty days before you must join the union to continue working on union projects. During that period the actor need only bring his or her pay stub or Taft–Hartley report to the membership offices of SAG-AFTRA in Los Angeles, and pay what is currently a $3,000 initiation—for many an impossible sum to pay in one lump. The union does offer a low cost twenty-four-month payment plan through its credit union, but others suggest patience. A savvy talent agent can often negotiate the payment of that initiation fee, by the production company, on a second booking as a condition of accepting the role.

Some actors prefer to stay on the outside of the union, declaring themselves FI-Core or Financial Core by submitting a written request to the legal department of SAG-AFTRA. A Supreme Court ruling in 1963 and again in 1988 established that employees who wished to leave the union could not be terminated as a result, though they were required to pay a fee for the administrative costs. A FI-Core actor can continue working nonunion projects as well as the occasional union gig.

For some that is a big deal. Others see them as scabs or free riders, undermining the very union that protects their rights. Likewise, "right-to-work" states allow individuals to apply and work union jobs without the requirement to join the union. The unions view such legislation as an attempt to undermine their jurisdiction.

Can I Continue to Do Nonunion Work if I am a Union Member?

Turning professional tends to realign employment opportunities into two distinct categories: union and nonunion casting, one acceptable and one now forbidden. Global Rule One of the SAG Constitution and Bylaws states that, "No member shall work as a performer or make an agreement to work as a performer for any producer who has not executed a basic minimum agreement with the Guild which is in full force and effect." Every union performer agrees to abide by this, and all the other union rules, as a condition of membership of the Guild. This means that no union members may perform in nonunion projects once they become members of the Guild (SAG, *Constitution*, ¶1).

ACTOR'S FORUM

If you're not booking something, it rarely it has to do with you not being good enough or good looking, etc. It has to do, for instance, with commercial auditions, with what the client is looking for. I lost a job that I was called back for because the guy in the story board looked like one of the other guys who came in, replete with a widow's peak which was drawn in the picture. He looked just like the guy, and that's the guy the client had in his head. It can be a million different variables why you don't get a role, and actors have to realize that when they say don't take anything personally. That's not just an axiom. You can't take it personally because the minute you start taking it personally, you're really in the wrong business. It could hurt your feelings, of course, but then you let it roll off of your back and move on.

MICHAEL GABIANO

The more tools you have in your toolbelt, the more useful you are to a producer. Often, they'll want you to do a number of voices if they possibly can. They're not going to bring in an actor for every different character. Become versatile. Practice. Play with it. Just like if you're doing an improv and you're just learning to play different characters. A lot of people do it in front of the mirror and just do a funny face and see if that doesn't lead to character ideas. Then see if you can flesh it out. The same with your voice. Play with it. Learn what you're good at. And then focus on what you're good at. Don't neglect the other stuff because as a secondary character, they'll say, "I want you to be a New Yorker." I'll do my damn best to be a New Yorker for that secondary character. So, I'm hirable. I don't typically submit myself, however, I know some voice actors who are very good about looking at all the stuff that's in production film and tv, looking at everything that's in post-production, figuring out who's doing the sound on post-production and then trying to figure out which group leader do they use to cast their additional voices.

PETER LAVIN

Motion capture breakdowns are mixed in with the regular acting breakdowns, so I let my agent or manager know to keep an eye out for that. You can give that to your agent and tell him, your job is to look for jobs for me. LA Casting has come a long way. I've just learned how to do a breakdown. I help cast motion capture projects. That's one of the bonuses of taking my class is that I connect you to the other studios and the other people. No one was doing it, so some people refer to me as the grandfather of mocap. We had to create it ourselves because nobody did it for us. I got a stunt agent who sent me out on that first audition. And then you have a casting person who has never done motion capture before, so they're not even aware of what's needed. Most of the time the motion capture studio will hold the audition. They're working now as the casting director.

RICHARD DORTON

8 THE CASTING GAME

Casting sometimes is fate and destiny, more than skill or talent, from a director's point of view.

STEPHEN SPIELBERG, Nashawaty, *Entertainment*

Casting can be heartbreaking. Dealing with the disappointment is the hardest part.

STOCKARD CHANNING, Horowitz, *"Stockard"*

ACTOR'S RESOURCES
Electronic Casting Services

Showfax/Actors Access
(310) 385–6920
 Los Angeles, CA 90028

NowCasting
60 East Magnolia Boulevard
Burbank, CA 91502
(818) 841–7165

Backstage Casting
(web only)

Casting Frontiers
6565 Sunset Blvd #200
(323) 300–6129

LA Casting/Casting
Networks
Los Angeles Kiosk
200 S. La Brea Ave.

Los Angeles, CA 90036
(213) 201–8100

Anyone who has ever been on the other side of the audition table will testify that casting is at best a guessing game. Casting directors never make choices with 100 percent certainty and often base them on intangible gut-feelings, as well as tangible qualities such as talent and experience. Simultaneously, actors play a game of "Guess what the casting director wants." Age? Hair color? Ethnicity? An attitude? A look? Actors are like commodities bought and marketed in this marketplace. And while talent agents do earn their commission promoting an actor, no one should be better at selling you than you are. But, in order to do so, one must know how to play the game. For that reason, actors must first get to know the gatekeepers, the casting directors.

Who Are Casting Directors?

Casting directors are not talent agents, producers, or directors, but specialized personnel, hired by the studios, networks, or production companies during the preproduction phase of a project to oversee the casting process from start to finish. They filter through the army of actors that have applied in response to a casting notice. They assemble several possible choices for each role for the producer and/or director, who will make the final decision. Producers depend upon the casting director's knowledge of the talent pool available and their ability to understand a director or producer's vision.

But, gone are the days when television networks and the major studios employed in-house casting directors. Today, most casting directors freelance as independent contractors and maintain their own offices. The cost and pressure of maintaining such a business has led to the unionization of casting directors and associates through Local 399 of the Teamsters who have bargained and successfully won concessions regarding health and pension benefits and working conditions in an agreement with the producer's guild (AMPTP). Some casting directors have padded their income by sponsoring casting workshops for actors who pay a fee to audition for them. This practice gained the attention of the Los Angeles City Attorney's office who filed criminal misdemeanor charges against five casting directors for violating the Talent Scam Prevention Act of 2009 which prohibits charging a fee for a job interview.

What Happens During the Casting Process?

Once a project has been greenlit, a producer chooses a casting agency to oversee the tedious work of screening thousands of actors to find the kind of talent desired for a project. Name actors may already be attached to the project or courted. Breakdowns for open roles are posted and after actors and talent agents have responded with submissions, casting assistants sift through and organize the faces. The casting director scans the fruits of their labor to choose approximately thirty to one hundred actors to audition for each role. Casting assistants then make phone calls to set audition times for reading and taping during the following few days. The casting director reviews the tapes, sometimes with the producer, and selects a small group of actors for callbacks. Casting associates again make appointments for the callback readings, often held with producers, directors, or writers in attendance. Often a casting director makes the final casting decision but always contingent upon a producer's approval.

On a typical day, casting directors pore through thousands of headshots and electronic submissions; audition hundreds of actors; attend casting workshops, showcases, and local theater events; and keep both eyes open for talent with striking looks. Finding both in the same package can make a career. To do this job, casting directors hold:

General Interviews

When time allows, casting directors interview actors who have caught their interest. It is an opportunity to chat and become familiar with the actor for possible future auditions.

Initial Auditions

Thirty to one hundred actors are selected to read or be interviewed for each role after casting associates have screened thousands of submissions.

Callbacks

Out of the initial auditions, a list of between five and ten actors are called to return for additional readings, sometimes in pairs or groups.

Final (Producer's) Auditions

A complete cast is presented to the producers who may rubber stamp the casting director's choices, make changes, or decide to start from scratch.

Are Casting Directors Licensed?

While neither California nor Los Angeles has any formal requirements for licensing of casting directors, the possible conflicts of interest or the misuse of the casting process has led to the formation of two organizations dedicated to setting professional standards: the Casting Society of America, established in 1982, and the Commercial Casting Director's Association. Conflicts between producers and casting directors over health benefits has also led to the unionization of Los Angeles casting directors and associates by the Teamsters Local 399. Many casting directors are former actors themselves or have arrived at their position by way of a theatrical or production background. They view their relationship with actors as collegial and their role as empowering and not as judgmental arbiters of talent.

Is the Casting Process the Same for All Projects?

Different kinds of projects require different approaches.

Commercial Casting

Casting associates shepherd hundreds of hopeful actors through the casting offices each day searching for some special look or talent; a spokesperson, a character actor, someone to wear a costume, mime a voice-over, or portray some humiliating, stereotypical public Joe. A laugh, a quirky smile, a dry wit, or the ability to fall down convincingly may seal the deal. Commercials often involve little or no dialogue but require strange talents for comic situations. Polaroid photos may be taken that might be used for measurements for costuming or prosthetics. The actor may be given time to familiarize themselves with a prop of some kind. Commercial casting directors often employ improvisation and role-playing games to screen potential actors. Actors may have to demonstrate an action or skill such as pratfalls or stage combat. Sometimes casting directors only need a look-see, satisfied to simply interview and tape a conversation with the actor. Commercial casting can be slow with continual consultations between the triumvirate of client, advertising agency, and casting agency with actors caught in the middle.

IN THE BOX

I had gone through three days of grueling auditions for a principal role in a new Los Angeles-based television soap opera. The casting had been overseen by an in-house television network casting director and all that remained was for the producers to approve the completed casting. I thought I'd finally made it and had already gotten out the party hats. Then my talent agent called to inform me that the meeting had been canceled.

"Rescheduled?" I asked. "No," he confided. The casting director had been caught in a compromised position with one of the actresses he had cast. "They fired him," he explained. "What did this have to do with me?" I asked. "It poisoned the well," he explained. "They've blacklisted everyone he cast. You can't even submit again." It was the first but not the last time I learned the lesson that what Hollywood gives, Hollywood can, just as easily, take away.

Television Casting

Television projects usually have tighter budgets and so must complete casting quickly. An hour episodic breakdown can be posted and cast within a five-day workweek. Casting directors usually stick to a strict schedule of five-minute audition slots and prepared sides, specially prepared excerpts from the shooting script. Casting directors have little time for interviews and no time for role-playing. Before the end of the week they must provide the producer with a tape of their preferences for each role. Usually three actors are chosen for each role with callbacks a choreography of scheduling and chemistry. The process can be excruciating and tedious, except for those who end up with principal roles in a network series.

Pilot Casting

Each pilot season casting directors carefully screen actors for television pilots. A successful television series does not happen by accident. Ensemble casting requires chemistry and casting the right actors the first time around. Scripts and characters may still be somewhat amorphous. Casting directors may even assemble dual casts, envisioning two competing stylistic directions of the project. Hundreds of actors may be read for each role, competing for the opportunity to become a breakout star. Few will be successful and even those who get cast will discover that only a handful of greenlit pilots make it to series.

Reality Show Casting

To be certain, reality shows audition contestants in much the same way as actors for scripted shows and will rely heavily upon improvisation and role-playing. But, that is where the similarity ends. Be prepared for the ten-page application form, an on-camera interview, and an intense background check before being offered a contestant contract and a scary confidentiality agreement to sign, neither of which is covered by union jurisdiction. Accepting employment on such programs requires considerable deliberation as a career decision since reality show stars rarely move on to any other substantial project. Far from unscripted, reality programs fall into several categories.

Contest

Actors are hired not as actors but as contestants in some kind of increasingly bizarre game show where they will win prizes, not paychecks.

Feel Good Shows

These reality shows perform a "good deed" for somebody, and thus make viewers "feel good." Producers hire actors to host, co-host, or participate in the restoration, transformation, or reformation of something or somebody. The carpenters, dressers, fixers, and hair stylists of these programs often have acting aspirations.

Re-Enactment

These programs dramatize past events such as medical emergencies, court proceedings, historical events, or police activity. Sometimes casting directors, armed with only a photograph, must accurately match the actor to a real-life counterpart without placing acting technique secondary. Some auditions require more intense preparation and technique than a historical re-enactment or a documentary. Casting directors may request that actors show up to auditions in period costume or another specific type of clothing.

Film Casting

Larger budgets often mean extra time for casting. Film casting directors plan a lengthy process of sifting and matching actors to match and balance a film cast. Actors may be asked to read three or four times in front of casting associates; an assembly of creative personnel such as directors, writers, and producers; or just to the camera.

Performance Capture

Gaming projects look for actors with excellent body control. Less emphasis may be placed on their facial looks or voice as these will mostly be provided by other actors. Auditions generally involve the casting director giving directions for specific movements or situations for the actor to pantomime and callbacks often include the actor performing movements in silhouette

Voice-Over

Actors are typically given time to familiarize themselves with a short script to read into a microphone with a stopwatch set at thirty seconds or so.

Stage

Theatrical auditions still rely mainly upon either cold readings or an actor's prepared monologues as an initial screening process but may easily turn to improvisation and informal rehearsals for callbacks.

Cattle Calls

Occasionally a project will announce an open audition to cast a high-profile role with an "unknown" actor, usually as a publicity stunt to gain notoriety for the project. Most recently, eighteen-year-old high school student Nikki Blonsky found herself cast in the film *Hairspray* out of 1,100 hopefuls who auditioned nationwide during open auditions.

Extra Casting

Agencies that specialize in the casting of background extras (see Appendix B) rarely hold live casting sessions unless they are in search of a particular skill. Instead, they rely upon a database of actors who have registered with their service. Actors call in each day to hear a prerecorded message listing the projects available and then leave a message if they are interested. Actors who meet the casting specifications receive an email with booking information. Those who respond first get work.

How Does an Actor Get an Audition in Hollywood?

Unlike stage projects that commonly hold open auditions, film and television casting directors hold private auditions scheduled by request only. Thus, an actor's first challenge is to get into the casting room.

The casting director must first contact the actor or the actor's talent agent to schedule an audition. Some actors do yearly mass mailings of their headshot and resume to the casting directors in Hollywood—all 600 of them. Many electronic services and bookstores sell packets of names and addresses. But general submissions mostly go into a pile that will sit for months until the summer hiatus or the Christmas break, when casting directors also hold general interviews with actors who have been recommended to them or who have attracted their attention in some other way. But, if an actor really wants to be considered for a specific project he/she must submit for that specific project.

How Does an Actor Learn What Projects Are Being Cast?

During preproduction, a casting breakdown for the project will be posted on Breakdown Services, a subscription service for talent agents, who peruse these notices posted by casting agencies and then submit their clients for appropriate roles. For an actor, access to those casting breakdowns to find out about roles which match their characteristics, remains fundamental.

Can Actors Subscribe to this Service?

Breakdown Services is a subscription service only for license and bonded talent agents, who receive these daily breakdowns electronically. Each morning an agent peruses the notices, makes notes on which roles match individual talents and then prepares electronic submissions. The contact information for those submissions to a casting agency is confidential and held closely by the talent agent as this is their edge. But, some actors have found exceptions and may make deals with their agent to self-submit. Others have found sources for breakdowns, copied, and sold a day or two later, but usually too late to be of use.

Are There Legitimate Electronic Casting Websites an Actor Can Subscribe To?

Breakdown Services, aware of the black marketing of their service, provides an internet portal for actors called Actors Access, listing all the nonunion and union breakdowns for projects that producers have cleared for wider distribution.

Actor's Access

Actor's Access and other electronic casting services provide a free service, up to a point. They provide free access to some casting breakdowns, but each electronic submission requires a nominal charge or a paid subscription. Nonmembers can review casting breakdowns and upload and manage photos and resume information, but any contact information remains confidential. These nominal charges can add up, and this provides the motivation for actors without an agent, who use the service on a regular basis, to subscribe and receive unlimited submission privileges. Membership also provides other services, such as posting an actor's reel or video online or giving advance notification of suitable roles. But do not be fooled into believing you have access to the complete breakdowns.

The success of Actors Access has spawned dozens of entrepreneurial internet services across the country, some legitimate and others that have opportunistically exploited the lure of fame and fortune, to anyone who fancies themselves an actor. Those sites promise access to legitimate Hollywood breakdowns, but in truth, list mostly nonunion projects or duplications of projects copied from other legitimate services, usually posted too late for submission. Some post breakdowns with suspicious origins about unconfirmed projects or from disreputable sources. Others have gone so far as to post fake projects just to entice hopeful young talent in Kansas to buy a year's subscription with the promise of a film or television role. The legitimate websites allow prospective subscribers to examine the casting notices in advance of subscribing. The following electronic casting websites are commonly used by legitimate casting directors.

LA Casting/Casting Networks

Once only used for commercials, LA Casting/Casting Networks has challenged Breakdown Services' monopoly on union projects. Commercial talent agents usually require their clients to register with LA Casting for represented actors; this service provides free registration, does not charge a yearly fee, and allows two free photo uploads and one free media clip or charges $25 for the first added photo and $15 thereafter.

Casting Frontiers

Also specializing in commercials, this site has grown to include theatrical, short film, and internet projects, though mostly nonunion. Represented actors will find the same basic services provided free of charge and subscribers will enjoy much the same benefits as LA Casting.

NowCasting

A few years back, when this service debuted, experienced actors had hoped this new business in Burbank would provide competition to Actors Access, but a cursory view of it shows mostly nonunion projects being posted. It does provide more information about the many services that cater to actors in Los Angeles and a great deal of helpful information through newsletters and online articles from casting directors and working actors. The breakdowns are the same as found on Actors Access, with the occasional inclusion of some exclusive breakdowns.

Backstage

This Hollywood trade publication has always published casting notices, especially stage casting. When it went digital years ago, it added an electronic casting service that lists breakdowns for independent and student filmmakers as well as theater projects.

The web abounds with many other electronic casting sites, each providing more or less the same services and fees. The casting services listed earlier provide legitimate casting notices and provide a reasonable value. Most represented actors follow their agent's advice, set up free accounts with those designated, and then monitor the notices, communicating to their agent(s) their requests for submissions. But for the unrepresented actor with limited funds, the monthly subscription fees or submission fees will add up quickly. If you want to subscribe to any of these services, monitor the sites for a week or two, paying attention to notices duplicated, and then choose the one or two that serve your needs.

Are There Other Sources of Casting Notices?

SAG-AFTRA

Their union web portal does offer actors access to limited casting notices, but more importantly they provide an important source of information about "Do not work" notices, which warn actors of production companies that violate union or employment standards.

Craigslist

This internet forum expanded its list of classified ad categories to include "TV/Film/Video." Open and unrestricted, Craigslist does provide fertile ground for scammers and fraud schemes. The validity of the postings varies from city to city, but in the Los Angeles area they range from legitimate job postings for nonunion talent and crew to solicitations for "adult actresses." Actors should beware and ask lots of questions when contacted after responding to an ad. But, music artists have been known to solicit actors for videos, as have famous directors and actors with boutique projects that could never get financing as a union project.

What Information Do Casting Notices Provide?

Electronic casting notices provide a host of information that will help the actor decide if the project meets their criteria.

Posting Date and Time

Casting notices can be posted on any day at any time, but once posted, the clock starts ticking. Casting directors face deadlines and normally choose actors for auditions before the end of the day posted. Most serious actors peruse the electronic casting sites early in the morning and then monitor them all day, either texting their agents with submission requests or processing their own submissions. Either way, the date and time stamp help an actor to determine if submitting to a project is a lost cause.

Project Type

Notices divide into categories, such as:

- television—pilot, episodic, reality, promo, infomercial, music video, public service announcement (PSA)
- film—feature, short, student, industrial, educational
- commercial—national, local, spec, online
- theater—play, musical, variety, staged reading
- internet—new media, web series
- interactive
- print

Character Description

Specifies character's name, gender, ethnicity, age range and/or vocal range, characteristics, any specialty skills required, and a brief synopsis of the character's role.

Union Status

SAG-AFTRA, SAG eligible, AEA, or nonunion.

Production Information

Casting notices often specify the name of the production company as well as its producers, writers, directors, and casting director. Audition dates may be listed as well as the pay rate, start date, location, and deadline for submission, all information an actor should take into consideration.

Submission Information

Casting directors want different things. Most want demo reels and clips, but will specify how to submit them.

Tagline

A brief description of the story.

How Do You Know if a Project is Legitimate?

No electronic casting service guarantees the legitimacy of the breakdowns posted. As with everything else in Hollywood, the reader must beware of both union and nonunion projects. Nonunion projects, such as music videos and local advertisements, are inherently suspect, but even union projects can fall apart at any point in the preproduction process. A talent agent has access to considerably more information on union projects and can advise an actor on submissions, but for nonunion projects, an actor is largely on their own. Follow your professional instinct and gather as much information about the project as possible. Electronic casting notices do provide the actor with a lot of information that will help, such as the names of the director, writers, production team, production company and any actors already attached to the project, all information that can be checked out on IMDb for legitimacy and past track record.

IN THE BOX

I remember wasting three weekends auditioning for a film company with a high-rise Hollywood address and fancy offices. No one seemed to be in charge. Audition times had been long forgotten. I spent an hour rehearsing one role only to have the associate casting director (really the author of the screenplay) ask me to read for a different role. In the end, I never got to read for either role, but for still a different one. Callbacks the next week were even stranger. I was paired off and given an hour to rehearse a scene. Two hours later I was finally called in to read, but not for that role rehearsed, but for the original role with a partner I had never seen. Imagine my surprise when I booked the project. I was told to clear the next weekend for rehearsals and wait for a call as to where and when. That call never came. Nor were any of my messages returned. In fact, I never heard from them again. But, a year later I noticed a film project in the breakdowns that just didn't seem right. I checked the production information and sure enough . . . the same team. I passed this time.

The union's website lists all union signatory productions and additional information can often be gleaned from checking the trades. The web also abounds with actor's forums where a simple question about a producer or production company can result in eye opening responses. One red flag involves the audition, callback, and production dates. If these dates are to be arranged (TBA) this suggests that this project may be still more of a hope than a reality. Finally, the notice should list the type of contract, the contract status, the rate of pay, and the film format. Once again, the less information given, the more suspicious one should be of its reliability.

If Everybody Uses Electronic Casting, Why Do I Need Hard Copy Headshots?

For film, commercials, and print auditions, it is less common to need a hard copy, but it is never a bad idea to bring one, especially if it is the first time you are being called into a particular office.

1   **Casting directors usually request actors to bring a hardcopy headshot and a resume to auditions.** Sometimes two copies. After seeing dozens of actors in the course of a day, the headshot helps the casting director to remember the actor. Even if you do not receive a callback, the photo may be filed if they liked your look.

2   **You never know who you will meet and where.** Always carry a headshot in the car just in case. A casual conversation can end with a request for a headshot, especially at industry events like showcases and screenings.

3   **Soliciting a talent agent or personal manager for representation.** Most talent agents first require a headshot and a resume before deciding whether to interview you.

4   **Many theaters still cast the old-fashioned way.** Electronic casting still dominates, but some theater productions request headshots and resumes be sent into their office for consideration, and for open calls, you will still need to bring your headshot and resume.

IN THE BOX

I was at the closing night of a play in Los Angeles on New Year's Eve. The theater planned a special party after the performance. Champagne flowed and the mostly industry crowd mingled and schmoozed. Suddenly a woman recognized me from a play I had performed twenty years earlier. She introduced herself, talked about a play she was directing, and asked for a picture and a resume. I remembered I had one in my car and quickly retrieved it. Several weeks later I found myself rehearsing a play written by the legendary Broadway producer, Stewart F. Lane, directed by that same woman for a special benefit performance honoring him. My performance was seen by hundreds of industry professionals and eventually led to other projects.

ACTOR'S FORUM

The number one audition mistake is going in unprepared. You've got to be prepared for cold readings where you are handed sometimes copious amounts of dialogue, and if you are not a good cold reader, your head is going to be buried in the page. Memorize as much of the script as you can, and then go in and make a choice. Make it you. Don't assume unless you're specifically told at the audition that they want this specific kind of character and this specific kind of voice. Your imagination is one of your best assets. Never apologize. Never make excuses for anything that happens. Nobody wants to hear you're sorry, they just want to get on with the business day. If you screw up, just go back, or ask for another take if it's that bad. We always think that everything has to be perfect. That's a hard lesson for young actors. And don't ever go in with an attitude. No matter what happened outside that door; someone could have been terribly inappropriate before you walked into that room, all hell could be breaking loose, something very traumatic could be happening in your life. They don't care. You're there to do a job. It's a chance to perform. Don't treat it like it isn't.

MICHAEL GABIANO

A voice-over audition is pretty straightforward. Now, you can audition in your bedroom, submit it, and you might have a decent chance if they listen to it and they like it. Most voice actors now have a home studio. You need to find a space or create a sound resistant space, somewhere where you can get a really good clean vocal track without any room noise or street noise. You spend several hundred dollars to buy a good digital microphone and your software so you can edit what you do because you cannot send in every take. You need to go through it yourself and edit it down to a couple of good takes. You look at the characters, you prep that character, and you bring that script to life. It's acting. You make choices. One good thing about voice-over, it doesn't matter how ridiculous you look as you're making your choice. You don't need to worry about how you're contorting your face or exaggerating. Don't be too proud. Go for everything that you could be right for. Give it everything you can, but don't expect to book them all. You will book a tiny fraction of the auditions you do no matter how great your submission sounds because there are a lot of good actors out there, and with the dissemination of recording technology, a lot more people can submit.

PETER LAVIN

There's two different types of motion capture. There's the in-game, meaning what you do inside the game as you're playing as a character. Then there's the cinematics. That's just like a regular audition, regular acting. You'll get a scene to read with somebody, and it's the narrative, so you treat that like you would any TV or film audition. The in-game audition is where we're checking your physicality, your skill. Most of it you're using your imagination as an actor. When you do an in-game motion capture audition, they're looking for your walk. Improv skills are very important, but it's not just improv or speaking skills, it's knowing your own body. You have to know your body physically and what works for you. People are very awkward. You don't know that you're pigeon toed, or you're left foot sticks out in a duck walk. You don't know that this arm is swinging funny. You have to be able to control those elements all the time.

RICHARD DORTON

9 AUDITIONING IN HOLLYWOOD

If there are nine guys auditioning and they're all gorgeous, I have an advantage, because gorgeous guys are a dime a dozen. But if they need someone else—a goofy guy with bad hair who is just okay—then that's me.

TOM HANKS, *Oprah*

ACTOR'S RESOURCES

Out of the Closet Thrift Stores—Hollywood
6210 W. Sunset Blvd.
Los Angeles, CA 90028
(323) 467–6811

Junk for Joy
l3314 W. Magnolia Blvd
Burbank CA 91505
(818) 569–4903

Quartermaster—Police Equipment, Security & Military Uniforms
2543 W. 6th Street
213–351–9632

LA Police Gear
28704 The Old Road.
Valencia, CA 91355
661–294–9499

SAG-AFTRA Foundation
5757 Wilshire Boulevard, Mezzanine
Los Angeles, California 90036

An audition is a job interview, plain and simple. It lasts less than five minutes, will be videotaped and involves a collection of industry professionals observing, scrutinizing, and yes, objectifying every minute of it. An invitation has been delivered, a date, a time, a location, an opportunity, a *business* opportunity. Your submission, electronic or hard copy, has reached a set of eyes that discerns something worthy of closer inspection. Actors prepare auditions for casting directors no differently than someone who prepares a sales presentation for a perspective business client. The form may change but the intent remains the same—to sell a product. An audition should be viewed no differently.

What Information Should I Receive with an Audition Call?

Talent agents usually receive audition requests late afternoon for the next day's appointments. This gives one little time to prepare. Much must be done and much will be expected. Take note of the following:

Role/Rate

Day player? Guest artist? Background? Make certain you understand the pay rate structure and any restrictions. Whether union or not, no one likes surprises when it comes to a paycheck. Make certain you understand the terms to your satisfaction. Confirming the audition infers agreement to accept the role if cast. Be certain you are comfortable with it, as playing "Princess of the Underworld" could well end up your legacy.

Audition Date and Time

Note how much time you have to prepare.

Location

Special directions may be emailed to you, such as maps and parking instructions, or you may be directed to log onto an online service, such as Basecamp that provides confidential logistic information.

Sides

These excerpted pages of the script may be emailed directly to the actor or made available on an electronic casting service.

Dress

Actors may be directed to dress in a certain manner or to wear a particular item of clothing. Otherwise, dress appropriately for the character without going overboard.

Special Requests

The actor may be requested to bring something or prepare in some way, usually in reference to some special skill that he or she must demonstrate, such as a martial art or a language.

How Should I Prepare for an Audition?

Innumerable books, seminars, workshops, and classes provide different perspectives on successful auditioning, much of it contradictory.

- make strong choices / play it safe,
- be yourself / become the character as soon as you enter the room,
- memorize the sides / don't memorize the sides,
- create a specific character / be yourself.

They all do agree that the more successful actors arrive well prepared for the audition. As such, observe the following standards:

1 **Arrive on time.** Carefully consider the audition location and travel time needed. Take into consideration traffic, parking, and wrong turns. Be sure to allow prep time for the reading. Casting directors schedule auditions every five to ten minutes. When it is your time, you need to be there. If you are late, call the casting office to alert them. While arriving early may earn you an earlier slot, arriving late brands the actor as unprepared and unprofessional.

2 **Don't memorize—"know" the sides.** Sides may or may not be provided. Some projects, such as music videos and some commercials, may just involve action but no dialogue. If sides have been provided in advance, the casting director will expect the actor to be familiar with the lines and not to rely entirely upon the script. Casting directors do not expect a

word-perfect audition and may actually exhort the actor to throw the script aside and to improvise. But, casting directors do expect actors to know what they are saying and why.

3 **Research the project.** Find out everything possible about the project and its producers, director, writers, or other actors. Current television programs have web links to sample videos. Go online, watch them, and strategize how to fit in. Trade references may also pop up, as well as past episode summaries. Check the producers' or director's IMDb pages to familiarize yourself with their work. Know what other projects the casting director has worked on. Will I be taped or filmed? Walk into the audition having done your homework and knowing exactly for whom you are auditioning and for what kind of project.

4 **Create a character.** Having learned as much about the project as possible, you may begin to develop certain aspects of the character. This process evolves just like a theater audition. As with any audition, look for clues in the sides to social status, educational level, profession, health, or anything not obvious from the dialogue. Consider vocal inflections, accent, and rhythms. Look for emotional range and the character's objectives. Making a strong choice admittedly is a gamble, but most casting directors prefer actors who make an impression over those who play it safe.

5 **Rehearse, rehearse, and rehearse.** One should not just be predominantly off-book, but know the scenes inside and out. Work on presenting the dialogue in a variety of ways. Casting directors often rely upon improvisation techniques. Consider how the character might react to a variety of stimuli or circumstances. The casting director may give you direction to read again in a different manner or style. Be ready for whatever may be thrown at you.

6 **Do not over dress for the role.** Casting directors seem wary of actors who arrive having over-accessorized or made conscious costuming choices about the character. They want to audition actors, not costumes, and the actor runs the risk of being upstaged by his or her own outfit. Actors should dress for the role, but make subtle choices using your own wardrobe. On occasion casting directors do request actors to wear particular types of clothes, perhaps specifying casual, conservative, or outdoor wear or even in period or uniform dress. Los Angeles's many goodwill and vintage clothing shops provide actors with a variety of resources in these cases. As a general rule, avoid white, shiny material and loud patterns, which do not film or videotape well.

7 **Do not bring props.** Unless specifically requested, props only get in the way and most likely will not be seen by a camera focused on your face.

What Should I Do When I Arrive for the Audition?

Take a deep breath. Even experienced actors feel anxious before an audition. You may fear arriving late. Sides may have been changed. Parking instructions may be complicated. Studio security guards may require a driver's license or other picture ID for entry. Directional signs may be posted but confusing. A maze of studio buildings and hallways must be traveled in search of some phantom room or wing. The more seasoned actors arrive early and relax into the role.

Eventually you will locate the small office suite where a casting associate with an ominous clipboard greets each actor on arrival by taking their headshot and resume and providing additional instructions. Listen carefully as these may be complicated. Ask questions if you are confused. Use this time wisely to ask questions concerning any pronunciation or ambiguities in the sides, but do not waste the associate's time playing twenty questions and do not be rude. That associate may be asked for their input later regarding an actor's attitude.

Sign-in

Somewhere should be posted a sign-in card or form (see Appendix C). SAG-AFTRA signatory projects must submit an audition report that documents each actor's name, talent agent, call time, time in, and time out. The form asks for a Social Security number or union membership number, the latter being preferred as Social Security numbers have potential issues regarding identity theft.

IN THE BOX

I was sitting in the casting offices for Fox's *The Shield*. I had done due diligence in preparation and found myself sitting there fairly relaxed and enjoying the opportunity to participate at this level. I surveyed the other actors in the room, all characteristically dark, good looking and middle-aged like me. Some nonchalantly read the morning paper or did crossword puzzles. Others sat in stony silence. Still others recognized each other from a film shoot not quite a year ago and chatted quietly. Some desperately familiarized themselves with the sides they had just received, while the rest of us who had gotten them yesterday, sat holding them patiently. Suddenly a short, bald man emerged from the men's room. Sweating profusely, he dabbed at his face and neck with a handkerchief as he surveyed the handsome faces of his competition. He then began to pace up and down the hallway with increasing panic until he bolted for the men's room once again. Five minutes later he emerged, only to repeat what he had done. By the time he was called to read, he had reduced himself to an exhausted, physically stressed, and psyched out wreck. Perhaps a brilliant actor, I could see he had fallen victim to his own insecurities rather than overcome them, the first real test of your aptitude for professional life.

The Waiting Room

The waiting room for the audition normally has a zen-like atmosphere, so complete any vocal, physical, and emotional warm-ups prior to arrival. If you are unable to do this, find an innocuous hallway to prepare. Otherwise, sit quietly and wait. Actors often chat with each other and share stories and information. This collegial time occurs incidentally, yet it often leads to new friendships, contacts, and sometimes work. Also, take a second to scan the competition. Certain personal similarities should appear obvious, offering a small glimpse of the casting director's vision of the character. On the other hand, do not psych yourself out by worrying about having a different look. Your uniqueness may be the edge you need.

What Happens During an Audition?

On Deck

When called, the actor follows the casting associate into the audition room to be greeted by between one and a dozen individuals waiting to observe the audition, which begins the minute the actor walks into the room. Actors must "own" the room and fill the space without appearing cocky or overbearing. Out of politeness the casting director usually introduces each of the other participants in the room. Do not move to shake a hand unless one is proffered due to possible health concerns when seeing up to sixty actors per day. Take the hand if offered, but otherwise do not touch anyone, unless directed to.

Reading the Room

Learn to read the room, to understand the dynamics involved and to adjust accordingly. Casting sessions vary; they can be hot one minute and cool the next.

This producer's not happy; this director wants to chat; this casting director seems cold; this one jokes and encourages. An actor must follow the casting director's lead, think on their feet, react accordingly, and keep focused.

The Reading

Usually filmed, the casting director will direct the actor to stand on a mark on the floor in front of the assembled group. Notice the camera—its placement and distance. Some instructions may be given: where to look, who to read with, and so forth. Feel free to ask any intelligent questions regarding characterization, pronunciation, or about the instructions, but rhetorical or fawning questions only waste time and gain nothing but the casting director's annoyance. You will be asked to slate for the camera, stating your name and the audition role. Take a good strong beat, pay attention to your posture and general appearance, and then begin, observing these guidelines:

1   No matter how secure you may feel with the script, always carry it. No worse sin exists than dropping a script with some bravado, and then going up on your lines.

2   Treat the camera as the audience, as if in an intimate theater venue and adjust volume and performance according to its distance from your mark.

3   Listen carefully to any suggestions or adjustments given before doing a retake. The casting director may test your ability to listen and follow directions. Take a moment to consider them, and then attempt the reading once again.

4   If you are not happy with your performance, ask to repeat the reading. Although strictly at the prerogative of the casting director, most will grant a second attempt. But, be prepared for your request to be denied, an occurrence that can rattle less experienced actors. Never let them see you sweat, and never let them see you cry!

The Exit

A polite "Thank you," will indicate that the casting director has seen enough. Thank the casting director in return and then promptly and professionally leave. Do not complain, make excuses, criticize the script, or offer suggestions. Refrain from asking questions like: "Did I get the part," or, "When will I hear back?" They will view any additional soliciting as desperation which will only serve to magnify your pathos—not the most professional impression to leave behind. On the other hand, a confident and unobtrusive demonstration of talent and a humble exit accentuates your professional competence. Finally:

- have fun with the role, even as the second spear holder,

- be patient and ask questions to clarify pronunciation, characterization, or instructions,

- bring extra headshots and resumes in case others in the casting office ask for them,

- be friendly but not overly chatty; make every word count for something,

- be nice to everyone from assistant casting associates to fellow actors in the waiting room,

- you never know what star will rise tomorrow—or fall.

IN THE BOX

I received an audition request for *The Office*. As I was not aware that an American version of the British show was currently under development, I assumed the audition was for the British show. I dutifully practiced the rather short sides with my best working-class London dialect, all along a bit confused as to why the BBC would be casting in Hollywood. The next day, arriving line- and dialect-perfect for the audition. I took my mark, and dropped my script, confident in remembering the several simple lines. As I waited for the casting director to set the camera, I casually asked, "So this is for the BBC?" "No, dear," she replied. "It's a pilot for NBC." I was stunned. "I suppose the British accent I worked on all night is unnecessary?" She smiled blithely and said, "Yes, it is. Are you ready?" I wasn't as I made mental notes to change the voice and accent to an American working-class character. Gone was my focus. Gone was my concentration. I went up on the lines so badly that I finally had to reach down and humbly pick up my sides from the ground and find my place. I couldn't leave quickly enough. Needless to say, I didn't get the part.

What Should I NOT Do During an Audition?

Actors have been known to display some very bad manners and habits in the audition room. Always remember that this is a job interview, no different than any other job interview, and you should always demonstrate professional courtesy.

- Avoid excessive perfume or cologne. Casting personnel often see hundreds of actors a day, and the cumulative effect can be sickening.

- Props are unnecessary unless requested. Warriors need not arrive wearing samurai swords, and military personnel may leave their assault rifles at home.

- Never touch or physically involve anyone else in the casting office in the scene reading, including your reading partner. Doing so could be misinterpreted as casting associates have experienced assaults and unwanted advances.

- Watch bad habits such as clicking the tongue, smacking lips, playing with hair or chewing gum unless making character choices.

- Never bring flyers or other publicity materials for other projects.

- Never bring friends, relatives, or pets to audition calls, even just to wait in the lobby—that is, unless you have concerns about the legitimacy of the audition. Then by all means bring a friend to sit with you.

- Never ask to read for a different role than the one for which you have been invited.

- Do not talk yourself out of a job. Some actors never know when to be quiet, and casting personnel can smell desperation at the door.

- Never make excuses. Self-deprecation is not a strategy. If you think you can do it better, then ask to do the reading again. Otherwise, leave your personal life at the door.

What Should NOT Happen During an Audition?

- Auditions should happen in offices, never in hotel rooms, private residences, or secluded locations. If you are ever directed to report to a questionable location for an audition, bring a friend, preferably a fatherly type.

- Nudity of any kind, male or female, even if mandated in the script, may not be required during initial auditions as per the SAG-AFTRA Basic Agreement (SAG/AFTRA, "2005 Basic Agreement," 105). If a role involves nudity, prior to callbacks an actor will receive a Nudity Rider that spells out exactly the extent of the nudity in the film, giving the actor time to make a decision. Nudity may then be expected during a callback. When filmed, the set must be closed to all non-essential personnel and photography prohibited without the actor's consent. An actor may withdraw consent at any time if he or she deems the situation unacceptable. Union policy remains very clear on this point, and all but the sleaziest nonunion projects treat this as standard.

- Professional actors never pay-to-play. If anyone at any time during the casting process discusses money changing hands as a prerequisite to obtaining employment, it is time to say goodbye.

What Should I Do After an Audition?

Always sign out before you leave. Your talent agent or personal manager may place a follow-up call to solicit feedback. Many actors maintain a journal or computer spreadsheet to document each audition, date, time, project, mileage, and outcome. This is a practice that proves invaluable not only as professional documentation, but also for tax purposes. While sending gifts to a casting director is discouraged, a polite thank you note will be appreciated.

Now the waiting starts. The casting process can transpire in either days or months and for actors, hope always springs eternal. Only those cast receive notification in the form of a booking. When too much time has elapsed, hope must turn to resignation. Letting go becomes the hardest aspect of an audition process. All actors second-guess their performance, and in the high-stakes drama of Hollywood, it is an obsession. Friends can help you navigate the rejection, but the entertainment industry does not nurture actors. Business drives all decision making, especially casting. The better actor may be passed over for a bigger bustline, a smaller waistline or a bigger name. One never knows exactly why the phone does not ring. Learn to let go . . . unless the phone rings with a callback, and then it all begins again!

A callback represents success in a way, a giant step toward achieving a booking. The casting director now has seen your work, has pitched it to the client, who now wants more input. Remember, accepting a callback means accepting the role if cast, and second thoughts after casting can result in ostracization. Callbacks repeat the audition in much the same way, but most likely before a different or larger group of people and sometimes with new directions. Casting directors occasionally utilize a more game-oriented or role-playing technique during callbacks. Sometimes the actor may be asked to cold read a new side, to improvise a scene, or to scene read with another actor. A callback raises the bar, and the actor must be prepared to meet that expectation.

If the phone rings with a booking offer, no matter how small the role, the universe suddenly becomes possible once again. But if not, then the practice of auditioning must be its own reward. Ask your agent to call the casting director for feedback. Any constructive criticism can help during the next audition or project.

Can I Self-Tape My Audition?

Technology has made all things possible, but more importantly, it has globalized the auditioning process. While auditioning in person is still preferable, your inaccessibility should not be an impediment to submission for a project. Actor Steve Zahn recently auditioned via Skype for the role of Bad Ape in the film *War for the Planet of the Apes* while working in Puerto Rico. "Really, anything of value, anything that's good, you need to fight for. So, I did this crazy Skype audition," he explained (Reisman, "Steve Zahn. Seriously"). Whether utilizing Skype, YouTube or a casting director's email, anyone with an iPhone, iPad, or video camera can now produce an acceptable audition tape if requested to do so, thus breaking down regional barriers and helping actors take more control of their careers. Ideally, an actor should establish a dedicated space as a taping studio, but in a pinch, the outdoors or a living room can become an audition room. But, like so much technology today, an audition tape can be done badly and harm an actor's career. To be sure, video equipment can be expensive, but depending upon your budget, setting up a video-taping studio need not be.

What Equipment Do I Need?

Camera

The cheapest camera is the one you borrow, but your own smartphone can be used quite effectively in the landscape mode, though the memory capacity may limit your attempts. A digital single-lens reflex camera (DSLR) or handycam can be purchased for around $400 and will produce high-quality video, with all the bells and whistles of a professional grade camera that would set you back twice that amount. Auditions need only be filmed at 720p HD and no higher as doing so will eat up memory and make your file difficult to email. A tripod is also a necessity as handheld audition videos look far from edgy. For those who self-tape on a regular basis, a professional quality camera may make sense, but before you spend the money, make certain you have the chops to pull it off.

Lighting

The cheapest lighting equipment is the sun or a household lamp. Natural light can be the best option, but outdoor filming presents other issues and can produce unwanted shadows that distract from your performance, or wash out all the contours of your face. Lamplight is more easily controlled but can create an eerie unattractive yellow glow. An inexpensive reflector on a tripod for ten or twenty dollars can solve both problems. Always start with your key light, which, if outdoors would be the direct sunlight. With your subject facing away from the sun, one well-placed large, white reflector in front of your subject would then bounce that sunlight back into your subject and produce a soft fill light. A large, white, foam board will do the same thing, and if you add a gold rim reflector, a more natural warm glow can be created. Indoors, window-light may be used as a key light, utilizing the same equipment. But, if artificial light is needed, LED film lights can be purchased for about $100 and will help you create a truly professional taping studio.

Backdrop

An old wrinkled bedsheet is not a backdrop, nor curtains or blackout drapes. A blank wall or door can suffice in a pinch if it is a pale, plain color, but purchase a professional photographer's white backdrop and stand if you plan to self-tape on a regular basis.

Microphone

The built-in microphones on iPhone, iPads, and even handycams and DSLRs may suffice for viral videos, but not for a job interview. In addition, outdoor noise and indoor echoes can ruin what might otherwise be a stellar audition. First, identify someplace in your home that is isolated and quiet and then consider purchasing a shotgun microphone to get the same sound quality as casting directors do in the audition room.

Editing

The most expensive professional equipment in the world cannot help if you edit the results poorly. Depending upon the format, use iMovie for Macs or Adobe Premiere Pro for Windows, all inexpensive and user-friendly software packages, and purchase the training DVDs as well. Of course, if you want to edit like a pro, Final Cut Pro remains the cutting-edge standard. But, if these are beyond your resources, an actor can utilize the computer lab and video recording equipment at the SAG-AFTRA Foundation's Actor Center in Hollywood.

How Do I Self-Tape a Professional-Looking Audition?

Before you can tape your audition, a few more issues must be addressed. Choose solid color clothes, without stripes or busy patterns. Avoid excessive jewelry and, if you must wear makeup, make sure that it is appropriate for the brightness of your light source. If you tape outdoors, find a plain background rather than a recognizable location. The camera should be placed on a tripod at eyeline height whether sitting or standing. Make certain the camera frames you properly from the top of your shoulders to the top of your head, focused squarely on your face. Check your camera for any lighting presets or white balance settings while using the autofocus feature. The casting office may give you specific self-taping instructions regarding lighting, framing, sound file names, and your scene reader that should be followed to the letter. You will need to slate yourself to the camera as per the standard slate: name and character. Make it confident and upbeat. Then begin. Just like a live audition, though, do not look into the camera while doing your lines. Have your scene reader close but out of camera range and choose someone who can help you to establish mood and pacing. Finally, follow the instructions given for labeling and sending your audition file to the casting office, and then follow-up to make certain it was received.

Are There Audition Scams I Should Avoid?

As a job interview, follow this simple rule for auditions. If money must exchange hands to be considered for casting, you are paying for a job interview, a violation of the Krekorian Talent Scam Prevention Act, a Californian labor law (BizParentz Foundation, "Advance"). Modeling agencies do often require prospective models to attend classes, and exceptions may be made for talent contest entry fees or pre-audition classes, but any audition or submission requirement must be disclosed in the audition notice or it is considered a "bait and switch" scam. Fraudsters continually find new ways to scam naïve newcomers to Hollywood, but some tried and true scams never die. Here are a few common scams to avoid.

Extra Casting Agencies

Newcomers to Los Angeles will soon discover notices stapled to telephone poles advertising extra casting: "Begin your career today. Just call this number." Of course, many legitimate extra casting agencies exist in Los Angeles (see Appendix B), but the fraudulent ones require the actor to purchase a "special" photo package, often costing hundreds of dollars. Hollywood has seen many variations on this theme. To be fair, legitimate extra casting agencies often do charge a one-time registration fee to process the actor into their database, but these agencies actually do casting, rather than sell photographs.

Management Companies

Again promising employment and even fame, these fast talkers pledge access to auditions for a fee for photos, postage, envelopes, portfolio, etc. These promotional packages range from basic to "the works," costing naïve actors their life's savings. Legitimate management companies never ask for an up-front fee. They make their investment back on a commission from the actor's earnings, just as talent agents do.

Casting Workshops

These workshops have grown in popularity. Sponsored by acting companies or entrepreneurial actors, they feature well-established casting directors and associates who observe scenes performed by actors who have paid a fee to participate. The casting directors commonly make opening remarks about their work and then pair off the actors to rehearse sides given to them. One by one each group performs. The casting director observes and critiques each group respectively, but the obvious added inducement derives from the hope that the casting director will remember the actor and call for a future audition. Truthfully, this does happen, but the union has deemed this a violation of its Rule 11, prohibiting any financial inducement for the right to audition (Robb. "SAG/AFTRA Warns"). Most recently the Los Angeles City Attorney filed charges against five prominent casting workshop firms, owned by prominent casting directors, for allegedly violating the Krekorian Talent Scam Prevention Act, resulting in several plea deals and convictions (Baum, "Two Casting Directors"). While the value of the casting director's critique may justify an actor's participation in a workshop, one cannot deny that the implied allure to actors remains the hope that their performance may open a door that might otherwise have been closed.

Other casting directors have chosen a different strategy; opting to teach informational rather than participatory workshops, often in collaboration with an organized non-profit weekend seminar or similar concept. This brings legitimacy to their purpose and satisfies the union's Rule 11 since actors, presumably, do not audition for the casting director but listen and learn from them.

Reality Casting Calls

The growth of reality programming has spawned its own scam artists. Watch for open calls for reality programs or talent search programs that require a "refundable" registration fee. Good luck getting that refund.

Financing Scams

Legitimate films have their financing in order before casting and production is greenlit. But in the dark world of nonunion projects, the next breakout film epic with your starring role only needs a few more thousand dollars to begin production. Needless to say, this film project probably does not exist. That might seem basic, but you might not recognize this scam when a producer offers a leading role in a movie in exchange for help financing the film, since film stars often participate in the financing of films. Except, those films have legal underpinnings and, generally, make a profit. Otherwise, the actor pays to play and, even if the project is legitimate and the risk seems to be shared equally between all parties involved, be assured that the producers will most likely emerge from this project richer, and you poorer.

More creative fraudsters use a common check cashing scam by offering to pay the actor in advance, citing travel, clothes, and so forth. A check may arrive, usually for more money than agreed upon with the producer asking for the additional money to be wired back via Western Union. Of course, the check will bounce and the "additional funds" wired by the actor will be picked up by an anonymous individual (Kagan, "Beware of Casting Scams").

The Casting Couch

This one does not take much explanation. Any nudity requirements for a role must be mentioned in the casting notice. Union projects may only require nudity after the second audition, but recent events involving high placed entertainment industry executives exposed for the sexual harassment of women prove that union projects are not safe from predators. Nonunion projects remain fertile ground for this as well, and men are not immune. Beware of projects that require nudity for an online audition, locations that are in private homes, or questionable circumstances. If you have suspicions, take a friend with you.

ACTOR'S FORUM

You should read every contract. You really should. Sometimes they look incredibly long and tedious, but you really should read what you're agreeing to do because you're signing it. Your agent isn't signing it, you are. But your agent is negotiating, and if you trust your agent, that's half the battle anyway. The only thing that happened to me, before I became union, I had done a nonunion commercial when I first moved here where they wanted to use a bit of it in the Midwest. It was like $1,000 and they were going to give a "plus" 20 percent to my agent who didn't negotiate the original contract. My agent at the time said to just say no. I said, "But we can both make money. It's money being offered to you with no work involved." Needless to say, I'm no longer with that agent.

MICHAEL GABIANO

Everything's on a time contract. You as an actor have so many hours on a given day for the contract. The technicians, the engineer, the studio space. It might be a Paramount movie, but it might record at Warner Bros. So, they're subcontracting space, and they're paying a lot of money to do that. If there's some issue with the sound quality of what was recorded on the set or on location or they'll want you to change some words. That happens throughout the post-production process in every TV and film project. Often actors won't want to redo their own performance, so they'll bring in other actors. But it's work, and it's a union contract, and with union contracts come residuals. If you're lucky enough to get an acting career off the ground, much of what you earn in any given year is residual payments from previous work. It's an excellent way for a young actor or an older actor to get good union work with full pension and health benefits and residuals. It's one of the few real ways to do that, And, you can do it with no credits, if you have skill. If you have something that the director or producer needs, they don't really care whether you've done this before as long as we can bring you up to speed. That's how I got into voice-over.

PETER LAVIN

The interactive contract also covers voice-over and singing. There needs to be a separate mocap contract. That's the problem when its bunched in with other stuff, it gets lost. There are more voice-over actors than mocap actors. So, you go to these meetings, and its ten voice-over actors and one mocap actor, and we just get drowned out. Everybody wants the same thing. Everybody wants more money; voice actors scream for four hours, but I get punched in the face for ten hours. I want a stunt coordinator on-set to watch my back. But for production, that's another body, another contract. . . . You're under a heavy non-disclosure agreement on a video game. They don't tell you everything. That's part of the argument with the union too. Voice actors don't know the characters they're voicing, so they don't know what game they're working on. I show up to a game shoot, and I don't know what I'm working on until I get there. I have to be super skilled. I might think I'm doing swords, and no, you're doing guns today. In a mocap audition you have to ask a lot of questions because they're not telling you anything.

RICHARD DORTON

10 HOLLYWOOD CONTRACTS

I wish to be cremated. A tenth of my ashes shall be given to my agent, as written in our contract.

GROUCHO MARX

If your audition has impressed the right people, you will receive a phone call from either your talent agent or manager, or if you are not represented, from the casting director who will offer a contract for work, referred to as a booking. A description of that work and the rate of pay remain the critical details. Whether you negotiate your own contract or rely upon the professional services of a talent agent, your name will be on the contract and it will be you who is held accountable for fulfilling its terms—not the talent agent. As such, an actor should understand not only the contractual terminology used, but the extent and scope of what a producer may or may not require of you. Nonunion contracts serve well to illustrate that difference.

What is the Difference Between a Union and a Nonunion Contract?

Under the terms of a union contract, a production company hires an actor as an employee with all the rights and benefits afforded employees, such as health care, pension, and profit-sharing (residuals). Under a nonunion contract, an actor is hired as an independent contractor with, commonly, no benefits provided. Union actors make a minimum wage of between $500 and $1,200 per day; a nonunion actor between $100 and $300 per day. As employees, production companies must abide by the Occupations Safety and Health Association's (OSHA) workplace regulations, whether in the studio or on location, while independent contractors must arrange their own health and liability insurance. Union actors on location receive reimbursement for meals and lodging, if not provided for by the production company. Nonunion location shoots may provide a small stipend but rarely cover an actor's real costs. Union shoots limit an actor's work day to eight hours after which overtime begins. Nonunion shoots are over when they are over with no provision for overtime unless negotiated for in the contract. Other significant differences exist between union employment and independent contracting, many involving tax reporting, residuals, and personal integrity that will be discussed below.

But, until an actor joins the union, nonunion projects provide the primary training ground for new actors to Hollywood. From spec commercials to music videos, and from internet projects, to bare budget vanity projects, Hollywood harbors as many would-be screenwriters and film directors as it does actors. Many legitimate projects begin as nonunion projects. For others just beginning their careers as directors or actors, they represent stepping stones. But whether working as a union or nonunion actor, always understand the terms under which you will be working.

What Kind of Contract Information Will I Receive for a Booking?

At the time of the booking, the casting director should also provide call information such as dates, times, and places. This booking may first take the form of a verbal offer, which may be canceled up until noon of the day preceding the start date. A booking slip or an offer letter should follow either to you or to your agent, indicating the role, the number of guaranteed days of work, and the salary. Sometimes these documents even precede the phone call if the talent agent and casting director have already engaged in some one-to-one negotiation over salary, work duration, travel, and expenses during the course of auditions. Depending upon the shooting schedule, daily or weekly contracts may follow. In more advanced scenarios where the actor participates in some other aspect of the production, such as being an associate producer, the actor receives a deal memo, specifying the salient business details agreed upon by the negotiation.

Nonunion bookings are considerably more informal. Often the exact times or locations of the shooting may not have been secured when the booking is made. The contract itself may be only a one-page "memo of understanding," specifying only a set daily salary for a guaranteed number of days and with a start date. If the actor is required to provide a costume, the contract usually provides for a small cleaning allowance, but any other remuneration usually requires negotiation.

Once the booking offer is tendered, whether union or nonunion, the casting director will request confirmation of the following information:

Dates of Hire

The booking may be contingent on the scheduling of a variety of work dates and report times for:

- costume fittings,
- rehearsals,
- makeup or prosthetic fabrication,
- on-set filming/taping,
- travel to location sites,
- retakes, and
- dubbing/re-dubbing.

Once scheduled, the actor has agreed to report on a given day(s) and time(s) to a certain location for their work assignments. Changes do not occur without great angst which could lead to the booking being withdrawn. At that time, an actor may have to choose between a booking and a daytime job that pays the bills. Even worse, an actor may also be given an "on or about" start date, creating uncertainty. But, a start date cannot be moved backward once agreed upon, it can only be moved forward.

Work Rate

A rate of pay will be offered, negotiable in some cases, depending upon the size of the role and the experience of the actor. Union contracts define a hierarchy of principal acting roles and specializations, normally based on the number of days contracted with a minimum scale or rate for each workday. When possible, your talent agent negotiates a higher rate of pay for you on which they earn their commission.

What Should I Expect of a Union Contract?

In 2014 SAG-AFTRA and the Producer's Guild negotiated a Basic Agreement that provides the master contract for all film, television, and commercial productions. It delineates the responsibilities of the producer and the actor, as well as the expectations for both. All production companies that have signed on as a union signatory must issue a union compliant contract to actors booked onto the production with either a standard union supplied form or a negotiated version. It creates one unified set of expectations, such as:

- performer minimum rates,
- residuals,
- number of mandatory union background actors employed before nonunion actors may be engaged.

In addition, this Agreement sets forth specific requirements for, among others:

- **Hours per workday**—A normal workday consists of eight hours and ends at 5 p.m. If these limits are exceeded, overtime begins.
- **Drop and pick-up**—After the completion of filming (six months for film and four months for television) the producer may recall an actor to film additional scenes without payment for the intervening time.
- **Overtime pay**—Most actors receive time and a half for every hour beyond the normal eight-hour workday.
- **Rest periods**—As filming frequently exceeds the eight-hour workday, most union contracts require a twelve-hour rest period between call times on consecutive filming days so that actors and crew are not working and traveling every day on limited rest.
- **Meal periods**—The union requires a thirty-minute meal period given within six hours of the call time under penalty regardless of the filming circumstances. Nevertheless, a producer faced with expensive equipment rentals and a complicated setup may force actors to work beyond this limit and will pay the penalties set by the union.
- **Safety requirements**—These specific and non-negotiable workplace accommodations required by the union are due to hazardous conditions, such as working in smoke or extreme weather.
- **Transportation**—This relates to a myriad of situations regarding location shooting. For example producers must provide first-class air transportation unless six or more performers travel together.
- **Travel time**—An actor may be compensated for the time required to travel to and from locations.
- **Overnight accommodations**—Contractual requirements involving "studio zones" and the "sixteen-hour rule" require producers to provide housing and or pay for an additional day's work if filming outside of the studio zone. Housing must consist of single room accommodation.
- **Use of extras**—Contractual requirements regulate the number of union extras required and their use (SAG-AFTRA, *2014 Theatrical and Television Contracts Digest,* "Background").

Background or extra casting often involves no signed agreement, only an email and a confirmation, but a booking of a principal usually requires a talent agent's services to negotiate the best possible contract with all of its clauses and its stipulations. Like most legal contracts, the language favors the employer. In order to understand exactly what has been agreed to, a few contractual clauses bear clarification.

Name and Likeness

Most contracts give the producer the right to use the actor's name and likeness for the purposes of promoting the project in perpetuity (meaning forever). This provides consent for the use of the actor's name, image, and voice commercially throughout the life of a product.

Merchandizing and Commercial Tie-Ins

An actor grants the producer certain rights unless these are separately negotiated. Does the actor participate in the profit-sharing of those highly lucrative entertainment transactions? That depends upon the contract negotiated. An actor's concern is twofold. First, for an actor used as a spokesperson for products or for endorsement of products, such as toys or clothing associated with the project utilizing an actor's name, image and voice, the actor should be appropriately remunerated. Second, actors must protect against overexposure lest it damages their own marketability with overexposure or charges of "selling out." As an example, Sir Lawrence Olivier was seen by many to have tarnished his legendary reputation by acting as a spokesperson for Polaroid. In addition, one must guard against unwanted publicity or overuse of your name or image. Many producers skirt this issue by selling product placement to brands who pay a fee for their product's prominent placement on-camera. In these cases, the actor receives no compensation even though associated directly or indirectly with the product.

Conflicts

Commercial contracts contain an automatic renewal after twenty-one months unless the advertising company receives a letter from the actor, sent no later than sixty days before the twenty-one-month expiration, revoking his or her consent for use. Why would an actor cancel a commercial? Conflict. Commercials fall into categories and if an actor appears in one pharmaceutical ad, it disqualifies him or her from appearing in any other pharmaceutical ad for the life of that commercial. If the producer wishes to retain the rights to air the commercial and wants to hold a performer exclusive to the product, a holding fee is paid to the actor for every thirteen-week cycle (SAG-AFTRA, *2013 Commercials*, "Use," 26).

Insurance

Investors in a film mostly require insurance to protect their investment. If a film's success is contingent upon a named actor, the producer may also purchase insurance covering the actor's life and health as a condition of employment. If the actor fails the medical exam or is denied coverage for any reason, the actor may be terminated. In addition, the insurance company will have the right to restrict or prohibit the actor's activities as a condition of coverage. As such, a studio can legally bar an actor from sports activities, such as skiing or mountain biking, or from traveling. Pregnancy represents another issue. In the past, an actress could actually be forced to obtain an abortion. Today, producers have claimed that the ensuing weight gain represents a "material change in appearance," as a reason for termination, but some courts have judged this reasoning as spurious (O'Neill, "Actress Fired," *Los Angeles Times online*). To be certain, an actor is insured for any type of air travel and/or driving a vehicle on-camera either as a principal or an extra (SAG-AFTRA, *2014 Basic Agreement*, 93).

Promotion and Publicity Services

A producer may require the actor to consider any "reasonable request" to participate in promotional activities such as photo sessions, interviews, premieres, or television, or radio appearances. Actors usually receive some compensation for these obligations. But, what constitutes a "reasonable request," and how much notification an actor should receive in advance of such activities lies in the negotiated details.

Assignment

This clause gives the producer the right to sell or assign a contracted actor's services. A delay in filming or a change in ownership of the film rights represent two examples where an actor's contract can be reassigned. More than one actor has woken up to discover in the morning trades that they have a new employer.

Favored Nations

Not always found in a contract, this clause provides that a principal actor will receive equal contractual treatment to others on the project in terms of billing, accommodations, or any other contractual provision. Though intended to prevent long tedious negotiations, this clause occasionally backfires on the producer when an actor takes a gamble and holds out for a better deal, perhaps unintentionally providing all the other principal actors a simultaneous upgrade.

Breach of Contract

This clause relates to an actor's work conduct—for example tardiness, incompetence, drug or alcohol use, medications, and any behavior or practice that might hinder an actor's ability to perform. The drama surrounding Charlie Sheen's on-set behavior on the sitcom *Two and a Half Men* stands out as a high-profile example. The producer must give warnings and a twenty-four to forty-eight-hour notice of termination or suspension, but producers rarely take such action for fear of bad press. A "newbie" may safeguard against such an occurrence by understanding that landing a guest actor role does not entitle the actor to suddenly demand star treatment and make outrageous demands.

Employee Conduct

The agreement may contain moral clauses that prohibit the actor from violating public conventions of "decency, morality or social propriety," or from behaving in ways "tending to result in scandal, ridicule or contempt to the Corporation" (Litwak. *Contracts for the Film and Television Industry*, 110). In the past, these clauses kept homosexual actors in the closet or restricted an actor's political involvement with the implied threat of termination. Today, producers have less leverage, but one must assume that actors whose sudden public apologies for inappropriate comments or publicized excursions to rehab clinics have not always been voluntarily.

Termination or Suspension

If a producer wants to fire an actor, a reason will be found. Loosely written, this clause allows the producer to fire or suspend an actor if his or her behavior "provokes any retaliatory action or boycott against himself or the Company" (Litwak, *Contracts*, 117). An actor's bad manners or behavior in the press can lead to the ridicule and disdain of a production company. This clause allows that production company to sever ties with the actor to cut its losses.

Exclusivity

An actor under contract may not work under a competing contract until the term of the preceding contract expires. For instance, an actor in a television series my not work with a competing network, series, or film unless the producer signs a "loan-out agreement" or reassigns the actor in exchange for some form of compensation. But with fewer episodes and work days for a television series, this limits an actor unreasonably. As such the *2017 Theatrical and Television Contract* limits a producer's option period, releasing an actor to pursue additional employment (SAG-AFTRA, *2017 Theatrical/Television Memorandum of Agreement*, 8).

Contracts may also include language about the following:

Studio Zones

In the past, production companies took their film companies outside of Los Angeles' city limits to escape stringent city and union rules. The union eventually created the studio zone, an area with a thirty-mile radius using the intersection of Beverly Boulevard and North La Cienega Boulevard as its center, to determine rates and work rules for union workers and granting less restrictive use of background actors when beyond a certain radius of the studio's operational base. In other cases, studio zones may require rest periods and overnight accommodation for actors filming far outside the studio zone (SAG-AFTRA, *2014 Basic Agreement*, "Studio Zone," 286).

Per Diem

Production companies largely provide craft services, but when not possible, the actor may receive a set amount of money to purchase their own food or pay for location lodgings.

Wardrobe Allowance

An actor who has been asked to bring wardrobe or even prop items for use in the project receives compensation. Extras receive a set compensation amount for each wardrobe outfit requested, whether used or not, while principals receive compensation only for the outfit actually worn.

Consecutive Employment

The number of consecutive days in which an actor works is used to compute salary and residuals, but this may or may not include rehearsals, holidays, or days in which an actor is on hold.

Night Work

Specific rules apply to filming from 8 p.m. to 6 a.m.

Sign-In Sheet

In some cases, actors may be paid for auditions and the required sign-in sheet serves as documentation.

Weather-Permitted Call

An actor may be released four hours after the call time due to bad or unsuitable weather and receive a reduced rate of pay for the day, usually half a day's pay.

Residuals

Calculation of residuals is based on formulas that take into account such things as the contract in place during the production, the time spent on the production, the production type, and the market where the product appears, whether it be television, video or DVD, pay television, or basic cable.

Undirected Scenes

This area provides that non-professional actors may be filmed in public or at public events without payment.

In addition, the contract should specify the services and compensation rates for fittings, rehearsals, post-production dubbing, or various other specified production time requirements. Nonunion projects mostly utilize the same terminology but not the same compensation rates, which usually range from approximately one-half of union rates to merely "copy, credit and meals," meaning that the actor will get a finished copy of the project with his credit attached and a free meal while working.

Usage

Though not always definitive, the contract should delineate the following:

Platform

Is this film for theatrical release or to be sent direct to DVD; live action or animation for television or cable; direct to DVD; New Media for the internet, webcast, or podcast? Is the commercial to be aired on television, radio, the internet, for foreign use, for Spanish broadcast, or for New Media? All have different pay rates and expectations.

Range

On what basis will it be released (nationally, regionally, for syndication, internationally, locally)?

Usage Rate

The usage rate refers to the residual compensation the actor will receive per television airing. In other words, actors receive compensation for each rebroadcast or use of the project in which they appeared as a principal performer. Television actors receive residuals once a show begins re-airing or is released to video/DVD, pay television, broadcast television, basic cable, or new media. Film actors receive residuals once a film appears on DVD, basic cable, free or pay television, or basic cable. Commercials have a complicated system based on the number or times the commercial airs, usually within a thirteen-week cycle. Nonunion commercials often contain a buyout provision, offering the actor a flat fee for the commercial's unlimited usage. SVoD residuals are based on the service's number of subscribers.

Screen Credit

Whether or not an actor receives screen credit, and its placement in the opening credits and advertising, requires negotiation and knowledge of the industry standards. An actor has truly reached celebrity status when his or her name is listed above the project title. But, until then, it is best to be satisfied seeing your name on the interminable credit crawl that flies by.

Each of these items requires expertise in negotiation. Unrepresented actors may find themselves faced with negotiating any or all of an offer, though it is unwise to do so without the services of a talent agent or manager. If not represented, a simple phone call to almost any talent agent will resolve the problem. Few agents would turn down an easy commission.

What Changes Occurred With the New 2017 Theatrical/Television Agreement?

In 2017 the union negotiated a new agreement that amended the *2014 Basic Agreement* between the union and the Producer's Guild for motion pictures, scripted primetime dramatic television, and New Media productions. In addition to increases in basic rates, the following improvements were agreed upon:

- The union secured significant improvements in the residuals rate paid to performers for exhibition of their performances on streaming platforms, like Netflix and Amazon, based on subscription levels.
- Actors should receive residuals for exhibition on subscription video-on-demand platforms after ninety days instead of one-year.
- A 3 percent increase for all minimum rates beginning on July 1, 2019.
- A 0.5 percent increase in pension and retirement contributions.
- A new foreign residual for work shown on affiliated platforms abroad.

- Double overtime for background actors: The eleventh and twelfth hours of the day to be paid at double time instead of time and a half for West Coast work.

- Additional increases for background performers including a boost to the photo double rate—an upfront increase of nearly 17 percent—as well as a new, standard voucher to protect against identity theft.

- Improved provisions for travel for television performers, including the setting of minimums that significantly increase relocation allowances.

- Guaranteed airfare to performers traveling for work taking place in Los Angeles.

- A reduction of the number of "idle days" that may be negotiated, from three to two with an increase in pay for those idle days from $75 to $100.

- A safe travel commitment from management to provide either transportation or lodging for performers who do not believe they can drive themselves safely due to exhaustion or inclement weather.

What Are the Contractual Differences Within the Various Kinds of Projects?

The union has a direct stake in encouraging signatory participation by as many production companies as possible. As such, SAG-AFTRA developed modified agreements to accommodate independent and experimental productions as well as for emerging technologies.

Film

While the major studios may churn out tentpole blockbusters with multimillion-dollar budgets, not all film projects have the resources to provide the generous employee accommodations required by the union. As such, the union has focused on extending union signatory participation to more independent filmmakers by modifying contract accommodations, based upon budgetary levels and providing incentives for participation. This allows smaller budgeted films to work with union actors without having to conform to the ridged requirements for compensation required of larger budgeted projects.

Diversity in Casting

Producers meet this requirement when members of these four protected groups comprise 50 percent of the total speaking roles for 50 percent of the total days

	Standard theatrical	Low-budget	Modified low-budget	Ultra-low-budget	Short	Student film
Budget	=/< $2.5 million	=/> $2.5 million	=/> $700,00	=/> $250,000	=/> $50,000	=/> $35,000
May be increase if agreeing to casting diversity*	N/A	$3.57 million	$1,050,000	N/A	N/A	N/A
Theatrical use	N/A	Required	Required	Entitled	Festivals academic showcase	Classroom only
Must shoot film in US	N/A	X	X	X	X	X
Day performer rates	$985	$630	$335	$125 per day	Deferred	Deferred
Reduced overtime	N/A	X	X	Pro-rated	Deferred	None
Minimum No. of background players	Feature-57 Television -21	30	Incentive for three	Negotiated	None required	None required
Residuals	% of distributor's gross receipts	Lower %	Lower %	Lower %	None	None

CHART 10.1 SAG-AFTRA Contract Comparison

Source: SAG—*Film Contract Digest 2005*

of employment: (1) women, (2) senior performers (sixty years or older), (3) performers with disabilities, and (4) people of color (Asian/Pacific Islander, Black, Latino/Hispanic, and Native American Indian).

Work Rate

An actor's compensation rate is determined either by the number of days an actor is booked or by his or her particular skill, not necessarily by their billing.

- Performer (Day, Weekly, Term, Multiple Picture)
- Background/Special Ability Background
- Dancer/Singer (Day or Weekly)
- Swimmer/Skater
- Stand-Ins/Photo Doubles
- Stunt/Stunt Coordinator

Residuals

After a theatrical release, residuals are due if the movie appears on video or DVD, which includes internet rental and/or download, basic cable, and free or pay television, calculated on the distributor's gross receipts.

Television

The 2012 merger of SAG and AFTRA and the *2014 Basic Agreement* have simplified contractual agreements with the AMPTP by creating a unified set of contractual expectations. While legacy SAG and AFTRA contracts predating July 1, 2012, still may be in effect, all existing television contracts moving forward must comply with the negotiated improvements noted earlier as part of the 2017 Theatrical/Television Agreement, including programming for free and pay television, basic cable, subscription-based or advertiser-supported VOD.

Work Rate

An actor's compensation rate is determined by a variety of factors:

1 The length of time their booking slip guarantees the performer; day player, three-day, weekly, term, or major role.
2 The length of the program filmed from a half-hour to two hours in half-hour increments.
3 The number of episodes guaranteed based on a standard of thirteen episodes.

In addition, a separate side agreement covers animated television programming voice actors that dictates minimum compensation rates based on the length of the filmed segment covered, the number of voices provided, as well as sessions for pick-up lines, lead-ins, lead-outs, bumpers, and wraparounds.

Residuals

Residuals for television are calculated using a formula that utilizes the number of runs and a percentage of the minimum rate of compensation for the actor. Residuals for foreign telecasts of the program use an entirely different formula based upon the distributor's foreign gross.

Commercials

The union defines a "commercial" as a "short advertising or commercial message made as a motion picture, 3 minutes or less in length," intended for use on television, foreign, theatrical, radio, internet, or new media. The 2016 contract includes infomercials, public service announcements, and specific waivers for non-professional actors in specialized commercials such as "Live Events," "Man on the Street," and "Hidden Camera Commercials."

Work Rate

An actor's compensation is determined by a variety of factors:

- the role designation either as a Principal or part of a Group, on-camera or off-camera,
- the classification (A, B, C, or Wild Spot) of the commercial based on the number of cities in which the commercial will air with some cities weighted more heavily than others,
- the intended market such as cable, Spanish language, or foreign use with internet and New Media offered a digital low budget waiver for commercials with budgets under $50,000, and
- the length of the commercial with fifteen second and thirty second commercials commanding a lower rate schedule.

In addition, an actor may receive compensation for "Creative Sessions," auditions in which the actor has been asked to improvise a scene.

Residuals

Actors receive residuals for each time the commercial airs over a thirteen-week cycle which can be renewed over a maximum of twenty-one months, the maximum period of time or cycle for which a commercial may be used. During this time, an actor may also be paid a holding fee to prevent him or her from filming a commercial for a competing product. Public service commercials command their own special rate structure.

Finally, advertisers often run edited versions of the same commercial. A principal or featured actor may receive a "downgrade" during a new cycle, meaning that the commercial has been edited and their face no longer appears or is recognizable in it. Payment may still be issued but at a reduced rate. Consequently, an actor may also receive an "upgrade" in which, after editing, the actor's face is featured, thus requiring additional compensation under union rules (SAG-AFTRA, *2013 Commercials Contract*, 37).

New Media

What has become known as "New Media" refers to the world of cell phones, tablets, watches, BlackBerrys, and whatever comes next to supplant the television. The union's New Media Agreement covers original and derivative dramatic and non-dramatic entertainment productions intended for initial exhibition via the internet, mobile devices, or any other new media platform. Clearly intended to draw younger independent producers into the signatory process, this contract also provides an additional door into union membership for nonunion actors who may wish to produce their own original content. Would-be actor–producers need only overcome three obstacles in order to apply for union signatory status and be eligible to join the union: they need a script, a budget, and at least one union member who has signed on as a principal performer. In addition:

- no minimum budget is imposed,
- initial compensation may be negotiated (although state, local and federal minimum wage laws still prevail),
- payment may be deferred,
- producers may hire union and nonunion actors, and
- the project may be distributed beyond New Media after initial release.

In order to assist potential New Media producers in completing the online signatory process application, the union has created a New Media Entertainment Contracts Department (SAG-AFTRA, *2014 New Media Agreement*).

Interactive Media

To create a character in interactive media one actor may be the face, another the body, and another the voice. Video games have quickly become a significant component of an actor's potential job market with the advent of motion capture and the mobile gaming market. Too quickly, perhaps, as actors' health and safety issues have also become a significant concern. The 2017 Interactive Media Agreement that ended a one-year strike in the industry took a step in the right direction. In addition to a 3 percent increase in session fees, the agreement resolved several issues, but left several others under review.

Transparency

As video game producers must keep their new game scripts secret, performers routinely work without knowing what game or role they could be performing prior to their call. The *2016 SAG-AFTRA Interactive Agreement* has provided union voice-over actors with a set of required disclosures so the actor and agent can make informed decisions about negotiating fair compensation, such as:

- name of the game and a full and forthright description,
- length of performer's role,
- use of unusual terminology,

- use of profanity,
- content of a sexual or violent nature,
- racial slurs,
- whether memorization is required,
- whether cue cards or other prompting devices will be used,
- whether stunts, fighting, or demanding physical action will be required (including a description of the action and the frequency it will be required to be performed), and
- whether yelling, screaming, accents, singing, and/or creature noises will be required.

Residuals

The producer's argument against residuals for video games has been twofold: Firstly video games are more expensive to produce than films, and secondly the "pay per play" compensation structure used for television is unworkable. The union confronted those concerns by negotiating a bonus structure that compensates the actor after every two million game units are sold up to a total of eight million and based on the number of sessions worked.

Vocal Stress

Voice actors often find themselves confronted with multiple sessions of yelling or creating deep-throated battlefield characterizations. Breaks or pauses in the session may be few and far between as session costs are expensive and producers are under time pressure. Union contracts now require a ten-minute break after each hour of work. Voice actors had hoped for more flexibility but instead must be content with a committee to study the issue.

Stunt Coordinators

Performance capture actors largely have more in common with mime artists, but as the market feels pressure to produce bigger and better games, producers expect more from mocap actors which often falls into the category of stunt work—even though mocap actors are not necessarily trained stunt performers. Under any other agreement, the producer would be required to have a stunt coordinator on-set to plan, setup, and coordinate the stunt. For now, mocap actors must also be content with a study committee (SAG-AFTRA, *2017 Interactive Media Agreement*, 2).

Music Videos

Prior to 2012, music videos were filmed as nonunion projects with few, if any, protections, and union actors risked sanctions for working outside of a union agreement. The recently updated historic agreement between the union and music labels provides basic health and safety guarantees; minimum daily rates; grievance and arbitration provisions; and contributions to retirement plans. Utilizing a tiered schedule based on the project's budget level, the agreement covers actors, announcers, dancers, singers, swimmers, skaters, puppeteers, voice-over performers, motion capture actors, and stunt performers as principals. In order to improve service to its members, the union has also formed a new music department to bring sound recordings and music videos under one umbrella (SAG-AFTRA, *2012 Music Video Agreement*).

Industrial/Educational

Corporations often produce in-house training or promotional videos. Educational institutions may create documentary films to chronicle research or scholarly investigation. SAG-AFTRA's *Industrial/Educational Films and Videotape Agreement* provides compensation and work accommodations, such as prompting devices for scripts containing medical or technical terminology, but also additional compensation should these videos ever find their way into theatrical or television distribution (SAG-AFTRA, *2015 Corporate/Educational and Non-Broadcast Agreement*).

Stage

Actors Equity has abandoned its ninety-nine-seat, Equity-waiver plan that served it so well over the years. This permitted union actors to perform in stage productions in Los Angeles County in venues with ninety-nine or fewer seats, with little or no pay, as a form of showcasing talent for potential talent agents or casting directors. In 2015 AEA announced a new 99-Seat Plan for Los Angeles that mandated minimum wage payment ($15) for rehearsals and performances, put limits on the run of the production, and retained the "Scheduling Flexibility Clause," the original codicil that provided actors with an automatic out, sans penalty, if a more lucrative offer were to present itself.

Secondly, AEA dealt a serious blow to "membership" theaters, non-profit organizations partially funded by the actor's monthly membership subscriptions, labeling it "pay for play." Nevertheless the AEA does allow for "self-production," permitting a group of actors to coproduce a project without the benefit of a union contract. In other words, they could collectively own the production as partners, not members, whether incorporated as a non-profit or not. The distinction is significant in that Equity would prefer that its members invest in their own art rather than someone else's. Actors may also encounter LORT agreements, a consortium of larger non-profit regional venues that produce quality productions and pay actors somewhat below commercial rates, but pay nonetheless (Actors Equity, *Los Angeles Transitional 99 Seat Transitional Code*).

What About Background Actors?

Background actors find their way into every genre of film. Once relegated to second class citizenship within the film community, the union has negotiated wages and conditions for background actors across the contract board that treats extras as human beings, not chattel. In general, they receive:

- a set pay rate for an eight-hour day,
- individual chairs,
- gender-specific dressing rooms and, for extraordinary circumstances, additional compensation for:
  - handling hazardous materials,
  - extreme weather conditions,
  - suffering physically demanding costumes or makeup application.

In addition, specific accommodations are provided for the following:

Work Rate

Fee schedules include rates for general background performers, special ability background actors, stand-ins, photo doubles, and omnies. Additional compensation may be provided for hazardous work, working with smoke or water, and for the use of body makeup, as well as overtime and penalties for breaking the sixteen-hour rule.

Wardrobe Allowance

Producers often request that background actors bring at least three different wardrobe selections to the set. Production assistants may take advantage of naïve actors by counting only the wardrobe pieces actually worn for compensation, but the contract stipulates that each outfit schlepped to the set by the actor counts for separate compensation.

Prop Allowance

Handbags, luggage, sports equipment, books, cameras, and electronic equipment, and so forth qualify as a prop. Background actors, if asked to use their own props, receive compensation at set rates listed on the standard contract.

Mileage

When required to report outside of a thirty-mile studio zone, the actor must be paid a mileage reimbursement.

Automobiles

Actors often register their automobiles with an extra casting service for use in a parking lot, a congested highway or other possible filmed scenarios, especially those actors with vintage or period-specific vehicles. But whether registered or not, the union stipulates that the producer must pay mileage to and from the set as well as a specific daily rental rate for use of an actor's personal vehicle.

Vouchers

Union signatory producers must hire a minimum of union extras which varies depending upon the type of contract. Beyond this number, nonunion actors may be hired. But, if a booked union actor fails to show up, a nonunion actor may be "bumped" to union status for this day only. For this they receive a voucher that firstly increases their pay rate substantially, but also serves as the first of three such attainments that eventually would open the door to union membership (SAG-AFTRA, *2014 Theatrical and Television Contracts Digest*).

Extras filmed in commercials also require special consideration, as with film. Individual extras may be contracted, but only under commercial contracts; producers may lump background actors into extra groups and request waivers for special compensation. For instance, crowd scenes, often a staple of commercials, may employ a number of non-professional unpaid extras to fill out large groups. Undirected scenes, or individuals filmed as part of crowd scenes, public events, or accidentally as part of a street scene, may be asked to sign a release form that waives payment to them if they are not members of the union (SAG-AFTRA, "Background Actors," *2014 Theatrical and Television Contracts Digest*).

Are There Other Legal Documents an Actor Must Know About?

Actors toil, in what too often becomes a legal minefield, in which success often leads to litigation and legal histrionics. Other legal documents may be required of you that may be difficult to understand. If so, do not hesitate to ask for legal advice before signing. Others, such as the following are more common and straight forward.

Nondisclosure Agreement

Studios and producers zealously guard scripts and the results of unscripted projects such as reality programs before they are aired. Any actor who auditions for principal roles may be required to sign a nondisclosure agreement as a condition of receiving an advance copy of a film or television script. These also apply to actors who participate in a reality program and may know the final results. These agreements contain severe financial penalties for violation of its provisions. Make no mistake, they mean it! So, read it carefully. Premature disclosure of a script ending or the result of a reality program contest can result in incalculable financial losses to a studio or producer who will take out their angst on the culprit, with help from their considerable legal resources.

Nudity Rider

This amendment to a contract obligates the actor to appear nude, semi-nude and/or to perform simulated sex acts on-camera. The emphasis here focuses on the word "simulated." The union requires strict adherence to its guidelines. Union signatories must follow these guidelines:

- An actor must receive notification prior to auditions if the role requires nudity.
- An actor may wear panties and a G-string during the initial audition or interview.
- The actor receives at least a $500 increase in pay.
- The actor must receive, in advance, a general description of the extent of the nudity and physical contact.
- The actor must provide written consent.
- The actor may remain clothed during rehearsals.
- The film set must be closed with all non-essential personnel removed.
- No still photos can be taken without the written consent of the actor.
- The actor may request a body double if they are uncomfortable with the situation.
- The actor may not revoke consent after filming has been completed.

  (SAG-AFTRA, *2014 Basic Agreement*, "Nudity," 110).

ACTOR'S FORUM

Respect everyone and be kind. What I hear from other actors who do guest star roles or are regulars on a series is that very often when they are in the middle of a scene, some background actors will just latch on and start a conversation between takes and start talking about personal things. There's an appropriateness on set. Too much conversation can be uncomfortable for the actor who has a lot of lines to remember. Let's be honest here, sometimes background people have an incredibly hard job, but they may not understand that this actor has to be on their "A" game in five seconds and in character, and the background actor may not realize that. So, I think every actor no matter what you're doing in a scene on-set should respect everyone's space, should respect what everyone has to do because you are working. This is not a social occasion. Once you've wrapped or you break for lunch and you're all around the craft table, sure you could say hello, especially if they're amenable to talking with you, fine; but always be professional. Respect their time.

MICHAEL GABIANO

You have to sustain a voice for a long period of time. If you are working on a project that's got a lot of yelling and screaming, you've got to figure how do I do this and not kill my voice. You have to learn techniques. I bend my knees so that I'm using more diaphragm than I am other muscles. I lubricate my voice and warm up my voice before I even start work. I continue to do that throughout the session so that there's constantly a mucus coating on my voice to protect it from making harsh vocal sounds. You have to learn how to sustain your voice and how to protect it because as an actor, that's your bread and butter. You've also got to be prepared to miss work. I'm going on vacation tonight. I've already missed two jobs next week. That's a thousand dollars a day that I've walked away from plus residuals. You've also got to look after your instrument. If you need some time off to be with family, that's important too. Obviously don't miss the opportunity of a lifetime. Make yourself available but have a life. . . . Don't be one of those actors that just sat in their studio apartment waiting for the phone to ring. Create work. There's so many more opportunities now with the internet. There's so much animation. Create some voices. Create some work.

PETER LAVIN

If you can do stunts and you get a chance to do acting, motion capture is a great blend of those two skills. I have played every race, color, size. I've played women because there weren't a lot of women doing motion capture when I started. There's no down time in game shoots. We're trying to capture between 200 to 300 moves in that eight-hour shoot day. It ranges from running forward, backwards, right, left, on the diagonal. Then doing it with a knife, then doing it with a gun, then doing it with a rifle. Climbing, jumping, falling, getting punched, getting shot in the head. Most of the times, you're going to have markers on your wrists so your hands look like paddles. The animator goes in afterwards and animates all the hand stuff you're doing. Or, if they pay more, they can put markers on your fingers, but every time you add somethings, it's more and more expensive. It's a collaborative art. I might be the body, you might be the voice, this guy might do the stunts, and this guy will be the face; and then all of that goes to twenty animators who are fixing our performance, correcting it, and making it pretty.

RICHARD DORTON

11 WORKING IN HOLLYWOOD

I can't say I have enough experience with Hollywood to feel that I've encountered racism there. I can tell you that I did about five fruitless years of auditioning for voice-overs where I did variations on tacos and Latin accents, and my first screen role was a bellhop on The Sopranos. It was actually an amazing experience.

LIN-MANUEL MIRANDA, *"Finding Originality"*

MAJOR HOLLYWOOD STUDIOS

STUDIO	STUDIO PARENT	ADDRESS
Columbia Pictures	Sony Pictures	10202 West Washington Blvd. Culver City, CA 90232
20th Century Fox	Walt Disney Company	10201 W. Pico Blvd. Los Angeles, CA 90064
Universal Pictures	NBC Universal (Comcast)	100 Universal City Plaza Universal City, CA 91608
Paramount Pictures	Paramount Group (Viacom)	5555 Melrose Avenue Hollywood, CA 90038

Walt Disney Pictures	Walt Disney Company	500 South Buena Vista Street Burbank, CA 91521
Warner Bros. Pictures	Time-Warner	4000 Warner Blvd. Burbank, CA 91522

Congratulations! You are a working actor. You have a call time at a studio or location because someone has offered you money for your acting skills. Whether for a lead in a new series or an extra in a street scene, certain standards of conduct are expected as in any profession where time is money.

What Should I Bring With Me to the Set?

The production crew usually reports to the set an hour or two before the actors, and they have little patience for actors with tardy excuses. Rule #1—be on time and prepared. You should always bring:

1 **The production company contact number**—Traffic happens, as do accidents and confusing directions. A preemptive call eliminates the need for a panicked call to one's agent and all the ensuing embarrassment and explanations.

2 **Driver's license** (or an additional form of identification)—Studio security requires an acceptable form of photo ID, regardless of the role.

3 **Union membership card**—Although not a requirement, this is a good idea.

4 **Paperwork**—Any paperwork you have received regarding this call may be helpful. In addition, bring a pen and a journal to make notes regarding work hours; per diem received; contact names; and telephone numbers for future reference.

5 **Cell phone**—This would seem to be a no-brainer, but production companies often ban cell phones from the set for a variety of reasons, such as celebrity privacy, script security, or to prevent an otherwise perfect take destroyed by a ringing cell phone. But, for many reasons an actor may need to contact their agent, manager, babysitter, husband/wife/significant other, or day job. Turn it off upon arrival and, if possible, leave it in a secure location with your other personal items.

6 **Change**—Parking may require feeding a meter. A parking garage may require payment in advance, although you should receive a refund before the day's end.

7 **Laptop/books/iPod**—Filming often turns into a hurry up and wait syndrome with large swaths of down time between setups. Actors often sit around and share their "war stories," but others put the time to better use. Production companies provide principal actors private and secure dressing rooms or trailers to keep personal items, but extras are entitled only to a rest area with chairs, not secured dressing rooms. You might wish to inquire in advance as to whether the production company provides a secure location before bringing anything of value onto the set.

What Should I NOT Bring?

1 **Food**—Unless you are on a special diet, leave your lunchbox at home. Production companies provide elaborate and generous craft services.

2 **Friends or relatives**—Everyone has a friend or relative who would love to see what happens on a film set, but bringing them with you is never appropriate unless you have been given permission in advance.

3 **An attitude**—Leave this at home along with your acting awards and degrees. No one cares how many films you have done or how you would direct the scene. They care about you hitting your mark, saying your lines correctly, and staying out of the way when not needed. Even if someone else pulls attitude, remember your professionalism. If you are disrespected, report any ill treatment or inappropriate request immediately to your agent or on-set representative.

What Should I Do When I Arrive On the Set?

1 Report to the assigned contact person and sign in. All extra casting services will have an on-set representative. Principal actors will report to a production assistant usually bouncing between each arrival with an omnipresent clipboard.

2 Fill out any paperwork which may include a W–4, and an I–9, a release form, and a payment voucher.

3 Wait. Costuming and makeup follow a tight schedule as does filming. Whether waiting in a trailer, dressing room, or holding room, an assigned production assistant keeps actors informed and on task.

What Set Etiquette Should I Observe?

What you may have experienced in community theater or student filmmaking has little relevance to an industry in which every wasted minute amounts to thousands of dollars. An actor's responsibility lies in not contributing to any delay.

1   Be fifteen minutes early to your call time.

2   Arrive with your lines learned.

3   Do not touch anything unless asked to.

4   Be silent during filming. "Quiet on the set" means exactly that.

5   Stay calm, boisterous adolescent behavior does not go over well with producers.

6   Do not give unsolicited advice to anyone.

7   Learn the names of the crew members. They can make an actor's day a dream or a nightmare.

8   Thank everyone, twice!

9   Do not throw anything away. Keep and file all call sheets and production information for reference.

10 Promptly return any props and hang up your costume once you are wrapped for the day.

11 Fill out all necessary paperwork before signing out and leaving the set. The union cannot help an actor without completed vouchers or production time sheets. The producers must submit a Production Time Report to the union as an official record for payment. Your signature confirms your hours worked. Bring any mistake to the attention of a production assistant or call the union if you believe the report is in error.

What Different Work Environments Will I Encounter?

Background

Bruce Willis, Ben Affleck, Clint Eastwood, and Sylvester Stallone all launched a successful acting career by first working as an extra. Whether to make ends meet, to get into the union, or to be discovered, in hierarchical terms, background actors represent the bottom tier. Often required to bring their own clothing, extras can be seen hauling some type of overnight bag or suitcase to the set. Herded like children from holding rooms to the set, an extra alternates between "hurrying up to wait" mode and complete idleness. Holding rooms can be hot or cold, may have cushioned or hard metal chairs, and food which is fresh or leftover. Far from glamorous, hours can be long with overtime only observed on union projects. Work conditions can be hazardous, involving moving vehicles and stunt work. Principals rarely mingle with extras except, perhaps, at the craft table where a strict hierarchy is observed: Principals eat first, then crew, then background. Daily pay rate can vary from "copy, credit and meals" to $195 depending upon the union status, the production contract, and the actor's status (special ability, stand-in, etc.). Additional pay may be received for hazardous work and for furnishing wardrobe, personal props, or vehicles. The union has established basic standards for work conditions, dressing rooms, and meal periods while nonunion projects remain a gambit (SAG-AFTRA, "Background Actors").

Some actors report annual incomes of six figures working exclusively as background extras. Others have found it a stepping stone to developing their career by keeping in contact with production members who can often recommend an actor for future shoots, sometimes even channeling small principal roles to them.

1   Check-in online with the production assistant before leaving home for the set in case of a cancelation or weather-permitting call.

2   Follow the instructions you are given at booking, especially regarding parking.

3   Check-in with the background production assistant, and promptly report to the second AD when instructed.

4   Fill out the paperwork promptly and correctly.

5   Be helpful, accommodating, and friendly with the crew, especially costume and makeup.

6   Listen carefully to instructions and remember people's names, especially ADs.

7   Be patient during long periods of idleness and bring something to keep you occupied.

8   Keep your energy up all day.

9   Stay in the background, don't bother principals while they are working, and do not take photos . . . ever.

Voice-Over

Some actors specialize in voice-over for animation, video games, and automated dialogue replacement (ADR). But, principal actors often find themselves in a recording studio staring at themselves on a big screen, lip syncing to their own performances because the sound quality had been compromised by off-camera noise of some kind. For them, the work environment may seem alien and the vocal requirements stressful. Professional voice-over actors know to avoid sugary drinks prior to working and to bring water and lozenges to keep their vocal cords lubricated, but traditional actors may find the pace daunting and working with different microphones tedious. For them, experience is the only teacher.

For those who wish to specialize, a voice-over career usually begins with voice-over classes, creating a demo reel, and then finding a voice-over agent, who will help them break into what has become increasingly competitive and somewhat of a closed shop. Technology has now provided voice-over actors the ability to submit for work in this $15 billion industry via website apps such as VoiceBunny, and then audition via home recording studios from almost anywhere. Successful voice-over actors can quickly find themselves in the union and in great demand as voice-over occurs in most projects whether they be automated dialogue replacement; voice acting in animation and video games; or commercial announcements. Voice-over actors who land gigs on video games and animation can expect little transparency regarding their roles, a heavy nondisclosure agreement, and a work environment devoid of props, wardrobe, makeup, and in some cases, even a scene partner.

Performance Capture or Motion Capture (Mocap)

When actor Andy Serkis first appeared onscreen as Gollum in the 2001–3 *Lord of the Rings* trilogy, few recognized this 3D animation technology as a game-changing approach to bridge the gap between animation and live-action film. Since then, Serkis has built a career playing nonhumans, while actors Tom Hanks, Mark Ruffalo, and Sigourney Weaver have also donned the odd-looking body suits that use ping-pong ball sensors to digitally capture an actor's performance. Inspired by the early 1900s animation technique of rotoscoping, the United States military briefly tested a form of electromagnetic motion capture to track the head movements of pilots. Disney Studios eventually developed it as a platform to create movement for its animatronics. Today's optical motion capture technology now samples the actor's sensors many times each second and creates a database of 3D points, with which an animator can build a character. New facial motion capture technology utilizes facial dots assigned to specific muscle groups that provide sophisticated sampling of an actor's most important tool, their facial mask, necessitating the change of terminology to performance capture. Finally, real-time monitoring, where the actual animated character can be dropped into the monitor in real time, has freed motion capture from the green screen CGI environment and into the realm of live-action cinema ("Prepare", *Screen Actor,* 24–28).

The bulk of performance capture work still occurs in stuffy green screen rooms known as volumes, located at specialized studios not necessarily found along the usual paths beaten by the entertainment industry, where body-suited actors mime all sorts of movement sequences, against nonexistent adversaries, using imaginary props. Most mocap actors are trained stunt people with experience in martial arts, swordplay, extreme sports, or the military, but as performance capture continues to demonstrate cinematic success, actors of all types may find themselves wearing the skin-tight Lycra body suits that are not for the modest. Filmed in 3D or 360 degrees, the need for different camera angles has been eliminated, and, with no sets or lights to move, sessions are fast-paced and physically exhausting. As with voice-over, ten-minute breaks are mandated by the union's *Interactive Agreement,* and though stunts comprise the bulk of the work, acting is still an essential component with classes now stressing a Stanislavski-based acting style along with physical training.

Television

Weekly television series represent an important source of an actor's potential income with some estimates predicting over 500 scripted shows in 2019 between broadcast, cable, and streaming services. Aside from coveted series regular roles, co-star, and guest star roles denote a stepping stone in an actor's career and a somewhat different work environment than film or commercial shoots. Structured around either a one-week or two-week cycle, actors first meet for a table read before progressing to blocking, rehearsals, run-throughs, and eventually filming. Sitcoms often shoot before a live audience using a three-camera setup, while dramas alternate between the studio and locations utilizing a single camera. Hours can be long and actors still complain about the lack of rest time between work days, but not as much as crew members who work even longer hours. Scripts may go through many rewrites as network suits and producers force changes, and scenes with guest actors are lumped into one day to minimize cost. Often close-knit and familial, the regular cast and crew function as a well-oiled machine. Guest actors will be welcomed in but only peripherally.

What Can I Expect From Nonunion Projects?

Unfortunately, when calculated against the total volume of all film, television, and commercial casting in Los Angeles, nonunion projects represent the greater number. They fall into five categories.

- We have a good script and some money.
- We have a bad script and some money.

- We have a good script and no money.
- We have a bad script and no money.
- We haven't a prayer of ever getting this project produced.

An actor must learn to differentiate between each category and to know when to say, "No thank you." Some projects, such as the first two categories, have the right intentions but simply lack resources and may represent true opportunities for nonunion actors. Others merely seek to exploit an actor's good intentions. One learns to tell the difference by noticing certain warning signs. Do auditions proceed chaotically? Is information posted incorrectly? Are questions answered evasively? All these are omens that portend ill for the working conditions, and more importantly, for compensation. Union actors must abide by SAG Global Rule One and accept work only from union signatory producers, but, if you are not yet a member of the union, these projects represent an important training ground. When you are offered a nonunion role, ask questions and then trust your instincts. Beginning actors should familiarize themselves with Californian labor laws that, at the bare minimum, provide some sense of a safety net (California Department of Industrial Relations, *California Labor Code*).

What Kind of Nonunion Projects Will I Encounter?

Films

The good—Occasionally, a director or A-list actor, for reasons of intellectual or artistic collaboration, may prefer to work in anonymity and outside of the traditional boundaries of the industry. Shooting is done discretely, often over many weeks or months, and the film commonly exhibits for film festival consideration or goes directly to DVD. *The bad*—The bulk of these projects tend to be youth-oriented high school/summer camp/forbidden sex/slasher films with bad scripts, uncomfortable location conditions, long waits between takes, and nonexistent craft services. *The ugly*—Actors will encounter a half-written script, endless rehearsals, and incessant promises before the director quits and the producer's cell phone number becomes inoperable.

Television

Basic cable airs many nonunion serial and episodic television programs. Their production companies, though reputable, prefer to function outside of union jurisdiction to produce cheaper products for an insatiable market. They do not employ actors but provide them with a stipend as an independent contractor that is considerably less than union scale with no provisions for overtime, residuals, or workman's compensation if injured on the set. Still, national airtime is national airtime. A principal role entitles an actor to bragging rights, an IMDb credit, announcements to casting directors, and eventually, key acting clips for an actor's reel.

Internet

The union's New Media Agreement has reduced the number of nonunion internet projects considerably, but a great many television pilots do begin as short, low-budget prototypes, filmed on-spec as sales presentations. Everything is bare bone. Actors participate in the hope of participating on the ground floor of the next great sitcom. Sometimes this does pay off by being re-shot as a network pilot, though not always with the same actors.

Commercials

Nonunion commercial filming prospers in Los Angeles and represents a frustration for union actors. Commercials filmed under union jurisdiction not only provide for minimum wages but for residual or buyout payments as well. Nonunion projects largely only offer a one-time stipend payment or a speculative promise, if the intended sponsor buys the finished project. Unfortunately, commercial sponsors easily exploit loopholes in the unions' jurisdiction and FCC oversight.

Reality Programs

Known as "unscripted projects," reality programs generally fall into three categories:

1 feel-good makeover shows,

2 contests of some (or little) skill, or,

3 a "real world" group of people forced to live with each other.

Once again, these programs do not employ actors. They select contestants, or participants. The real reality is that actors comprise an enormous contestant pool for these programs, most of which find their "contestants" through breakdowns to casting services. The selection process even mirrors theatrical casting, but at its end, the actor is offered a contestant or participant contract, rather than a performance contract, which stipulates the "prizes," cash or otherwise, but not wages or terms of employment.

Whether these are a curse or boon to a career, an actor who opts to participate in a reality program must prepare to perform without a safety net. These programs mostly operate outside the jurisdiction of the union and producers have little incentive to work through talent agents or managers. For instance:

- An actor may be asked to agree to submit to humiliating and potentially dangerous scenarios and may have to pledge not to sue if plans go awry and cause bodily harm or death.

- An actor must submit to a background check as a condition of participation. Past experiences on several notable network programs, such as *Big Brother*, have necessitated careful screening for potential embarrassment and to guarantee the safety of the other participants.

- An actor must fill out a rather long and detailed, multi-page, application form. Producers may contact friends, family, and employers as a condition of participation and may obtain the actor's personal and financial records within the lax legal boundaries prescribed by law.

- The producers may require exclusivity rights, and require the signing of a very scary nondisclosure agreement that threatens financial ruin if violated.

Music Videos

Once mostly operating outside the jurisdiction of the union, music video production companies pay actors and performers small stipends or an hourly wage while constantly pushing the boundaries of safety and erotica. The union's *Music Video Agreement* has helped to bring more of the music video projects under a union banner with the safeguards and wages spelled out more clearly.

Stage

Los Angeles is primarily a film town and theater serves as a tool for actors to gain exposure. Nonunion theater in Los Angeles unfortunately too often resembles community theater, complete with dueling egos and artistic vacuity. Many actors involved may never have experienced performing on stage live. Imagine the shock when fresh out of the box from the University-of-Wherever a trained actor discovers that not everyone understands theater etiquette and ethics the same way. When you read the casting notices, remember that "nonunion" also means "non-professional," and too often, "no theater experience." I have learned the hard way that as a theater professional, I need to work with professionals, especially those who do not waste my time. Equity-flavored productions have the distinct advantage of being professional. If you are a union member, you will be paid for a change, and if you are not, you will at least be with good company.

What Workplace Issues Might I Encounter?

On-Set Safety

Harrison Ford, Tom Cruise, Jake Gyllenhaal, Sylvester Stallone, Daniel Craig, and Dylan O'Brien; a few of the high-profile actors who have recently suffered serious injuries while filming despite current OSHA and union protection. The *Los Angeles Times* has documented 251 catastrophic injuries and forty-four deaths between 1990 and 2014 (Schileuss, "Film set accidents," *Los Angeles Times*). These, and more recent accidents, have led the SAG-AFTRA National Board to create a President's Blue-Ribbon Commission on Safety to investigate among other issues extended work hours, inclement weather protection, and travel demands.

But, the safety issues extend into the realm of stunt and hazardous conditions, as productions continue to push the boundaries of an actor's skills during extreme action sequences in an increasingly competitive live-action market. Actors in union productions have certain protections and options that nonunion actors lack. Both workplaces must comply with OSHA requirements, but union standards and protocols exceed OSHA's and extend into areas of aerial safety, firearms, water hazards, fog, and other artificial effects and stunts.

While most stunts are performed by trained stunt actors, any actor may be called upon to participate in an action sequence that may contain a degree of danger or hazard. Under union jurisdiction, protocol requires at least one safety meeting that includes the actors, prior to rehearsal. A stunt coordinator, who has supervision over all aspects of the planning, set-up, rehearsal, and execution of the stunt, will then brief everyone as to the sequence of events and their responsibilities. At this time, at least one rehearsal will be conducted before filming. At any point, an actor has the right to refuse to perform any stunt or hazardous activity that places them in danger. If this happens, an actor should speak up, and then call their agent and/or manager, who represent(s) the actor's first line of defense in such matters. The union also provides a hotline number, (844) SAFER SET, to report workplace concerns. Still, as an actor, you bear the ultimate responsibility for your own safety on the set and must ultimately bear the consequences if you agree to a request. As such, actors should ask questions and take note of the Safety Bulletins available on the union website (SAG-AFTRA, "Safety Bulletins"). In addition, actors can protect themselves by making certain that:

- a medic with visible ID is on-set when a performer is working under hazardous conditions,
- first aid equipment is readily accessible,
- fire extinguishers and exits have been identified, and
- a vehicle equipped with a stretcher and first aid equipment is standing by.

Vocal Stress

Voice-over actors often find themselves spending a work day making vocally stressful screams, requiring their full vocal range, especially for video games. Though union contracts set limits on what an actor may be required to do, the union reports receiving an increasing number of complaints of these provisions being violated, causing medical problems for actors including vocal nodules, cysts, polyps, and vocal cord hemorrhaging that can cause career-ending vocal cord paralysis. The union has fought back by filing unfair labor charges with the National Labor Relations Board and has asked the California occupational safety regulators to investigate the videogame industry for unsafe work practices. Again, though, actors bear the ultimate responsibility for their own safety. Following some basic advice can mitigate these issues.

- Learn to release excess tension in the body and throat muscles.
- Learn diaphragmatic breath support techniques.
- Bring plenty of throat lozenges and/or water to each session to maintain vocal lubrication.
- Avoid caffeine, alcohol, smoke, and air conditioning prior to a work session.
- Pay attention to warning signs, such as hoarseness, and seek out a qualified laryngologist.
- Always warm up your voice prior to any work session.
- Seek out a qualified voice teacher to learn proper vocal technique.

Motion Capture Stunts

The expanding market for video games has been a boon to union mocap actors, who grind out the movements and sequences needed to satisfy the animators. Increasingly these sequences cross into a realm that on a film set would require a stunt coordinator. But as this is animation, no such requirement exists. The issue was raised during negotiations of the union's *2016 Video Game Agreement,* but video game companies have been reluctant to bargain on this issue for fear of opening the door to other live-action protocols. Both parties agreed to continue discussions.

Sexual Harassment

The union spells out its zero-tolerance policy towards sexual harassment to all union signatories and talent agents, including their employees, agents, representatives, contractors, subcontractors, and vendors, in its Affirmative Action/Diversity Policy and Anti-Discrimination and Sexual Harassment Policy (SAG-AFTRA, "Production

Notice & Resources"). Still, sexual harassment happens—both to women and to men. We all know it; we have seen it; we may have experienced it. The public shaming of high-profile Hollywood actors and producers with the #MeToo movement has shone a bright light on Hollywood's dirtiest secrets. In the future, abusers will find their victims more sophisticated and prepared to resist. Actors should take note of the toll-free number provided to report any incident and of the process required to make a formal complaint (SAG-AFTRA, "Discrimination & Harassment Policy"). Unfortunately, the actions of those who abuse their positions often results in collateral damage where projects get canceled and innocent actors lose work.

Discrimination

An audition is a job interview and the same state and federal hiring laws that govern job interviews apply to auditions. As such, regardless of the specific requirements stated in the breakdown, actors may not be asked questions during an audition about their age, ancestry, religion, sex, sexual orientation, gender identity or expression, pregnancy, national origin, citizenship, marital status, disability, medical condition, veteran status, or any other characteristic protected by state or federal laws whether a union or nonunion casting. Actors who feel they have been discriminated against may contact the union's toll-free number or contact their state or federal Employment Equal Opportunity Commission for redress.

Privacy

Most actors realize that the less the public knows about them, the more effective they can be as an actor. Actors may face a challenge separating their private life from their professional life, especially in an era of social media marketing in which every detail of your life can be fodder for gossip. At present, a California state law that barred IMDb from posting an actor's age has been declared null and void by a federal judge, citing it as a violation of the First Amendment. Employers may not provide personal employee information, but when living in the public eye, actors must make personal decisions about privacy that can affect their families as well as themselves. If exposing your private information while marketing yourself, remember that information on the internet remains forever.

Pay Equity

The issue of women's pay equity has just begun to gain attention as the disparity between female actors and their male counterparts has begun to be exposed. As performers at this level negotiate their above-scale rates through their agents, the union has little leverage other than to investigate the circumstances. The solution looks to be in shining more light on the issue.

ACTOR'S FORUM

Know how much money is coming in. I'm not a financial whiz at that, and I don't always budget perfectly for every particular month, especially when it's a lean month. I think basic financial skills, being able to put a budget together for what you need to do is important. For example, tax season is coming up. Know everything you can deduct and what you can't deduct. I think those things I've learned. My tax person says it to me every year, "office supplies." On a given year actors can go through an enormous amount of money on what could be considered office supplies. I've started keeping receipts for all of those where before I didn't do that. This is something that a lot of actors don't realize, especially union actors: your phone expenses, certain driving expenses, your cell phone bill every month. If you're a member of a credit union, you get a deduction every month from the cell phone company.

MICHAEL GABIANO

I don't really write off all of my throat lozenges though I probably should. I'm sort of the nice guy who always brings in tons of throat lozenges so everybody can use them because people forget, and it is crucial. A lot of the ADR work is team work, so you need the team to be up to snuff. Your home studio is deductible obviously. Any regular actor has a lot of write-offs that they can apply. Production of any demo materials is all tax deductible. Any education that you're doing. Typically, your cable subscription, your movie tickets, your theater tickets. Anytime you're going to watch any other performances is part of your education, and that's also tax deductible.

PETER LAVIN

I can deduct the cost of the gym, but a regular actor can't. I have a really good accountant. My expenses are for a lot of props for doing swords and light sabers, things like that. Every weapon moves differently. So, I have to have that in my arsenal to know what to use. I have a tool box of props because these motion capture places won't tell me what I'm working on until I get there, so I load my trunk up to be prepared. I work at a small VFX house; they have one gun, one rifle. I just went in and shot a piece where I played eight different characters, and they all had different weapons, so we took that gun and flipped it upside down and held it backwards. But I also said, let me go to my car. I have four more guns in my car that are resin props that I could hold.

RICHARD DORTON

12 FINANCE AND ACCOUNTING

The income tax has made more liars out of the American people than golf has.

WILL ROGERS, *Weekly, 1923*

ACTOR'S RESOURCES

IRS—Is Your Hobby a For-Profit Endeavor?

IRS—Self-Employed Individuals Tax Center

IRS Publication 587—Business Use of Your Home

VITA (Volunteer Income Tax Assistance)/Los Angeles site
Youth Policy Institute (YPI)
1075 Western Ave., Suite 110
Los Angeles, CA 90029
323–836–0055

IRS Form 3676-B—(VITA) Services Provided/What to Bring

IRS Publication 463—Travel, Entertainment, Gift and Automobile Expenses

IRS S Corporations

Mint.com—Personal Finance and Money Manager

The 2017 tax reform legislation passed by Congress presents a new problem for actors who, as employees, could previously deduct the considerable business expenses they incurred in the process of pursuing their career. Unfortunately, this new tax legislation eliminates employee deductions, potentially raising an actor's tax liability by 30 percent. Ironically, nonunion performers working as independent contractors may still deduct these costs as legitimate business deductions, but not union actors. Tax experts have suggested that professional actors, who work consistently and are high earners, consider incorporating themselves by forming their own S-Corporation or Limited Liability Corporations (LLC). Many name actors already do this to limit their tax liability. By doing so the actor literally becomes a business and may then continue to deduct expenses as previously (Internal Revenue Service, "S Corporations"). But as Sandra Karas, Secretary/ Treasurer of Equity counsels, "Those corporations cost money. They cost money to form. They cost money to have the taxes prepared. They cost money to run payroll through" (Karas, *2018: What Can We Expect*). Unfortunately, most actors cannot predict their professional earnings in advance, making this an extremely expensive fix in lean years. This new tax law also eliminates charitable contributions, medical expenses, and mortgage interest deductions, thus affecting many other taxpayers. Union leadership emphasizes that actors are not alone in this struggle and legislators are being pressured to make corrections. When, and if this will happen is anyone's guess, but in the meantime the best advice is to continue to document your expenses and consult a tax specialist before filing your taxes. The Volunteer Income Tax Assistance (VITA) program has been created by The Actors Fund, supported by the performing arts unions to assist income tax preparation for low to moderate income members of both SAG-AFTRA and Equity, by offering six days of free tax preparation. Union members should go to the VITA website to determine their eligibility and can access tax preparation worksheets on the Equity member portal. This chapter, thus, assumes an actor should still document business expenses as before.

When the Clinton Administration nominated actress Jane Alexander to chair the National Endowment for the Arts in 1993, she faced a monumental task in preparation for her confirmation hearings. The government required her to assemble the names and addresses of all her employers as an actress. "This was daunting, to say the least," she stated, "because of the numerous engagements I'd had as an actress; some had taken only an hour or two … and none, not even performing in a hit play, had lasted longer than a year. When the list reached more than three hundred, I began to give up" (Alexander, *Command Performance*, 19–20).

Actors rarely experience long-term employment and may work for a dozen or more employers during the course of a tax year. The added burden for an actor lies not in the 45,000 pages of the tax code, but in bookkeeping and knowing the tax liabilities inherent in this profession.

Do Actors Have Any Special Tax Liabilities?

Neither Congress nor the IRS have been sympathetic with the tax reporting burden faced by actors and artists of all stripes. Few taxpayers face reporting dozens of bookings during the course of the year and their corresponding deductions. The important division lies in union status. Actors hired under a union contract have been hired as employees. Thus, their income takes the form of a salary with residual, health benefits, and pension benefits. Union projects may pay directly to the actor or through the union, but in both cases taxes are withheld and Social Security and Medicare deductions are matched. Still other projects, principally national commercial projects, route through a central advertising booking agency that withholds taxes and then transfers the funds to the actor's commercial agent who deducts his or her commission before issuing a check to the actor. Either way, the actor as an employee, signs W–2s, receives 1040s at the end of the year from each employer, and files a tax return reporting this income.

But, actors rarely rely entirely upon union employment for all of their professional income. Actors new to Hollywood may find breaking into the union takes some time and must rely upon nonunion work in the meantime. Actors may also freelance as writers, directors, musicians, choreographers, print models, or designers. In these cases, unless a member of an associated union, the actor is hired as an independent contractor and the IRS considers these actors to be self-employed. Nonunion projects often pay with cash, for which the actor signs a receipt. Others will have the actor sign a voucher for a lump sum check (no deductions). At the end of the year, the actor receives an IRS 1099 form that declares the income. Many companies do not bother if the stipend was under $400, but they are required to if they paid an actor $600 or more during the course of the year. The actor at that time becomes liable not only for the unpaid withholding deduction, but, as a self-employed independent contractor, also the matching Social Security and Medicare payments an employer would have paid to the IRS. The 15.3 percent self-employment tax levied on this income reflects this liability.

In addition, the IRS may determine your acting income to be a hobby, not a career, and disallow deductions that exceed your acting income. For-profit endeavors are expected to be exactly that, profitable. Section 183 of the IRS code known as the Hobby Loss Rule states that any artistic endeavor that does not make a profit in three of the last five years should be classified as a hobby (IRS, "Is Your Hobby a For-Profit Endeavor?"). An actor new to the profession may go for many years when their costs far exceed their professional income and will rely upon the income from a survival job for many years before reaching an acting career level that self-supports. For this reason, actors should not deduct career expenses in excess of their acting income in consecutive years, but instead deduct only enough without showing a loss. Also, remember that equipment costs and other capital expenses can be depreciated over time rather than deducted all at once.

Does the IRS Offer Any Special Tax Incentives to an Actor?

Congress designated the category of qualified performing artist in the 1980s with a special tax status and some restrictions. But anyone thinking Congress might have found enlightenment should first look closely at those restrictions. The actor must have:

- worked for two or more employers during the year as an actor,
- received at least $200 in wages from each employer,
- job-related expenses of more than 10 percent of this income, and
- an adjusted gross income of $16,000 or less.

Actors who meet these criteria may deduct employee business expenses as an adjustment to income, rather than as miscellaneous itemized deductions. The main difference lies in the fact that for most, miscellaneous itemized deductions are subject to a 2 percent limit. A qualified performing artist is not subject to this limitation (IRS, *Publication 529: Performing Artists*).

What Deductions May Actors Take on Their Income Taxes as an Employee?

Hopefully, with professional union status comes income and with income comes taxes. But with taxes also come deductions, a small detail all too often overlooked by beginning actors who, more used to paying for the privilege, have developed a hobbyist's mentality. How many costume pieces, makeup items, or props have been paid for out of pocket in an actor's formative community theater years? An actor beginning a career in Hollywood will incur considerable start-up costs, as well as ongoing overhead, and future capital expenditures for items such as a computer, printer, camera, camcorder, etc. The costs of moving to begin a career or new job are also deductible as long as you maintain a paper trail of receipts.

Actors must also demonstrate the discipline to maintain normal business records. During my sabbatical year, I booked twenty-four roles. That meant twenty-four different employers, twenty-four different contracts, and theoretically twenty-four different W–2s or 1040s (if no taxes were deducted). Many of those production companies were structured as short-lived, limited partnerships that probably meant they were soon defunct or operating under the IRS radar. Still, I counted fifteen different employers that year. The tax preparation was laborious and tedious. Some studios often provide paperwork on location, but this can easily be lost and may be hard to read. Conscientious actors must keep a log of their work each year and retain all paperwork even if it seems insignificant. Sometimes a retrieved call sheet reveals the name or telephone number needed to secure the W–2 or 1090 that never came in the mail. I desperately tied together the pieces of my professional life from the assemblage of emails, contracts, vouchers, and receipts that documented my year's work.

Minimizing your tax burden requires careful bookkeeping and an understanding of what cost are applicable as tax deductions. In general, an employee's allowable work-related deductions fall under two categories: the cost of looking for work and non-reimbursed expenses.

The Cost of Looking For Employment

The IRS permits an individual to deduct costs related to the process of finding work, something that actors do every day and at great expense. Most bookings, regardless of pay, rarely last longer than a day to a week. As most union actors only work one or two jobs per year, this means the vast majority of an actor's time and money goes toward finding work, all of which is tax deductible.

Marketing Materials

Good marketing requires good marketing materials. Photos, resumes, postcards, and business cards must be printed; services such as photography, video editing and duplication, website design, hosting, and maintenance; even the purchase of tickets when showcasing for prospective talent agents or casting directors are deductible expenses. And, while clothing rarely qualifies as a deduction, the purchase of a uniform for an audition does. Actors may also try marketing gimmicks, such as t-shirts promoting a play or an ad in a trade publication. One actress in Hollywood has rented a billboard in Hollywood promoting herself for over a decade. Whether or not it has led to gainful employment, it is deductible.

Professional Registries

Electronic casting services have evolved into a mandatory business expense. The cost of registration for any service that legitimately registers and displays actors' marketing materials to elements of the entertainment industry serves an important business function and can be deducted.

IN THE BOX

I had just completed work as an extra. As luck would have it, I had been in the right place at the right time and had been given a line to speak on-camera. After filming I approached the assigned production assistant to inform her that I was a nonunion actor and that I wished to be Taft–Hartleyed into the union. She needed only to sign a form to confirm the fact. But would she bother? I called a local florist and ordered a bouquet of flowers to be sent to her office. I received that waiver form, and the next day I joined the union. I'll never know if the flowers made the difference, but it didn't matter. They were deductible.

Communication

The days of actors calling in to an answering service three times a day have long passed. Like everyone else actors carry cell phones and they serve as a lifeline. Talent agents must be able to reach an actor at a moment's notice. While most casting directors give twenty-four-hour notices of auditions, a talent agent must confirm it, make arrangements and then transmit the information to the actor. If booked, the agent must gather, transmit, and confirm information regarding wardrobe fittings, rehearsals, meetings and location. An actor out of touch quickly becomes an actor out of work.

IN THE BOX

One day I stopped by my talent agent's office to drop off photos. She was engaged in a frantic search for an actor who had just been booked as a possible recurring role on a television soap opera—a plum role and a steady commission for her. But soap operas tape on a tight schedule, and the booking was contingent on the actor making a wardrobe fitting that afternoon for the next day's taping. She had called his cell phone, his home phone, left messages everywhere, and had even called his evening work number. No luck. At 4:00 p.m. she called the casting director to turn down the booking. As it turns out, the actor was at home, sleeping off a late-night bender. When he woke and returned the message at 6:00 p.m., he learned a hard lesson: you snooze, you lose.

The purchase cost of a cell phone falls under equipment purchases and can be deducted or depreciated over a period of time. The monthly cost of cell phone, internet or email service can also be deducted as a cost of doing business, but not entirely. What complicates the issue is the percentage of use for work versus personal use. Most use a cell phone for personal needs as well which is not deductible. Most accountants suggest a 75 to 80 percent ratio as a business deduction, assuming that between 20 and 25 percent of your use is personal.

In addition, the IRS may allow the deduction of basic internet and phone service, but not for its bells and whistles, such as ring tones or iTunes. Indeed, some actors maintain two phones, one professional and one personal. Otherwise, billing statements provide a paper trail for tagging the exceptions.

Office Supplies

The cost of looking for work includes office supplies, lots of them. Printer paper, ink, postage, envelopes, mailing labels, and every other desktop item needed to maintain the daily production line of submissions to casting directors, prospective talent agents, or managers all count as marketing costs. Even those $2 receipts for staples or tape can add up. Of course, as any good office manager knows, buying in bulk saves money. Some office supply stores offer reward programs to keep them competitive with online services. Discounts kick in not just when buying in bulk, but progressively, as well.

Legal Expenses

A talent agent can negotiate most union contracts, but occasionally a contract's complexity exceeds the agent's expertise. And even though many top agents in Hollywood also exhibit legal credentials in entertainment law, in order to avoid a conflict of interest, they should refer the actor to a third-party consultant, such as an attorney specializing in entertainment law. Most standard performance contracts conclude in a pretty straightforward manner, but some, such as reality programs, stray into nonunion territory where punitive clauses and restrictions apply. Contracts may also make caveats about pregnancy, weight, insurance, or any number of other restrictions. Lawyers in these situations, though expensive, pay for themselves by negotiating better terms, defending your rights, and tying up the loose ends all of which might have cost you more without legal counsel. So, do not hesitate to involve professional advice if you feel the room starting to spin.

Travel

The cost of travel to and from auditions or callbacks in a personal vehicle may be deducted in terms of the mileage at a set amount per mile determined each year by the IRS. But, the IRS requires the actor to keep a logbook to document the date, location, and mileage to and from the site. Do not just estimate. Show the actual odometer readings. Online services such as MapQuest can provide accurate mileage. Print out the travel distance and then annotate it with your odometer readings. Keep this with all audition materials, such as the audition notices, email confirmations, and even the sides for the audition as documentation in case the IRS disputes it. The cost of public transportation as well parking fees and tolls are deductible, but once again, only with a receipt.

Travel to and from work falls into a separate category. No one gets to deduct the mileage for going to work, only for looking for work. But for many actors, professional acting work represents a second income, a second job, something for which the IRS does provide for mileage deduction. You cannot count the mileage to your first employment for the day, but from there, to the second and home again does count as deductible mileage if properly documented.

The deductibility of fares for public transportation seems more complicated. The IRS does not allow the deduction of a monthly or yearly Metro pass, rightly assuming that one uses public transportation for more than carriage to and from an audition. Only the fare for a particular audition, callback, or fitting may be considered. And, of course, all fellow travelers know that bus drivers love to stop and write out receipts! If you have the money, take a taxi, an Uber or whatever commercial lift you can find; they rarely complain about writing receipts.

If you are working on location where craft services may not be provided, production companies generally provide a per diem for meals and/or lodging. Keep all meal and lodging receipts to prove that this stipend was not income but reimbursement, keeping in mind that the IRS maintains a standard meal allowance that disallows lavish feasts. The IRS publishes Publication 463 to delineate this and other legitimate business travel expenses whether reimbursed by the production company or not (IRS, *Publication 463*).

Professional Development

An actor must be life-long learner. Every role provides new challenges with skills such as dialects, stage combat, training, makeup, or character research. How one pursues that quest remains an individual decision reflecting an actor's professional goals. Fencing lessons develop reflexes and stature; acting lessons hone technique; researching plays and films broadens one's perspective on the industry and the profession. Any legitimate professional development adds to an actor's skill set and improves their chances of a casting. The full tax deduction of professional development provides an extra-added incentive. So, learn Tai Chi, take high wire lessons with the Cirque du Soleil, or attain proficiency in weapons handling. An actor can justify any skill-building expense as long as it can be tied to the craft of acting.

Contract Labor Fees (Services)

Actors need other professionals to provide them with professional services such as photography, piano tuning, accountancy, or coaching to name a few. Any service that helps an actor prepare for and maintain their career falls under the heading of professional service, with the exceptions of gym memberships, physical therapy, and hair styling. But, whether it is the manager, the dialect coach, the accompanist, the photographer, or the acting coach, their service is indispensable to an acting career. Once a professional relationship has been established, a service provider should supply you with an invoice for your records. But others may not. A personal check to a private party does not suffice as proof of payment for services rendered, and a receipt for cash is useless. How does one prove this fee was provided for a service without documentation of the service? The IRS provides two forms on its website to facilitate this documentation: W–9 and 1099. The W–9 first establishes the professional relationship wherein the actor "hires" the service provider, and the 1099, issued by the actor at the end of the year, simply documents how much the actor paid the service provider for the year.

Commissions and Fees

All commissions, whether paid to a talent agent or a personal manager, represent a deductible expense. Most commissions will be paid to the agent out of an actor's gross pay along with their taxes, either by the talent agent or a disbursement service before issuing checks to the actor. An actor, though, may need to pay a manager. As agents and managers rarely contract a nonunion role, any commissions paid to them remain voluntary. But, all commissions paid by an actor directly to a talent agent or manager, out of his/her net income represents a legitimate deductible expense.

Equipment Purchases

Actors need all kinds of equipment, especially computers along with peripherals such as printers, scanners, and speakers. Actors also need digital technology such as digital cameras and camcorders for self-taping auditions. Learning new songs often requires a tape recorder, vocal and dialect work requires digital stereo equipment, and a host of other electronic gadgetry may be needed. Once again, the cost of these expenses may be depreciated over time rather than just in the year purchased. The IRS provides Form 4562 for this purpose, but consulting an accountant might be a safer approach. Even some software for film editing, accounting, Photoshopping, and any other business applications, or leased modules, can be deducted as long as one can legitimately point to its use for business whether purchased or as leased modules. Once again, the total cost may not be deductible, only the percentage used for business as opposed to for personal use. Some actors utilize a separate cell phone for their career while others use the standard 10 percent for business guideline over most general use equipment purchases. The IRS requires a high bar for documenting these expenses, requiring you to provide itemization of each item purchased, the date of purchase, the cost including tax, and the percent used for business.

Unreimbursed Expenses

Many employees such as teachers and police officers find themselves in the position of paying for required work-related items such as uniforms, books, and supplies. The employee may deduct these costs as long as they are required or critical to their work and appropriate receipts and notations are maintained.

Professional Supplies

Turning professional means never having to pay out of your pocket for the accoutrements of your profession. But, when you do pay, you may able to deduct the cost from tax. Wardrobe purchases must be tied to a specific paid project, except for uniforms or protective clothing for activities like fencing practice. Makeup and hair care only count during the work period. But so often the purchase of your supplies occurs on the fly, with cash, and with little thought toward maintaining records. An eyebrow pencil, a pair of glasses, a *Backstage West* each week at the convenience store—all of those cash transactions so easily forgotten and receipts so easily lost, add up over time. The only solution remains to organize your receipts with an accordion file that separates receipts by month (AEA, *Your Income Tax*, 4).

Research

Actors often do research for a particular role, either for an audition or for a booking. The purchase of books, movies, tickets, or any other item as legitimate research for a role is deductible. Keep all appropriate receipts that correspond to a particular role along with their documentation, for example a ticket stub along with the booking notice for the role researched.

Home Office Space

Actors renting, leasing, or owning a space with a dedicated room as an office may be able to deduct a percentage of the cost of their rent or mortgage and utilities. Actors, as such, do not qualify for this deduction, unless as a voice-over actor you maintain a home studio. The IRS requires that the office be your principal place of business or the space where you meet regularly with clients (IRS, "Home Office Deductions"). But, as actors often also work as writers, musicians, or designers, the cost of maintaining a home office, such as rent, mortgage, insurance, and utilities, may be deducted against income from this work. There are two methods for calculating the deduction: regular and simplified as explained in Chart 12.1. The regular method uses the square footage of the room divided by the home's total square footage. The resulting percentage is then used to calculate the percentage of the allowable expenses to calculate the total deduction. A simpler method, initiated by the IRS in 2013, allows the taxpayer to simply multiple the square footage of the room by $5. The space should not contain a bed and should be used exclusively for business. But, the IRS rarely shows up on your doorstep to investigate.

Simplified Option	Regular Method
Deduction for home office use of a portion of a residence allowed only if that portion is **exclusively** used on a **regular basis** for business purposes	Same
Allowable square footage of home use for business (not to exceed 300 square feet)	Percentage of home used for business
Standard $5 per square foot used to determine home business deduction	Actual expenses determined and records maintained
Home-related itemized deductions claimed in full on Schedule A	Home-related itemized deductions apportioned between Schedule A and business schedule (Sch. C or Sch. F)
No depreciation deduction	Depreciation deduction for portion of home used for business
No recapture of depreciation upon sale of home	Recapture of depreciation on gain upon sale of home
Deduction cannot exceed gross income from business use of home, less business expenses	Same
Amount in excess of gross income limitation may not be carried over	Amount in excess of gross income limitation may be carried over
Loss carryover from use of regular method in prior year may not be claimed	Loss carryover from use of regular method in prior year may be claimed if gross income test is met in current year

CHART 12.1 Simplified Option for Home Office Deduction
Source: IRS.

What Additional Deductions May Actors Take on Their Income Taxes as an Independent Contractor?

An independent contractor is considered self-employed and, thus, can deduct any legitimate business expense, including a home office, without qualification. Unfortunately, the concept of an independent contractor has been stretched without much pushback from Congress. One finds independent contracts mostly as individual plumbers, electricians, and carpenters who work out of a vehicle and have little need for an office or a business name (other than a DBA). But some corporations have exploited the vagueness of the statutory language to shed employees, such as sales, janitorial or marketing staff, and then rehiring them as independent contractors, thus saving on the payment of benefits and taxes, since independent contractors are responsible for filing and paying their own taxes quarterly. Under a union contract, the actor is an employee, but as an independent contractor, they are considered self-employed (IRS, "Independent Contractor Defined"). Actors routinely face this dilemma. We are both employees and self-employed depending upon the day of the week, the time of the day, and the particular artistic endeavor.

Location Costs

As an independent contractor, your income represents any additional monies a producer provides. On location, when catering's not an option, meals may be handled by distributing per diem funds—a set amount of cash, usually $50 per day—with which to purchase food. On a union shoot, as the producer has an obligation to feed the cast and crew, this money is nontaxable; but, during a nonunion shoot, the producer may add this amount to the actor's earned income. In addition, travel costs may provide "reimbursement" for transportation, or may provide "compensation." A reimbursement means the actor has paid out of their pocket while compensation refers to the cost paid up front by the producer. The former represents the producer's deductible cost of doing business and the latter represents the actor's. If you are compensated, as opposed to reimbursed, the amount may be added to your reportable earned income. The IRS will expect you to pay taxes on anything of value provided to you during the course of the project so keep all receipts, no matter how tattered or faded or poorly printed, especially if travel costs exceed the per diem provided.

Proper filing and bookkeeping, as with any business, provides the answer to this problem. Meal and grocery receipts, airline ticket invoices, and taxi vouchers must be retained. Tollbooth fares, private auto mileage, hotel costs, room service, valet services, and gratuities should be documented. Private auto mileage must be recorded. Hotel costs, room service, valets and gratuities should also be documented. A location shoot can be expensive, so whether you pay or the production company pays, you should keep comprehensive records in case you foot the bill in the end. And, if you find yourself touring in a stage production, check out the IRS Publication 463 for additional guidance.

How Do I Maintain These Records?

The amount of receipts and record keeping can seem overwhelming, but they are essential to minimizing one's tax burden. If you are audited the IRS will take exception to many actors' deductions. The onus is upon the actor to prove their claim. Using one debit or credit card exclusively for all business transactions provides an effective solution, by generating an electronic paper trail through the banking institution, but the IRS requires receipts during an audit, not credit card statements or bank statements. Unless you develop a strategy for handling receipts and keeping records, you will find yourself working primarily for your talent agent and the IRS. One useful strategy would be to separate your career and personal banking by establishing separate bank accounts with separate debit cards. An accordion file annotated by month is useful for all those paper receipts and paid bills, and keeping a log book and pen in your car facilitates accurate recording of your mileage. More organized actors opt for technological strategies to manage their finances. Computer software such as Quicken provides the most useful tool to maintain both records of income and of deductible expenses. Many successful actors use BlackBerrys to maintain records of work-related expenses, especially when they are on the road or on location. Maintaining a calendar, electronic or otherwise, helps to remember a booking, schedule of auditions, rehearsals, costume fittings, and filming.

Of course, there is still the problem of documentation. But whatever your strategy, remember if you are audited, the only documentation the IRS will look at are those receipts from the point of sale. When tax preparation time comes, report exact numbers, not rounded-up estimates (a big IRS red flag), collect year-end statements from contracted services, and hound production companies for your W–2s and 1099s. Union members can access helpful worksheets on the Equity website. If in doubt, though, have your tax return examined by a tax professional or take advantage of the union's VITA program.

What Should I Do if I Am Audited?

IRS agents have far bigger fish to fry than starving actors, but if you happen to be selected for an audit, the best offense is a good defense. In other words, stretching the truth or pushing the limits only tempts fate. Claiming thousands of dollars in entertainment deductions or trying to count your weekly massage treatments as a professional expense sends up red flags and only invites scrutiny. But if the IRS ever comes calling, do not expect them to understand the needs of an actor. Most IRS auditors would not know a legitimate acting expense from a manicure, which is a legitimate expense, in some circumstances. Immediately consult a tax attorney or specialist. First, organize your documentation, not by project, but by category, unless the IRS is disputing only one particular project. Bring the actual contracts to detail your financial involvement in each project. Do not provide estimations. Have concrete numbers and the paper trail to back them up. Answer the questions, and if more information needs to be gathered, ask the IRS for an extension. Do not offer information to the auditor. Let them ask for it.

What Mistakes Should I Avoid?

1 "I'll write it down later." These famous last words have been the failing of an actor at one moment or another. The truth is, you will probably forget, and your loss is the IRS's gain.

2 "It's only a $1.29 receipt." If I only had a nickel for every time I have used that excuse. Better yet, how about $1.29 for every time I didn't utter that excuse!

3 "I really do not need this piece of paper." The world is littered with little discarded scraps of paper that collectively could have provided a sizable refund to an individual. Save everything and train yourself to use a dedicated wallet, not a pocket, where receipts are soon to be forgotten and only remembered too late in the washing cycle.

4 "I needed a new pair of shoes anyway." That was always the excuse I used when purchasing items for a community theater production with no budget. It was pathetic then, but downright sinful as a professional.

5 "The production company will pay for it." Beginning actors often live in a dream world, and naively agree to pay for needed items, for which they believe they will be reimbursed. Remember, if you bought it, you own it and it should go home with you. Save the receipt, though, as you will need that.

What Items Are NOT Deductible?

The IRS allows deductions for "necessary" and "ordinary" business expenses, but what the IRS considers "ordinary" or "necessary" causes headaches for many actors if they are audited. Deductions for items such as clothing raise red flags for an auditor.

Clothes

No one, including actors, may deduct the cost of clothing for work, or even auditions with the possible exception of a uniform. Once again, document the audition with a notice to prove the purchase's legitimacy.

Makeup

The cost of makeup may not be deducted regardless of its necessity for an audition with the exception of preparing for a headshot photo or the purchase of stage makeup from a supply house.

Health Club Memberships

We all know that actors must all be beautiful and trim, but the IRS views the issue differently. The cost of your gym membership, including dance classes, may not be deducted no matter how necessary it is to your career, unless you are a stunt person or coordinator, or it is stipulated in a contract. A production company must make the actor's weight, fitness or physical training a contractual condition of employment for the IRS to consider this a legitimate employee deduction.

Hair Styling

The IRS considers the cost of hair styling for auditions or photography to be at the discretion of the actor, and, unless mandated by the producer, cannot be deducted. The final word on the subject: *document, document, document!*

ACTOR'S FORUM

Early in my career I worked with a company in New Haven, Connecticut, that had a professional improv company. Now, I never formally studied improv, but I worked with this company, I did shows with them, and I learned improv skills by doing. You can't always get that opportunity to learn by being thrown into something. I always think that it's like acting. You have certain skills or techniques that you studied, and some of them are just simply inbred. You're born with them. I always wanted to know if I could do improv because you'll see that very often on a call. "We're looking for people who are in Groundlings or this or that," which I never did. Now, I've actually recently considered spending some money and formally doing that. That's a talent that I probably should have cultivated a long time ago because it was always something that I liked.

MICHAEL GABIANO

Make sure you're watching everything there is to watch, listening to everything there is to listen to, and don't mute the commercials. Hear what kind of voices they're using, what kinds of characterization. Same with radio commercials and announcers. How are they announcing these shows? The styles quite popular right now are the totally underplayed announcements. Find out what's being hired right now, what kind of voices are being hired. Trends change all the time. In Hollywood and Burbank there's Kalmenson and Kalmenson that runs a lot of voice-over classes. . . . Use the internet. Read the reviews. Working in Hollywood, you'll find that people want to part you and your money over and over and over again. Most of it is not usable. You have to find out what's a good way of spending your limited resources to enhance your career potential. Don't just go to every workshop. Find out what's going to work. Obviously be open to experiences. Sample things, but don't start committing all your money to something that may be really no use to you.

PETER LAVIN

Take a mime class. Take a skills class. Mask work is really important. Workouts. You go to the gym. Most of the people doing motion capture are stunt people. You have to have the skill so you're training all of the time or keeping your body in shape. But there are specialized gyms you can go to. You're going to work out your martial arts skills, or working out fight and combat skills. It's not just working out. Acting lessons. You gesture more in motion capture because if we're just sitting here and talking and not moving, it's boring. I've started teaching on my own through the MOCAP Vaults because I'm getting too old to do this. I love sharing what I do because I want the next group of kids doing these games to only get better. Now with the change to VR (virtual reality), it has taken us closer to our theater roots because you're shooting in 360 degrees. You have to memorize longer scenes. You've got to memorize much longer segments than you do in film and television. You have to be more than just a good actor. You have to be well-rounded.

RICHARD DORTON

13 PROFESSIONAL DEVELOPMENT

It never stops, the studying. I'm always studying something: voice, singing, different disciplines with the body, clowns, masks. There's always something going on; it never ends.

OLYMPIA DUKAKIS, "Successful Actors," *Backstage online*

ACTOR'S RESOURCES

BackStage.com
www.backstage.com/

The Los Angeles Equestrian Center
www.la-equestriancenter.com/
480 Riverside Drive, Burbank, CA 91506 / 818–840–9063

The Internet Movie Database
www.imdb.com/

Samuel French Theatre & Film
7623 W Sunset Blvd—Los Angeles, CA / 1–866–598–8449
www.samuelfrench.com/bookstore

The LA Actor's Blog
www.dufflynsblog.com/

SAG-AFTRA Foundation Video Archive
sagaftra.foundation/video-gallery/

Mocap Vaults
www.themocapvaults.com/

UCLA Extension
www.uclaextension.edu/

Why Should I Continue With My Education or Training?

Actors of all ages, skill levels, and ethnicities arrive in Hollywood equally confident and ready to work. Their limitations lie within. Now as a working actor, carefully survey the professional landscape—the projects, the competition, and the casting process—and determine your own limitations. The bar has been raised. Every profession has its learning curve and the film industry in Los Angeles is no exception. Acting styles change, as do the skill sets. After Johnny Depp's *The Pirates of the Caribbean* premiered in 2003, hundreds of actors rushed to fencing studios to take classes in swordplay. Similarly, 2012's *Hunger Games* inspired many to take up archery. Tomorrow, westerns could be in vogue and horseback riding a necessity.

Today's actors find themselves competing in various arenas of their peers, defined by age, ethnicity, and gender, each with certain expectations of skill sets. They must be more than a pretty or handsome face, and even well-trained actors need to update skills or develop new ones to remain competitive. Actors with only stage training may find the transition to film acting formidable, and confronted with new technologies for which they have no training, for instance, performance capture and green screen technology. Actors may be expected to acquire specialized skills in gun handling or police procedures. Commercial and comedic actors will benefit from improvisational and physical skills such as gymnastics, mime, and role-playing. Breakdowns often specify language skills or sports skills, such as rock-climbing, skateboarding, incline skating, and, yes, even horseback riding. A working actor should also keep abreast of advancements in technology involved in filmmaking such as the use of robotics and drones. It even helps to sing and dance a little.

For college graduates who have just completed sixteen or more years of education, the thought of more schooling might seem appalling. So, take a break if necessary, but know that in Hollywood it is often more a matter of *what* you know than *who* you know. Sometimes at the end of the day, after all the auditions, the actor who fits the costume gets the job—or the actor that knows how to surf, speak several languages, holds a black belt in Tae Kwon Do *and* fits the costume. Not surprisingly, Los Angeles has a surplus of film industry related coaches, schools, and classes. Any personal professional development strategy should anticipate one's goals by developing the supportive skills they require. And **you**, as this business's only employee, must decide which pathway you should pursue.

What Are The Different Training Options for an Actor in Los Angeles?

Every actor competes in a niche market. Younger actors compete against other young actors. Male actors compete against other male actors. They must live up to certain skill related expectations. Every actor looks for whatever will provide that edge over the others. Los Angeles offers an array of possibilities from academic institutions to acting studios, offering classes, workshops, seminars, coaching, informal gatherings of actors and writers, and unlimited research resources with a daunting array of price tags to match.

Academic Institutions

Talent impresses casting directors, not academic degrees. Their value to an actor lies not in the credentials they confer but in the training the actor received and the professional relationships that emerged. But if an amateur actor seeks comprehensive training, Los Angeles boasts many extraordinary conservatory-style training programs with superior facilities, advanced technology and industry contacts. Admission is competitive and requires an audition of two contrasting monologues honed and ready for a performance.

Ranked first in the nation by the Princeton Review/Gourman Report, the University of California in Los Angles (UCLA) School of Theater, Film/Television, lives up to the sizable legacy of its alumnae by integrating the study of theater, film, and television within one program. It also nurtures a very successful collaboration with the Geffen Playhouse (UCLA, School of Theater, Film and Television, *About the School.* ¶4). In addition, the UCLA Extension offers a wide variety of entertainment industry classes. Not to be outdone, UCLA's territorial rival, the University of Southern California's (USC) School of Dramatic Arts offers internships, ranging from Audience Development, Management, Casting, Marketing, Costume Shop, Press, and Development, to Finance and Production (University of Southern California, "Professional Development"). More economical and perhaps less pretentious, though equally respected, Santa Monica College offers an Associate of Arts conservatory-style degree in traditional theatrical arts (Santa Monica College: Theater Arts, *About the Department*). Newly located in the old Charlie Chaplin Studios in Hollywood, the highly regarded American Academy of Dramatic Arts offers an accredited two-year conservatory for film, television and stage acting. Finally, one might wonder why the New York based American Musical and Dramatic Academy would open a campus in a city world famous for film. The many musical influences seen in today's popular culture such as in *Empire* and the film musical *La La Land*, indicates a rebirth in the movie musical genre has begun.

Acting Studios

For actors who have already obtained academic training and now seek to sharpen or refine their acting technique, the legacy of the Group Theater of the 1930s and 1940s still dominates actor training in Los Angeles. No fewer than three institutions eternalize its namesake's particular flavor of the "Method" school of acting. The Stella Adler Academy of Acting outlines a two-year program of sense-memory based acting concentration; while farther west the Lee Strasberg Theatre Institute's program offers traditional acting programs ranging from four-week intensives to a two-year conservatory certificate, in addition to Tai Chi workouts and a variety of dance and movement classes. Finally, the Sanford Meisner Center, now established in Burbank, supports a rigorous nine-month theater intensive pedagogy guided by Martin Barter, personally trained by Sanford Meisner.

But, living and breathing acting coaches also flourish in Hollywood, many touting recommendations and testimonials from celebrity actors. Some acting teachers, such as Eric Morris, do have strong, long-term reputations in Los Angeles, and their institutes offer a comprehensive acting program. But, Los Angeles boasts others whose studios have varying reputations that border on urban legend. As the teaching of acting is very personal, an acting teacher's approach and methodology, not to mention personality, will affect the rehearsal space dynamics. Actors need a degree of safety to experiment but discipline to succeed as well as the freedom to play without judgment and the discipline of performance for critique. Most acting teachers would prefer that a potential student audit a class or two to observe the class interaction and the teacher's guidance before they consider auditioning. Prospective coaches can be researched on IMDb.

Several specialized acting studios have gained industry attention as well, such as the Actor's Boot Camp that expands on the Meisner technique. Another, TVI Los Angeles, employs casting directors and associates of many well-known casting agencies to teach classes. Here a student pays for the instruction and helpful direction, but also, undeniably, for access to the industry's gatekeepers as well.

Still other acting schools specialize in career enhancement. Stage trained actors might have difficulty transitioning to the subtler style of film acting and might consider classes in on-camera technique or cold reading to improve their craft. Non-comedy trained actors should consider classes in improvisation with Los Angeles' many improv groups such as the Amy Poehler-founded Upright Citizens

Brigade Training Center or at legendary improvisational groups, such as the Groundlings or Second City. The latter offers a noncommittal two-hour Improv Drop-in class every Wednesday and Sunday from 12:00 to 2:00 p.m. Certifications from either of these groups places one in a category often specified in breakdowns. Or, actors might consider focusing on a particular niche in the industry by studying voice-over at Sound Advice or the Kalmenson and Kalmenson Studio, commercial acting at the Elizabeth Mestnik Studio or performance capture at the Mocap Vaults. For stage combat training in weapons and fight choreography, check out the Academy of Theatrical Combat or Swordplay LA. Quieter arts are taught at the Mime Theatre Studio in North Hollywood. And, at the Los Angeles Equestrian Center, one can even learn to ride a horse. More experienced riders should check out the Sunset Ranch at the top of Beachwood Drive for a close-up view of the Hollywood sign. Finally, entrepreneurial actors who utilize YouTube as a marketing or production tool can access training, resources, and workshops at YouTube Space near the Marina to further develop their production skills.

Actors might also expand their artistic horizons by developing other artistic skills. Writer's workshops provide a natural symbiosis between actors, writers, and directors in a collaborative environment that invites actors to read developing scripts. Scripts are often rough, but actors find the space to experiment and to work for the sake of the work. Friendships form, collaborations are forged, and an occasional project is honored. Often talented scriptwriters or directors emerge and recommend familiar actors for roles in future projects. At the very least, an actor will find a multitude of showcase opportunities at organizations such as First Stage or the Writing Pad LA East. New groups come and go and form through MeetUp.com wherever writers and actors meet and socialize.

Specialized Coaches

Actors may also turn to experts for one-on-one coaching. In order to prepare for an upcoming role or audition, an actor may choose to consult a dialect coach. Individual coaches can help actors familiarize themselves quickly with a particular sport, sharpen certain dance or martial arts skills, or remove an impediment through accent reduction or non-native English speaking lessons. Some actors may choose weekly vocal coaching or musical instrument lessons. Kinetic Theory Circus Arts provides training in aerial acrobatics and stunts.

Membership Theaters

Live theater in Los Angeles ranges from big splashy proscenium shows to tiny storefront performances. Many of these small storefront theaters survive through membership fees paid by the actors to provide the theater group a financial security blanket. In return, the actors receive the opportunity to experiment and showcase their talents. The practice sits on firm legal ground as long as the theater company exists as a non-profit corporation. Membership in such a theater company may be a prerequisite to casting in one of plays, but their value depends upon the value of the product. Research the theater company carefully, not only for artistic integrity, but for longevity and ethics. Too often someone gets rich from actors paying to perform. Perhaps the learning experience might justify the cost, perhaps not. Still, consider that any more than a short-term membership in such a theater group can become a security blanket that hinders, not enhances, a career.

What Other Kinds of Research Resources Will I Find in Los Angeles?

A new actor to Los Angeles will have much to learn but a plenitude of resources to consult. *Internet*. Much of the research for this book was conducted on the internet on specialized websites just as easily accessible to anyone who knows where to look. Every arts-related institution, studio, coach, or performance group in Los Angeles has its own website. Governmental websites provide municipal information. Industry trade magazines offer online editions. SAG-AFTRA can provide comprehensive workplace information and advice. Actors can utilize rental services, classified ads, Craigslist, and IMDb. YouTube has no shortage of entertainment industry professionals offering actors tutorials on every subject from basic acting skills to gun training, many by internet star wannabees, though, with questionable credentials. Industry media icons *Variety* and *The Hollywood Reporter* post many of their livestream events on YouTube and the venerable SAG-AFTRA Foundation provides an archived video gallery of their livestream events available for free to anyone on their website. Check out everything. One can truly find out anything if one knows how to utilize the tools at your disposal.

Trade Magazines

Most will recognize the august names of the *Hollywood Reporter* and *Variety*, but the trade publication most important to actors turns out to be *BackstageWest*. This weekly publication contains casting notices, trade advertisements, and acting-oriented articles. The casting notices tend to be mostly nonunion, but this periodical still provides an important resource even for union actors. Its seasonal actor-training spotlight editions offer a comprehensive list of actor-training options, supported by a host of advertisements.

This recommendation is not to say that the other trade publications are without merit. *Daily Variety* and the *Hollywood Reporter* provide detailed business information on the entertainment industry: mergers, financing, studio deals, story development, casting news, production information, and hiring and firings. Actors, to be blunt, lie pretty low in the Hollywood food chain, so only by keeping yourself knowledgeable about the industry do you keep from being eaten.

Bookstores

Like any large city, Los Angeles has its collection of venerable new, used, and specialty bookstores. The Samuel French Bookstore in West Hollywood provides the most comprehensive collection of scripts, books, and periodicals on almost any subject of the entertainment industry. Larry Edmunds Cinema and Theatre in Hollywood provides a more central outlet for much of the same. Studio executives browse alongside actors and writers at Book Soup on the Sunset Strip. The Last Bookstore downtown buys, sells, and trades used books, records, CDs, and DVDs, and The Skylight Bookstore in Los Feliz and Small World Books behind the Sidewalk Café on the Venice Boardwalk both epitomize the cozy neighborhood bookstore.

Libraries

The Los Angeles Public Library maintains an extensive collection of materials for download or checkout through its central facility downtown and an intra-loan program with dozens of satellite collections scattered throughout the city. The Beverly Hills Public Library and the Burbank Public Library both offer a well-stocked and accessible reference center. All provide short-term internet access, copy machines and typewriters in a pinch.

Network

Talk to friends. Arrange to audit a class. Watch, join in, or ask fellow actors about their experiences. Check internet blogs, forums, and resource pages for postings from other actors sharing their issues or experiences associated with a particular coach or studio.

In many ways success in Hollywood comes down to networking, making contacts, and reaching out to others from the first day one sets foot in the city. Developing a support system will help keep you on the merry-go-round with each revolution another chance at the gold ring. For many, the gold ring is not the goal. Success equals survival for most, the opportunity to continue pursuing a career as a player in the bigger pond.

APPENDIX A: LOS ANGELES CITY NEIGHBORHOOD STATISTICAL DATA

Los Angeles City Neighborhood Statistical Data

Community	Total Pop.	Pop. per Square Mile	% Renters	Median Rent 1 Bdm	Median Age	Household Income	% Under 18	% 65+	% w/ college	% w/o HS degree	% Foreign Born
Arlington Heights	17,618	21,423.00	81.60%	$1,371	31	$31,421	30.20%	8.60%	13.80%	46.60%	49.80%
Atwater Village	14,101	8,379.00	59.60%	$2,175	34	$53,872	24.80%	11.70%	22.60%	33.00%	49.30%
Bel Air	8,261	1,207.00	14.50%	$10,950	46	$207,938	19.60%	20.90%	66.10%	4.20%	24.10%
Beverly Crest	7,850	1,318.00	10.00%	$2,294	45	$169,282	19.30%	17.00%	67.60%	4.50%	25.00%
Beverly Grove	21,417	12,990.00	74.80%	$2,450	38	$63,039	8.40%	20.40%	50.00%	11.00%	36.30%
Beverly Hills	34,869	5,975.60	56.60%	$10,950	41	$96,312	20.80%	20.10%	54.50%	5.00%	38.20%
Beverlywood	6,080	7,654.00	29.70%	$2,022	39	$105,283	26.50%	16.50%	55.30%	7.40%	24.50%
Brentwood	30,964	2,059.00	48.40%	$1,785	39	$112,927	14.10%	17.20%	70.40%	3.00%	21.10%
Burbank	105,319	5,969.30	56.40%	$2,020	36	$64,416	23.30%	14.50%	29.00%	11.30%	31.10%
Culver City	39,717	7,475.00	45.60%	$1,966	39	$70,774	21.60%	15.70%	41.20%	7.80%	26.60%
Del Rey	33,829	11,420.00	55.20%	$2,801	35	$62,259	22.80%	11.90%	27.00%	2.50%	37.90%
Eagle Rock	31,610	7,644.00	43.90%	$1,480	35	$67,253	24.60%	12.30%	8.60%	21.60%	38.50%
East Hollywood	42,384	31,095.00	91.30%	$1,654	31	$29,927	28.80%	8.90%	13.40%	48.40%	66.50%
Echo Park	34,627	16,868.00	6.00%	$1,962	30	$37,708	29.40%	8.10%	18.00%	6.70%	53.10%
Encino	48,619	4,411.00	38.40%	$1,600	42	$78,529	18.50%	19.70%	46.80%	9.30%	32.80%
Fairfax District	9,681	10,122.00	71.50%	$2,192	33	$65,938	16.90%	14.20%	54.60%	9.50%	23.20%
Glendale	201,020	6,295.60	61.60%	$1,995	37	$57,112	23.70%	13.90%	32.10%	15.60%	54.40%
Hancock Park/La Brea	165,610	6,459.00	52.70%	$1,971	37	$85,277	19.70%	13.20%	56.20%	6.90%	26.30%
Harvard Heights	23,473	23,473.00	84.30%	$1,306	30	$31,173	30.50%	8.00%	10.30%	5.00%	57.80%
Highland Park	48,109	16,835.00	60.90%	$1,537	28	$45,478	32.70%	7.60%	21.90%	47.70%	45.10%
Hollywood	22,193	22,193.00	92.40%	$1,850	31	$53,694	20.30%	8.90%	27.50%	31.70%	53.80%
Hollywood Hills	21,588	3,063.00	56.50%	$1,983	37	$69,277	12.00%	11.70%	54.80%	6.70%	28.80%
Koreatown	115,070	42,611.00	93.00%	$1,604	30	$30,558	26.00%	6.20%	21.40%	40.90%	68.00%
Larchmont Village	3,769	17,747.00	72.90%	$1,850	34	$47,780	22.60%	8.30%	31.80%	24.90%	56.00%
Los Feliz	38,247	13,512.00	75.50%	$1,680	36	$50,793	15.40%	13.20%	42.70%	15.80%	44.50%
Mar Vista	39,431	12,259.00	60.60%	$2,009	35	$62,611	19.80%	11.70%	42.30%	16.30%	33.50%
Mid Wilshire	65,232	14,988.00	78.30%	$2,405	34	$58,483	17.90%	12.40%	45.20%	14.00%	33.90%
Mid-City	15,202	15,051.00	68.90%	$1,838	31	$43,711	30.00%	8.30%	16.80%	35.50%	35.10%
North Hollywood	132,512	13,264.00	75.40%	$1,576	30	$42,791	29.30%	6.70%	18.50%	39.80%	46.40%
Northridge	75,797	6,080.00	46.40%	$1,567	32	$67,906	24.20%	11.90%	34.90%	18.30%	31.80%
Pacific Palisades	24,303	1,048.00	17.50%	$2,707	43	$168,008	23.80%	17.40%	70.90%	2.30%	15.50%
Palms	29,572	21,870.00	86.90%	$2,025	31	$50,684	17.20%	6.50%	45.90%	12.00%	40.30%
Pasadena	141,023	5,366.00	54.00%	$2,324	34	$82,825	23.90%	12.00%	41.50%	20.40%	32.30%
Pico-Union	30,705	25,352.00	90.50%	$2,517	31	$26,424	32.70%	7.10%	6.70%	65.70%	64.60%
Playa del Rey	16,231	3,542.00	53.00%	$2,600	38	$91,339	12.40%	11.00%	59.20%	2.80%	16.20%

Sources:

2010 U.S. Census	http://www.census.gov/quickfacts/table/
Los Angeles Times	http://maps.latimes.com/neighborhoods/
RentCafe	http://www.rentcafe.com/apartments-for-rent/us/ca/

Demographic, geographic, and economic information for 55 actor-friendly communities within the city of Los Angeles

Los Angeles City Neighborhood Statistical Data

Community	Total Pop.	Pop. per Square Mile	% Renters	Median Rent 1 Bdm	Median Age	Household Income	% Under 18	% 65+	% w/ college	% w/o HS degree	% Foreign Born
Playa Vista	2,711	1,859.00	45.20%	$2,804	37	$68,597	19.50%	15.70%	26.50%	25.70%	31.10%
Rancho Park	8,741	7,169.00	45.60%	$2,200	36	$69,274	19.20%	12.60%	49.30%	7.20%	28.50%
Reseda	67,554	10,600.00	47.70%	$1,405	32	$54,771	28.80%	9.90%	19.00%	31.30%	43.10%
Santa Monica	93,220	10,663.80	70.20%	$3,205	38	$69,013	14.90%	16.10%	54.80%	4.70%	24.80%
Sawtelle	106,184	13,319.00	79.80%	$2,205	32	$57,710	12.40%	10.60%	49.80%	14.60%	39.00%
Sherman Oaks	66,696	6,687.00	58.90%	$1,810	37	$69,651	16.40%	13.50%	45.00%	8.00%	26.20%
Silver Lake	33,444	11,266.00	64.30%	$1,821	35	$54,339	19.00%	10.70%	36.20%	24.80%	41.10%
Studio City	38,836	5,395.00	55.90%	$2,127	38	$75,657	14.20%	13.20%	49.40%	4.80%	21.10%
Tarzana	34,506	4,038.00	41.30%	$1,445	38	$73,195	22.00%	15.20%	40.30%	13.60%	35.10%
Toluca Lake	3,984	6,393.00	62.20%	$1,936	37	$73,111	15.60%	10.10%	48.40%	6.70%	17.70%
Valley Glen	51,149	12,325.00	62.90%	$1,558	32	$46,175	29.30%	9.50%	21.30%	33.30%	49.00%
Valley Village	13,243	11,600.00	68.70%	$1,911	36	$55,470	18.30%	12.70%	36.50%	13.10%	28.90%
Van Nuys	93,258	11,542.00	73.90%	$1,422	28	$41,134	31.60%	6.70%	15.30%	43.10%	49.80%
Venice	32,625	11,891.00	68.80%	$2,758	35	$67,647	14.20%	8.60%	49.30%	13.10%	22.30%
West Hollywood	36,222	18,229.50	78.40%	$2,157	39	$52,855	5.70%	14.80%	46.80%	4.60%	35.90%
West Los Angeles	47,338	12,061.00	51.00%	$2,205	38	$86,403	13.20%	17.40%	60.40%	5.50%	28.00%
Westlake	56,934	38,214.00	94.90%	$1,720	27	$26,757	29.80%	7.60%	12.00%	58.90%	67.60%
Westwood	48,500	13,036.00	64.10%	$2,311	27	$68,716	12.40%	12.00%	66.50%	5.20%	31.30%
Windsor Square	5,275	8,255.00	59.00%	$1,705	38	$61,767	24.50%	12.40%	46.10%	13.20%	45.00%
Woodland Hills	69,044	4,040.00	36.90%	$2,065	40	$89,946	20.10%	16.10%	47.00%	6.40%	24.80%
LA County	10,170,292	2,419.60	N/A	$1,800	35.60	$56,196	22.40%	12.60%	30.30%	22.70%	34.60%
LA City	3,971,883	8,092.30	N/A	$1,895	34.90	$50,205	21.80%	11.20%	32.00%	24.50%	37.40%

2010 U.S. Census http://www.census.gov/quickfacts/table/
Los Angeles Times http://maps.latimes.com/neighborhoods/
RentCafe http://www.rentcafe.com/apartments-for-rent/us/ca/

Demographic, geographic, and economic information for 55 actor-friendly communities within the city of Los Angeles (continued)

Los Angeles City Neighborhood Statistical Data

Community	% Caucasian	% Latino	% African-Am	% Asian	Diversity Index	Non White	Property Crime
Arlington Heights	4.70%	56.60%	24.50%	12.90%	0.600	95.3	90.0
Atwater Village	22.20%	51.30%	1.40%	19.70%	0.645	77.8	104.2
Bel Air	83.00%	4.60%	9.00%	8.20%	0.301	17	89.7
Beverly Crest	87.50%	3.40%	1.70%	4.00%	0.230	12.5	75.2
Beverly Grove	82.00%	6.00%	2.00%	5.10%	0.319	18	282.2
Beverly Hills	81.80%	4.80%	1.40%	7.60%	0.320	18.2	NA
Beverlywood	80.00%	6.10%	4.20%	7.30%	0.348	20	88.8
Brentwood	84.20%	4.50%	1.20%	6.50%	0.283	15.8	129.7
Burbank	58.80%	24.80%	1.60%	9.20%	0.581	41.2	NA
Culver City	48.30%	23.80%	10.70%	12.30%	0.681	51.7	NA
Del Rey	34.00%	44.30%	4.40%	14.00%	0.666	66	88.5
Eagle Rock	29.80%	40.30%	1.90%	23.90%	0.690	70.2	103.6
East Hollywood	17.50%	60.40%	2.40%	15.50%	0.578	82.5	117.0
Echo Park	12.90%	64.00%	2.00%	18.80%	0.538	87.1	121.6
Encino	80.10%	8.50%	2.40%	4.90%	0.346	19.9	126.7
Fairfax District	84.70%	5.90%	2.20%	4.50%	0.277	15.3	295.7
Glendale	54.10%	19.60%	1.00%	16.30%	0.635	45.9	NA
Hancock Park/La Brea	70.70%	8.50%	3.80%	13.10%	0.473	45.9	204.3
Harvard Heights	3.30%	66.30%	16.00%	13.30%	0.517	96.7	146.6
Highland Park	11.30%	72.40%	2.40%	11.20%	0.449	88.7	66.1
Hollywood	41.00%	42.20%	5.20%	7.10%	0.644	59	194.3
Hollywood Hills	74.10%	9.40%	4.60%	6.70%	0.433	25.9	152.3
Koreatown	7.40%	53.50%	4.80%	32.20%	0.602	92.6	115.4
Larchmont Village	24.60%	37.20%	3.00%	30.00%	0.708	75.4	174.0
Los Feliz	57.60%	18.70%	3.70%	13.50%	0.610	42.4	143.5
Mar Vista	51.30%	29.10%	3.50%	12.80%	0.634	48.7	88.1
Mid Wilshire	33.60%	19.90%	22.70%	19.80%	0.755	66.4	137.6
2010 U.S. Census	http://www.census.gov/quickfacts/table/						
Los Angeles Times	http://maps.latimes.com/neighborhoods/						
RentCafe	http://www.rentcafe.com/apartments-for-rent/us/ca/						

Demographic, geographic, and economic information for 55 actor-friendly communities within the city of Los Angeles (continued)

Los Angeles City Neighborhood Statistical Data

Community	% Caucasian	% Latino	% African-Am	% Asian	Diversity Index	Non White	Property Crime
Mid-City	9.50%	45.20%	38.30%	3.90%	0.637	90.5	106.5
North Hollywood	27.00%	57.70%	5.00%	5.70%	0.586	73	149.2
Northridge	49.50%	26.10%	5.40%	14.50%	0.661	50.5	190.3
Pacific Palisades	88.60%	3.20%	4.00%	5.50%	0.210	11.4	83.1
Palms	38.30%	23.40%	12.20%	20.40%	0.739	61.7	93.7
Pasadena	39.10%	33.30%	13.90%	10.00%	0.706	60.9	NA
Pico-Union	3.00%	85.40%	2.90%	7.60%	0.264	97	99.4
Playa del Rey	72.60%	10.00%	3.90%	7.90%	0.451	27.4	112.2
Playa Vista	32.40%	34.80%	4.70%	21.20%	0.722	67.6	231.3
Rancho Park	58.30%	16.20%	3.60%	18.20%	0.598	41.7	324.8
Reseda	37.20%	43.50%	4.20%	11.20%	0.656	62.8	102.4
Santa Monica	71.30%	13.50%	3.50%	7.10%	0.465	28.7	NA
Sawtelle	49.60%	22.80%	2.60%	19.90%	0.659	50.4	146.0
Sherman Oaks	73.80%	11.80%	4.40%	5.00%	0.434	26.2	171.0
Silver Lake	34.00%	41.80%	3.20%	18.00%	0.676	66	151.4
Studio City	78.00%	8.70%	3.70%	5.40%	0.378	22	193.8
Tarzana	70.70%	15.10%	3.60%	5.00%	0.471	29.3	157.2
Toluca Lake	71.90%	14.00%	5.30%	5.00%	0.457	28.1	175.2
Valley Glen	39.50%	45.20%	3.90%	5.40%	0.632	60.5	126.3
Valley Village	66.70%	18.90%	5.50%	4.40%	0.512	33.3	152.7
Van Nuys	23.10%	60.50%	6.00%	6.40%	0.571	76.9	134.3
Venice	64.20%	21.70%	5.40%	4.10%	0.534	35.8	166.6
West Hollywood	81.20%	9.00%	2.80%	4.00%	0.330	18.8	209.4
West Los Angeles	76.70%	5.30%	2.40%	11.40%	0.393	23.3	170.1
Westlake	4.50%	73.40%	3.90%	16.50%	0.430	95.5	102.8
Westwood	62.90%	7.00%	2.00%	23.10%	0.543	37.1	71.7
Windsor Square	37.70%	14.80%	4.30%	41.60%	0.661	62.3	188.8
Woodland Hills	78.30%	7.60%	2.90%	7.10%	0.374	21.7	177.7
2010 U.S. Census	http://www.census.gov/quickfacts/table/						
Los Angeles Times	http://maps.latimes.com/neighborhoods/						

Demographic, geographic, and economic information for 55 actor-friendly communities within the city of Los Angeles (continued)

APPENDIX B: LOS ANGELES EXTRA CASTING AGENCIES

Alice Ellis Casting
(310) 314–1488

A Background Artists Casting Agency
12021 Wilshire Boulevard #632
Los Angeles, CA 90025
(310) 425–3460

Big Crowds/BeInAMovie.com
12400 Ventura Boulevard
Los Angeles, CA 91604
(818) 985–8811

Bill Dance Casting
4605 Lankershim Boulevard
North Hollywood, CA 91602
(818) 754–6634

Burbank Casting
P.O. Box 7106
Burbank, CA 91510
(818) 559–2446

Caravan West Productions (specialty western)
35660 Jayhawker Rd.
Agua Dulce, CA 91390
(661) 268–8300

Carol Grant Casting
(323) 390–9422

Sande Alessi Casting
28914 Roadside Dr. #200
Agoura Hills, CA 91301
(818) 964–1462

Central Casting
220 S. Flower St.
Burbank, CA 91502
(818) 562–2700

Creative Extras Casting
2461 Santa Monica Blvd. #501
Santa Monica, CA 90404
(310) 391–9041

Debbie Sheridan Casting
13547 Ventura Blvd., Ste. 311
Sherman Oaks, CA 91423
(800) 820–5305

Extra Extra Casting, Inc.
P.O. Box 279
Los Angeles, CA 90049
(310) 552–1888

Headquarters Casting
3108 W. Magnolia Blvd.
Burbank, CA 91505
(310) 556–9001

Idell James Casting
877 Via De La Paz
Pacific Palisades, CA 90272
(310) 230–9986

Jeff Olan Casting, Inc.
14044 Ventura Blvd. #209
Sherman Oaks, CA 91423
(818) 285–5462

L.A. Casting Group, Inc.
8335 W. Sunset Blvd., Ste. 332
Los Angeles, CA 90069
(213) 537–6083

Prime Casting & Payroll
201 N. Hollywood Way #208
Burbank, CA 91505
(818) 558–1200

APPENDIX C: DOCUMENTS

SCREEN ACTORS GUILD

CM2 Motion Picture-One Page TV/TH Agreement

This Agreement, is entered into at _____ between _____, the
                                    (print location of agency)   (print name of agency)

"Talent Agent," and _____, _____, the "Actor." (collectively,
                         (print performer's name)   (Social Security Number)

"the Parties").

The Actor engages the Agent as his sole and exclusive agent for the following fields as defined in the
SAG Codified Agency Regulations, a/k/a Rule 16(g), incorporated herein by reference in their
entirety, and the Agent accepts such engagement for [mark appropriate spaces]

  ☐ Theatrical Motion Pictures   ☐ Television Motion Pictures

The term of this contract shall be for a period of **one** (I) year, commencing on _____.
The Parties hereto agree to be bound by all the terms and conditions set forth in Rule 16(g),
including those contained in any full length SAG agency contract contained therein and incorporated
by reference here. The Parties further agree that they may not change, modify, waive or discharge any
aspect of this contract or enter into any other agreement that is violative of any provision of Rule
16(g) without the express written permission of SAG. All non-conforming contracts shall be
considered null and void.

Key Man Clause: With Actor's Permission:
Performer Enters One Agent's Name: Agency May Enter One Agent's Name:

_____   _____

The Actor agrees to pay to the Agent, as commissions, a sum equal to 10% of moneys or other
consideration received by the actor, subject to regional requirements for said payments, as
enumerated in Rule 16(g).

The Agent shall offer the following covenants, and the Actor shall accept them by initialing where
indicated:

_____ Actor has been offered a copy of the full length SAG Agency Contract for his/her review.

_____ By signing this document, Parties agree that it shall have the same full force and effect as
           the representational contracts contained in Rule 16(g). In addition, all Rule 16(g)
           arbitration requirements shall be incorporated by reference here.

_____ Performer will be provided a copy of this one page contract immediately upon signing.

Date:_____ | Date:_____

Actor (print)_____ | Agent (print)_____

Signature:_____ | Signature:_____

The content of this Form entitled "CM2 Motion Picture-One Page TV/TH Agreement" has been reviewed and approved
by SAG.

Sample Talent Agent Agreement for actor representation by a SAG-AFTRA franchised
talent agency

EXCLUSIVE CONTRACT
BETWEEN ARTIST AND TALENT AGENCY

1. I hereby employ you as my exclusive talent agency for a period of ___ years (not to exceed 7 years) from date hereof to negotiate contracts for the rendition of my professional services as an artist, or otherwise, in the fields of motion pictures, legitimate stage, radio broadcasting, television and other fields of entertainment.

2. I hereby agree that you may advise, counsel or direct me in the development and/or advancement of my professional career.

3. As compensation for your said services agreed to be rendered hereunder, I hereby agree to pay you a sum equal to _____ percent (___%); not to exceed maximum rate shown on fee schedule of all monies or things of value as and when received by me directly or indirectly, as compensation for my professional services rendered or agreed to be rendered during the term hereof under contracts, or any extensions, renewals, modifications, or substitutions thereof, entered into or negotiated during the term hereof and to pay the same to you thereafter for so long as you remain licensed. It is expressly understood that to be entitled to continue to receive the payment compensation on the aforementioned contracts, after the termination of this agreement, you shall remain obligated to serve me and perform obligations with respect to said employment contracts or to extensions or renewals of said contracts or to any employment requiring my services on which such compensation is based.

4. I hereby agree that you may render your services to others during the term hereof.

5. In the event that I do not obtain a bona-fide offer of employment from a responsible employer during a period of time in excess of four (4) consecutive months, during which said time I shall be ready, able, willing, and available to accept employment, either party hereto shall have the right to terminate this contract by notice in writing to that effect sent to the other by registered or certified mail.

6. Controversies arising between us under the provisions of the California Labor Code relating to talent agencies and under the rules and regulations for the enforcement thereof shall be referred to the Labor Commissioner of the State of California as provided in Section 1700.44 of the California Labor Code.

7. In the event that you shall collect from me a fee or expenses for obtaining employment for me, and shall fail to procure such employment, or shall fail to be paid for such employment, you shall, upon demand therefore, repay to me the fee and expenses so collected. Unless repayment thereof is made within forty-eight (48) hours after demand therefore, you shall pay to me an additional sum equal to the amount of the fee as provided in Section 1700.40 of the California Labor Code.

8. Subject to my availability, you hereby agree to use all reasonable efforts to procure employment for me in the field or fields of endeavor specified in the contract in which you represent me.

9. This instrument constitutes the entire agreement between us. Statements, promises, or inducements made by any party hereto that are not contained herein shall not be binding or valid, and this contract may not be enlarged, modified, or altered, except in writing signed by both the parties hereto; and provided further, any substantial changes in this contract must be approved by the Labor Commissioner.

10. You hereby agree to deliver to me an executed copy of this contract.

Dated: _____

Agreed to and Accepted by:

_____
Talent Agency

_____
Name of Artist

_____
Street address

_____
City   State   Zip

This form of contract has been approved by the State Labor Commissioner on the ____ day of _____, 20__

By: _____

DLSE 315B (Rev. 9/10)

Sample General Services Agreement for actor representation by a talent agency not franchised by SAG-AFTRA

SAG·AFTRA.

THEATRICAL/TELEVISION TAFT-HARTLEY REPORT
(PRINCIPALS ONLY)

Please be advised that it is the Producer's responsibility to complete this report in its entirety or it will be returned for completion. This report must be submitted to SAG-AFTRA within 15 days from the date of the first employment of a non-member (25 days if on an overnight location).

Resume
Photo

EMPLOYEE INFORMATION

*Name: _____ * SS#. _____

*Address: _____ * Date of Birth: (If minor) _____

City: _____ State: _____ Zip: _____

Phone: _____ Work date: _____

E-mail: _____

EMPLOYER INFORMATION

Signatory Name: _____ Phone: _____

Address: _____ City: _____ State: ___ Zip: _____

E-mail: _____ Contact Person: _____

*EMPLOYMENT INFORMATION

CONTRACT TYPE	ENGAGEMENT CONTRACT	PERFORMER CATEGORY	
Theatrical	Daily	Actor	Stunt
Television	3-Day (TV only)	Singer	Stunt Coordinator
	Weekly	Dancer	Other:

Work Date(s): _____ Production #: _____

Production Title: _____

Shooting Locations(s) (City & State): _____

Reason for Hire: **PLEASE COMPLETE REVERSE SIDE AND ATTACH APPROPRIATE DOCUMENTATION ***

Employer is aware of General Provision, Section 14 of the Basic Agreement, as amended, that applies to Theatrical and Television production, wherein Preference of Employment shall be given to qualified professional actors (except as otherwise stated). Employer will pay to SAG-AFTRA, as liquidated damages, the sums indicated for each breach by the Employer of any provision of those sections.

Signature: _____ Date: _____

Print Name: _____ Producer   Casting Dir.   Phone: _____

Note: Please forward the completed form to SAG-AFTRA in the city in which you are shooting or, if there is no local office in that city, to the SAG-AFTRA office nearest your location. Please see attached list of SAG-AFTRA local offices. If sending to the **Hollywood Office**, send to the appropriate department as follows: **Principal Performers for Theatrical** motion pictures – Attn: Theatrical Dept. **Principal Performers for Television** programs – Attn: Television Dept.

*Required Information

Taft Hartley Report Principals 6.1   Updated 8.27.15   1 of 3

Sample Taft–Hartley Report for actors newly employed as a principal actor by a union signatory producer

Reason for Hire
(Check Appropriate Box)

Member of recognized "name" specialty group (Attach documentation and photo)

Important, famous, well-known or unique persons portraying themselves (Attach photo and bio)

Background actor adjusted for non-script lines (Attach photo)

Military or other government personnel used due to governmental restrictions (Describe restrictions below)

Special skill or unique physical appearance. (Describe skill below or attach photo)

First employment of a person who has training/experience as a professional performer and intends to pursue a career as a motion picture performer (Attach photo and resume)

Child under the age of 18 (State age and attach photo)

Owner or operator of special or unique vehicle or equipment (Describe below and attach photo)

Employed as stunt coordinator (Attach photo and resume)

Employed as body double for scenes requiring nudity or sexual conduct (Attach photo)

Other (Describe reason for hire below and attach photo and resume

Sample Taft–Hartley Report for actors newly employed as a principal actor by a union signatory producer

NUDITY RIDER TO ACTOR PLAYER CASTING AGREEMENT

DATED AS OF _____
BETWEEN _____ ("PRODUCTION COMPANY")
AND _____ ("PLAYER") IN CONNECTION WITH THE ADULT FILM
CURRENTLY ENTITLED _____ ("PICTURE") Reference is made to
the Agreement dated _____ (the "Agreement") between
you, ("Player") and _____ ("Production Company") with respect to
your acting services in Connection with the adult film currently entitled _____
(the "Picture").

1. NUDITY SEX ACTS: It is understood between the parties that, with respect to the services to be rendered by Player, for the consideration set forth in the Agreement, such services shall require Player to appear nude and/or semi-nude, and/or perform designated sexual act(s), as the case may be, in the Picture. The general description of the extent of such nudity, and the type of physical contact required in such designated sex acts, is attached as Exhibit "A".

2. PLAYER'S CONSENT: Player agrees and consents to render the services set forth above and hereby affirms that the Player agrees to appear nude and/or semi-nude and to perform such designated sex act(s).

3. OWNERSHIP OF PERFORMANCE: Pursuant to terms and conditions of the Agreement, Production Company owns all results and proceeds of Player's services rendered pursuant to the Agreement and has exclusive right to use, license and exploit the Picture and Player's performance therein, throughout the world in perpetuity and any and all media whether now know or hereafter devised.

All terms and provisions of the Agreement remain in full force and effect without modification or change and the Agreement is hereby affirmed.

I acknowledge my agreement to the foregoing by signing below:

AGREED TO AND ACCEPTED:

_____
"PLAYER"

EXHIBIT "A"

1) _____ (Description of Sex Acts#1)

2) _____ (Description of Sex Acts#1)

3) _____ (Description of Sex Acts#1)

4) _____ (Description of Sex Acts#1)

5) _____ (Description of Sex Acts#1)

Sample Nudity Rider consent form delineating what sexually explicit action will be expected of the contracted actor

SAG·AFTRA

SAG-AFTRA THEATRICAL TELEVISION AUDITION SIGN-IN SHEET

PRODUCER: _____
PRODN CO: _____
PRODN OFFICE _____
PHONE #: _____
AUDITION DATE: _____

CASTING REP: _____
CASTING REP PHONE: _____
PRODUCTION TITLE: _____
EPISODE: _____
CASTING DIRECTOR SIGNATURE: _____

SAMPLE

(1) NAME	(2) SOCIAL SECURITY OR SAG-AFTRA MEMBER NUMBER	(3) ROLE	(4) AGENT	(5) PROVIDED? PARK	SCRIPT	(6) ARRIVAL TIME	(7) APPT TIME	(8) TIME SEEN (CAST REP)	(9) TIME OUT	(10) TAPED?	(11) ACTOR INITIAL

Audition Sign-In Sheet Theatrical Television 5.3

Sample Audition Sign-in Sheet used for all union signatory auditions

AN ACTOR'S FILM AND TELEVISION GLOSSARY

above the line costs Portion of the project budget allocated to a creative team of writers, actors, director, and designers.

A-List Top tier of actors who are paid the highest salaries.

ambient light Natural or available light for a scene.

anachronism Element out of the intended time and place of the scene.

ancillary rights Agreement over percentage of profits from film tie-in products such as CDs, t-shirts, or action figures.

angle A specific camera placement.

anime Distinct style of animation derived from Japanese comic books.

anthropomorphism The attribution of human qualities to animals or objects.

archetype Specific genre or classification of character, place, or thing such as the town sheriff, the drunk, the saloon owner, and the whore with the golden heart.

arc shot A film shot in which the camera moves by circling around the subject.

art director Member of the film's art department responsible for the overall look of the set and prop construction and dressing.

artifacts Damage to a film, such as specks, scratches, and defects printed from the film negative.

attached An agreement with name actors and/or a director to join a film production.

audio bridge Music or dialogue that connects two scenes by continuing from one to the other uninterrupted.

automated dialogue replacement/looping The rerecording of dialogue by *actor*s in a sound studio during *postproduction*.

B-film Refers to low-budget, independent films with unknown actors, gratuitous violence and sex, cheap special effects, and an uninspired script.

backlighting Lighting from behind the subject that puts the figures in the foreground either in darkness or silhouette.

back door pilot A two-hour TV movie that is a setup for a possible TV series.

back end Refers to the profit participation after production and distribution costs are recovered.

back lot Sector of a studio complex in which various outdoor sets have been built and maintained for continued film use.

back story Refers to the events and history of a character before the beginning of the film's storyline.

barney A blanket placed over a camera to dampen its operational noise.

basic cable Contractual term referring to cable stations that exist between the public airwaves, ABC, NBC, CBS, etc., and pay per view channels such as HBO.

beat A pause noted in the film script that interrupts dialogue, or in *mocap*, a move or take that is captured.

below the line costs Portion of the budget set aside for technical and production costs.

best boy *Gaffer's* assistant or apprentice.

biopic Biographical film.

bit-part Small acting role usually with one scene and only a few lines.

blimp A camera housing used to prevent sound equipment from picking up sound generated by the camera.

blue-screen Special effects technique in which an actor works in front of a monochromatic blue or green background, allowing computer generated or previously filmed footage to be added later.

blurb TV commercial.

body double An actor that temporarily replaces the principal performer for scenes in which specific body parts are filmed without facial close-ups.

Bollywood Center of the film industry of India. A combination of the words "Bombay" and "Hollywood."

bookends Framing device in which complementing scenes are used to begin and end a film.

boom Telescoping extension pole upon which a microphone or camera may be suspended above or outside of a scene during filming.

bounce board A large white card made of poster board or foam used to reflect light into a scene.

breakdown Character descriptions of the various roles in a film.

bridging shot Transitional film shot between two scenes.

buddy film Film genre in which mismatched or contrasting characters act as foils to each other.

bumper A brief announcement, usually two to fifteen seconds in length, placed between a pause in the program and its *commercial* break, and vice versa.

burka Hooded robe worn by *mocap* actors to shield makers from being captured.

buyout Contractual term, offering an actor the alternative of a one-time payment verses a long-term residual.

buzz track Natural or atmospheric soundtrack, added to a film to provide additional realism.

call sheet Schedule provided to actors and crew detailing the shoot schedule and who is required to report at what times.

cameo Special screen appearance of a famous actor or prominent person in a walk-on role of minimal lines and screen time.

can Film canister that holds the film for transport. A completed film is referred to as "in the can," and rerecorded footage referred to as "canned footage."

cap The maximum payment allotted.

casting couch Illegal practice of trading sexual favors for a role in a film project.

CGI Acronym for "Computer Generated Imagery," the technology that adds digital 3D graphics to create fantastical special effects on film.

character arc The emotional progress of the characters in the story.

chopsocky Slang term for martial arts films.

Cinemascope Trademark name for Twentieth Century Fox's widescreen process.

cinema verité Style of documentary that employs minimalist techniques often using handheld cameras, natural sound and grainy high-contrast, black and white film.

clapboard Originally a small, hinged chalkboard that displayed film identifying information such as scene, title, date, and take number, and was slated or clapped in front of the camera before each new shot. Now production companies use a digital version of the same.

Class A Commercial contract specifying sponsorship of a particular network program or series that runs concurrently in more than 21 cities for a 13-week cycle.

clean contract Contract in which no paragraph has been struck out and all affirmative boxes have been initialed by the actor.

clean speech A take in which the dialogue was performed without error.

cold opening A short segment before a television program's "opening credits" that serves to build dramatic tension.

coda Epilogue or ending scene to a film that provides a conclusion or closure to the story line.

continuity Process of documenting and recreating an exact scene for shooting on multiple days or multiple takes and angles.

contract player Any actor that is under contract with a production company.

Coogan's Law Landmark 1930s legislation that protects a child actor's earnings in a court-administered trust fund; named after child actor Jackie Coogan.

corral Farthest point outside the volume where usable data can be captured.

coverage Term referring to all the shots needed by a director to complete a scene or location of a film.

cowboy shot Film shot framed from mid-thigh up popularized for Westerns.

craft services Catering company or film studio department that provides food and beverages to a production company while on location.

cross-cutting Editing technique that alternates or interweaves two different storylines.

cross-over appeal Ability to appeal to two or more different demographic groups.

cue cards Cards on which dialogue has been printed to help the actor or announcer.

cutaway shot Brief scene inserted to interrupt the main action, such as a cutaway to a newspaper headline.

cyberpunk Sub-genre of science fiction that incorporates classic elements of *film noir*, including alienation, dehumanization, the presence of counter-cultural anti-heroes, darkness, dystopia, and corruption.

dailies/rushes Raw footage from the previous day, screened to preview film progress.

dark horse Industry vernacular for a film unlikely to succeed.

day player Actor contracted for one day's work, usually for a small supporting role.

deal memo Letter written to confirm the negotiated points of a pending contract.

deferred payment Agreement to work without payment until the time the project recovers additional production costs and turns a profit.

director's cut Director's final edited version of a film before editing by studios and producers.

discovery shot Sequence in which the camera suddenly discloses a person or object.

dissolve Transitional editing technique that blends one scene into the next.

diversity agreement Contract that provides financial incentives for films that employ a significant number of underrepresented actors.

dolly Platform or track on which a camera moves either in or out of the scene or alongside the subject.

double Person who stands in for a principal actor for stunts, nude scenes, or photographically.

downgrade Notification that an actor's contract status has been reduced as a result of editing.

drop and pick-up Contractual clause that allows an actor to be dropped for up to 10 days and then brought back to complete filming with no pay for the intervening days.

dubbing Act of recording a soundtrack of music, dialogue, or sound effects to match already filmed sequences.

Dutch tilt Camera shot made by leaning the camera to one side to film on a diagonal angle.

Easter egg An intentional reference to a movie, person, or event that is intended to be too subtle to be noticed on the initial viewing.

ensemble Large cast of actors in which all roles are equal with no true leading roles.

episodic Television program composed of weekly installments loosely related by plot and character.

establishing shot Long wide-angle shot providing an overview of the scene to identify the locale and characters involved.

exhibitor Movie theater owner.

experimental film Film, usually low-budget, that challenges conventional filmmaking techniques.

exploitation film Film designed to appeal to sensationalistic appetites of sex or violence in order to assure commercial profitability.

extras Actors hired for non-speaking, non-specific roles for crowd scenes or background. Often referred to as *background* or *atmosphere*.

eyeline match A technique, often a grip holding a pole, used to make sure an actor is looking at the "face" of the *CGI* character/creature to be inserted later.

favored nations Contractual term in which all actors are entitled to equal treatment in regards to pay, billing, and other designated provisions.

featurette Short subject film, twenty to forty-five minutes in length.

feevee Pay TV.

film noire Dark, sober films characterized by low lighting and black and white cinematography, depicting an underworld of crime and corruption.

final cut Final edited version of the film officially released.

First AD First Assistant Director is responsible for the preparation of the shooting schedule and script breakdown, tracking the progress of filming versus the production schedule, observing all rules related to union crafts, labor contracts and location agreements, maintaining safety on the working set, and working with the Unit Manager to keep operational costs within the budgeted plan.

first refusal Casting director's request for the actor to call before accepting another booking for the same time period.

fish eye lens Wide-angled lens with a short focal point that exaggerates and distorts an image as if through a glass ball.

fists of fury A hand calibration pose where an actor clinches their fists tightly.

flash frame Barely perceptible clear frame inserted into a scene to give the perception of a flash of white.

flying tpose A suspended *mocap tpose* used for wire harness stunts.

Foley artist Named after radio sound effect master Jack Foley, Foley artists create and synchronize the sound effects added to the film during the editing process, such as footsteps, slamming doors, and fight scenes.

force majeure Contract clause that sets or suspends certain financial obligations as the result of any catastrophic event that interrupts the progress of the film.

foreground Action closest to the camera, as opposed to background. Stage equivalent is downstage.

freeze-frame Optical printing technique that gives the illusion of the scene freezing into a still photograph.

gaffer Chief or lead lighting technician on a film crew.

generation Reference to the number of times a videotape has been reproduced from the master tape.

giraffe Mechanically extendable and manipulated *boom microphone*; a pole worn by a *mocap* actor playing a character taller than they are.

greenlight Industry vernacular denoting production approval.

grindhouse film Film genre characterized by more sex, nudity, and violence than actual plot, ranging from B-movie action-adventure films to slasher films and soft porn.

grip Film crew member responsible for setup and tear down of the film equipment, set pieces, and supplies.

guerrilla film Low-budget film created outside the rule of permits, unions, and corporations.

guillotined When an actor has gone above the *tentpole* where facial data cannot be captured.

hard deck The lowest down point in the *mocap volume* where facial data can be captured.

head-on shot Camera setup in which the action either moves directly into the camera or the camera moves directly into the action.

helm (1) To direct a film or TV program; (2) helmer—a director.

high-angle shot Camera setup in which the subject is filmed directly from above.

hi-def Slang for high definition television that increases the lines of resolution on a television screen, substantially increasing the level of detail.

hitchhiker A mocap marker that has transferred from one actor to another.

hitting a mark Actor's term that refers to executing the movement to an exact predetermined position during camera takes.

hold A conditional booking with a cancelation fee in effect.

hold over Contractual term that refers to an actor required to work more additional days than originally contracted.

holding fee Retainer paid to an actor in exchange for exclusivity rights for a fixed cycle.

honeywagon A trailer, or truck used as the dressing room for actors when on location shoots.

horse opera Originally referred to the singing cowboy films of the 1950s but more generally refers to all western films.

hot set A *set* where the placement of furniture and props has been finalized for a scene that is in the process of being *shot*.

hype Slang for hyperbole or exaggeration. The manufactured buzz generated through marketing and advertising programs.

IATSE Abbreviation for the International Alliance of Theatrical Stage Employees, the technical union for film, television and stage.

in the can Studio lingo indicating that the day's shooting or entire film has been completed.

indie Short for "independent films" or for a production company that is independent of major film studio financing.

infomercials Classification of taped programming that primarily promotes the attributes of a particular product.

iron cross A sitting *mocap tpose*.

jazz hands A *mocap* hand calibration pose in which an actor splays their fingers outwards.

jib A boom device with a camera on one end, and a counterweight and camera controls on the other that permits the camera to be moved vertically, horizontally, or a combination of the two.

jump cut Abrupt transitional editing device in which the action is advanced in time to create discontinuity.

juvenile role Role meant for an underage actor that, if hired, requires additional supervision and restraints.

key light Primary light of the scene.

key grip The *grip* in charge of camera movement whether on a *dolly*, camera crane or mounted on the hood or bumper of a vehicle.

kick-off First day of principal photography for a project.

kill stick/fear stick A large stick covered with foam used to hit *mocap* actors for reaction during filming.

Klieg light Carbon-arc lamp that produces an intense light; used principally for large-scale filming and movie premieres.

knee pose A kneeling *mocap pose*.

kudocast Awards show.

lavalier Tiny wireless body microphone clipped to an actor.

leadman Member of the art department often in charge of the set dressers.

legs Refers to a film with strong growing commercial appeal that will carry it forward for months.

letterboxing Process of reformatting a film to portray its entire width on a television screen, creating black bands above and below the film image.

line producer Individual responsible for managing the expenses and people involved in a production.

lip sync Synchronization of mouth movement on film with a vocal track.

live area The greater area of the *scene* in the *camera*'s viewfinder than will appear in the final product.

loan-outs Type of corporation setup by an actor or musician to "loan out" their services to a production company while protecting their assets and obtaining certain tax benefits.

location Anywhere other than the studio or studio backlot in which filming is conducted in order to lend a sense of realism to the scene.

lock it down Direction given by the *AD* for everyone on the set to be quiet, to move out of frame, and to secure the set against anything or anyone interrupting the shot.

logline Short summary of a screenplay provided on the first page of the script.

looping The process of rerecording dialogue by the actors in the recording studio as part of the post-production process.

Macguffin/weenie A term used by Alfred Hitchcock to refer to an item, event, or piece of knowledge that the characters in a film consider extremely important, but which the audience either does not know of or does not care about.

magic hour Time just before sunset or after sunrise that provides low level soft and colorful light.

majors Term used to refer to the major studios of Hollywood.

mark (1) Designation on the ground indicating an actor's final destination during filming. (2) The sound created by clapping the slate board used to synchronize the soundtrack.

marker Highly reflective balls or small bright lights attached to a special *mocap* suit that track the wearers movements by computer software that assembles the data into an approximation of the actor's motion. Active systems use markers that light up or blink distinctively, while passive systems use inert objects like white balls or just painted dots (the latter is often used for face capture).

marker doon A marker that has fallen off an actor during *mocap*.

martini shot The last camera shot of the day.

master shot A long film take that shows the main action of a scene in its entirety.

match shot A transition in which something in the scene that follows in some way matches a character or object in the previous scene.

megaplex Movie theater with more than sixteen screens.

miniatures Models photographed to give them a full scale illusion.

mobisode A short TV episode made for mobile phones.

mocap Slang for motion capture or performance capture technology.

mocap friendly Something non-reflective that can safely be brought into the *volume* without registering on the computer.

mocap ready When the *mocap* system is ready to capture another *beat*.

mockumentary Farcical documentary that may look like the real thing but in actuality mocks the subject matter.

money shot Scene that provides the audience with the pay off or climax.

monitor Small television screen used to oversee filming as it happens.

monkey paw *Mocap* hand calibration pose where the actor curls the first digit of their fingers and all the way down to touch the palm.

Moppet Term referring to a child actor.

morph Process of transforming one digital image into another using animation techniques.

motion capture technology Also known as "performance capture," this technology captures an actor's movement digitally via sensors, or *markers*, placed over the actor's body to be later animated or modified on a computer.

multiple tracking A rerecording by the artist(s) of an existing recording.

multiplex/megaplex Movie theater comprising more than two screens but less than 16.

MPAA Abbreviation for the Motion Picture Association of America, which represents the interests of the studios and responsible for rating commercially released films.

New Media Reference to the evolving and emerging media forms and platforms being developed for cell phones, tablets and technology still under development.

non-traditional casting Refers to an inclusive casting strategy to use people of color and persons with disabilities in roles not specifically requiring them.

NTSC Abbreviation for the National Television System Committee. It refers to a film format standard for North America and Japan.

off-net Network TV series repeats sold into syndication.

off-Hollywood Independent films made outside of the Hollywood studio system.

omnie Speech sounds used as general background noise such as party chatter.

on-spec Working without pay on the gamble that the project will lead to something else more profitable.

optical Any visual device that must be added during post-production.

option To secure the rights to a screenplay for a given length of time.

outtakes Film takes that have been edited out of a film's final cut.

outgrade Notification to an actor that his or her image or soundtrack has been completely edited from the final version of the commercial; required within 60 days after the completion date.

overcrank Filming technique in which the camera *speed* is increased, giving the impression of slow motion when played back.

overlap To carry over dialogue, music or sounds from one scene to the next.

over-the-shoulder Camera angle in which the camera films the action from behind the head of another character.

PAL (Phase Alternation Line) Film format standard adopted by Europe.

pan Abbreviation for "panorama," meaning to move the camera from one side to the other.

payoff Dramatic scene that provides an explanation or climax to the film's main plot line.

payola Terms referring to under-the-table payoffs.

pipeline A studio's schedule of film production *greenlit* for production.

pitch Sales proposal for a film project to obtain financial backing.

post-production Final stage in film production in which the film is edited and opticals, sound effects, dubbing and title sequences are added.

potboiler Reference to detective or crime thrillers.

preproduction Initial stage of film production in which the planning of storyboards, budgets, location scouting, design and the shooting schedule takes place.

prequel Film sequel that tells the *back story* of a character before the time of the original film.

principal performer Lead role.

principal photography Reference to primary filming of lead characters and main action sequences.

product placement Advertising strategy in which major brand name items are intentionally placed in a scene for recognition.

production value Refers to the level of perfection or quality expected by the director or producer.

prosthetic appliances Makeup additions made of a material such as latex or gelatin glued to an *actor*'s skin.

PSA Public Service Announcements

punked A *mocap maker* covered by a stunt harness.

Q-rating Advertising research rating that gauges an actor's household recognition factor.

reaction shot Cutaway shot of a character's reaction to another character's statement or action.

real time Actual time in which an event would take to occur.

rear projection Antiquated technique in which actors are filmed in front of a screen on which a background is projected.

redlight Opposite of *greenlight*, meaning a project has not been approved for production.

reissue Rerelease of a film project by a studio.

reshoot contingency Funds kept or saved by a producer in case reshoots are required after test screenings or decisions made by studio executives.

residuals Contractual term that refers to the payment of a royalty to each creative member of a project each time the project is shown or sold.

reverse shot A *shot* taken at a 120–180 degree angle from the preceding *shot*; used in dialogue scenes that alternates between over-the-shoulder *shot*s that show each character speaking.

revival house Movie theater dedicated to the exhibition of classic films.

rhubarb Background conversation by extras: Extras were often asked to mutter the word "rhubarb" to produce the effect of genuine conversation.

rider Amendment to a contract.

to ROM the actor Where a mocap actor moves through a series of movements used to calibrate the *CGI* character skeleton.

room tone Recording of the natural ambient "silence" in a *set*/location for the *sound editor*, who will use it either as a reference point or for when silence is required.

rough cut First edited version of the project.

rushes Previous day's rough takes, often called *dailies*.

safety An additional take filmed as a back-up.

scale Minimum pay for an actor.

scale plus 10 Minimum pay plus an additional 10 percent to pay the talent agent's commission.

schlock film Inferior, low-budget, exploitation film.

schmutz Anything that gets on a *mocap marker* to negatively affect its reflectivity.

screener Promotional DVD version sent to voters of a film award.

second banana Sidekick, foil or straight man to a lead comedian.

Second AD An assistant to the *assistant director* who oversees the movements of the *cast* and prepares *call sheets*.

Second Second Assistant Director An assistant to the *second assistant director* responsible for herding and directing the movements of *extras*.

second unit photography Smaller subordinate film crew from the principal photography unit that films crowd scenes, locations and other secondary film shots.

sepia tone Brown and gray tones added to a black and white image to enhance the dramatic effect.

serial Television show with a multi-episode storyline, such as soap operas.

set-up Placement of the camera, scenery and characters for a particular shot.

sfx Shorthand for "sound effects".

Shemp Actor whose face is not seen and who has no lines, such as *stand-ins* and *extras*; borrowed from Hollywood lore about a *stand-in* used to finish Three Stooges films after Shemp Howard's death.

shooting script Film script version in which scenes are numbered and camera directions inserted.

showrunner The writer or producer who is responsible for the production of a television series.

sides Script excerpts used for auditioning actors.

signatory Production company that has signed a union production contract.

silk A large section of translucent white cloth used to soften a hard-light source.

slate (1) Recorded identification of a film's *scene* and *take* numbers now done with a digital clapboard held in front of the camera. (2) Actor's filmed audition introduction, stating his or her name and the role to be read.

sleeper Project that unexpectedly attains great success.

soft focus Camera technique in which gauze or Vaseline covers the film lens to blur the image, create romantic effects, or to rejuvenate an actor's face.

spaghetti Western Low-budget Western made in Italy or Spain.

spec–script Script written before any agreement has been entered in hopes of selling the script to the highest bidder once completed.

speed Announcement made by either the *director of photography* or *camera operator* to the *director* that the *camera* is operating at the correct *speed*.

spoiler Specific information about a film's ending that if known will impair the dramatic effect of the film for the audience.

squib Small explosive charge taped underneath an actor's clothing that when activated, gives the impression of a bullet strike.

stand-in Actor who is physically similar to a principal actor and takes their place during camera set-up and focusing.

star vehicle Film customized to show off a particular celebrity's talents.

static shot Camera set-up in which the camera never moves.

Steadicam Special hydraulic, gyroscopic, handheld camera that allows the operator to move with the action without the need of a track.

stills Photographs taken during filming, later used for publicity, advertising or documentation and continuity.

stinger Surprising, last-minute bit of film footage that appears after the end credits.

stock footage Common or previously filmed footage such as tourist attractions, archived for future use.

stop motion Animation technique where 3D objects, filmed one frame at a time, are repositioned minutely each time, thus giving the illusion of motion.

story reader An individual hired by studios and production companies to read, analyze, and evaluate submitted scripts.

storyboard Sequential scene-by-scene drawing of the project, somewhat resembling a cartoon.

studio zone also known as the thirty-mile zone (TMZ) this area marked roughly around a thirty-mile (48 km) radius of the intersection of West Beverly Boulevard and North La Cienega Boulevard, which is used by the *unions* to determine rates and work rules for union workers.

stunt double A stunt *performer,* chosen to resemble an *actor,* who takes the actor's place during a *stunt.*

subjective point of view Narrative technique in which the camera provides a limited perspective, thus confusing the viewer.

super To "superimpose" one image over another, such as words over a filmed scene.

syndication Distribution deal providing television programming to independent commercial stations for airing.

syndie Syndicated television programming.

sweetening The addition of a new additional recording over the original recording.

sweet spot The center of the *volume* where there is the most camera coverage.

take Filmed sequence, often repeated until the director is satisfied.

take a header To seriously injury oneself during a take.

talent General reference to the actors in a film.

tpose Standing position taken by *mocap* actors at the beginning and end of a *beat.*

telefilm Made for television film.

tentpole The center or highest point in the "sweet spot" of the *mocap volume.*

thirty-mile zone Measured from the Beverly Center in West Hollywood, the radius in which a production company can shoot without paying travel expenses or a per diem. Also known as the *studio zone.*

tie-in Commercial project or products associated with a film.

tight on A close-up shot.

topline Top billing above the title of the film.

tracking shot Camera set-up in which the camera moves with the action along a preset track or a road, utilizing a truck or a *Steadicam.*

trades Daily and weekly periodicals that report the entertainment industry news.

trailer Short teaser or publicity preview of a film.

treatment Summary of a proposed project detailing the story line and characters that is designed to be a sales presentation.

triple threat Refers to an actor that can sing, dance, and act equally well.

tubthump To promote or draw attention to a film usually conducted by publicists, advertisers, and agents.

underground film Low-budget, noncommercial film, independently produced outside of the mainstream film industry.

vertigo effect Camera technique created by Alfred Hitchcock that involves tracking backward while simultaneously zooming in, making the person or object in the center of the image seem stationary while their surroundings change.

voice-over (VO) Off-camera recorded voice or narration.

volume/the grid The acting area that is within the camera's range where motion capture data can be acquired.

walk-on Brief but featured performance on-camera without dialogue.

walk-through First rehearsal day on a film set in which all technical elements are added.

webisode Short scripted film made for the internet.

wig-wag Red warning light located above each entrance or exit door on a film set sound stage, designed to flash (with a buzzer sound) to indicate when shooting commences or ends.

wild sound Scenes that are filmed without the sound being recorded at the same time to be dubbed in later.

wild spot Commercial usage assigned on a per city or region basis rather by program or network.

wrangler A person who is responsible for the care and control of vehicles or animals on the film set.

wrap Completion of filming for the day.

wraparound A short segment of a film or TV program that comes before or after the main part and provides an introduction, conclusion, or context for the main story or subject.

yawner Dull film that puts its audience to sleep.

zitcom Television comedy aimed at teenagers.

zoom To quickly change lens perspective from wide-angle to telephoto.

BIBLIOGRAPHY

Books

2017 Hollywood Diversity Report: Setting the Record Straight. Ralph J. Bunche Center for African American Studies at UCLA. February 2017.

2017 Studio Responsibility Index. Gay and Lesbian Alliance Against Defamation, 2017.

Alexander, Jane. *Command Performance: An Actress in the Theater of Politics.* New York: PublicAffairs, 2000.

Badgett, M.V. Lee and Jody L. Herman. *Sexual Orientation & Gender Diversity in Entertainment: Experiences & Perspectives of SAG-AFTRA Members,* SAG–AFTRA, the Williams Institute, 2013.

Caine, Michael. *What's It All About: An Autobiography.* New York: Ballantine Books, 1992.

Holden, Anthony. *Behind the Oscar: The Secret History of the Academy Awards.* New York: The Penguin Group, 1993.

Litwak, Mark. *Contracts for the Film and Television Industry.* Beverly Hills: Silman-James Press, 1998. 2nd Edition.

Motion Picture Association of America. *Theatrical Market Statistics 2016,*

Selznick, David O. *Memo from David O. Selznick.* (Ed. Rudy Behlmer. New York: The Modern Library, 2000.

Smith, Stacy L., Marc Choueiti and Katherine Pieper. *Over Sixty, Underestimated: A Look at Aging on the "Silver" Screen in Best Picture Nominated Films.* Media, Diversity, & Social Change Initiative: USC Annenberg School of Journalism, February 2017.

Smith, Stacy L., Marc Choueiti, and Katherine Pieper. *Inequality in 900 Popular Films: Examining Portrayals of Gender, Race/ Ethnicity, LGBT, and Disability 2007 to 2016.* Media, Diversity, & Social Change Initiative: USC Annenberg School of Journalism, July 2017.

Smith, Stacy L., Marc Choueiti, Katherine Pieper, Traci Gillig, Carmen Lee, and Dylan DeLuca. *Inequality in 700 Popular Films: Examining Portrayals of Gender, Race, & LGBT Status from 2007 to 2014.* Media, Diversity, & Social Change Initiative: USC Annenberg School of Journalism, 2015.

Thoreau, Henry David. *Walden and Other Writings.* Ed. Joseph Wood Krutch. New York: Bantam Books, 1981.

Where We Are On TV: GLAAD's Annual Report on TV '16–'17, Gay and Lesbian Alliance Against Defamation, 2016.

Woodburn, Danny and Kristina Kopić. *The Ruderman White Paper on Employment of Actors with Disabilities in Television.* Ruderman Family Foundation, July 2016.

Periodicals

Actors Equity Association. "You Income Tax," *Equity News*, March 2011, p. 1,4.

"Prepare to Enter a Strange New World." *Screen Actor,* Spring 2010, 24–28.

"Radio Artists Ask Closed Shop." *Los Angeles Times*, January 2, 1939, p.10.

Rogers, Will. "Weekly Article #17," *The New York Times*, April 8, 1923.

SAG-AFTRA. "Keeps the Pressure Up on SBS." *SAG-AFTRA Magazine*, Summer/Fall 2017, 11.

Shope, Keli. "The Final Cut: How SAG's Failed Negotiations with Talent Agents left the Contractual Rights of Rank-and-File Actors on the Cutting Room Floor." *Journal of the National Association of Administrative Law Judiciary*, March 15, 2006. Vol. 25: Issue 1, 128–129, 133, 137–142.

Zelenski, David. "Talent Agents, Personal Managers, and Their Conflicts in the New Hollywood." *California Law Review*, Vol. 76, 979, 979–1002.

Websites

Academy of Motion Picture Arts and Sciences. "History and Structure." http://www.oscars.org/academy-story (accessed October 16, 2017).

Actor's Equity Association:
"About Equity—Historical Overview." http://www.actorsequity.org (accessed October 16, 2017).
"Constitution." (accessed October 16, 2017).
"Los Angeles Transitional 99 Seat Transitional Code." (accessed December 28, 2017).

Baum, Gary. "Two Casting Directors Plead No Contest in Pay-to-Play Audition Scandal." *The Hollywood Reporter* online. October 5, 2017. http://www.hollywoodreporter.com/news/two-casting-directors-plead-no-contest-pay-play-audition-scandal-1046016 (accessed February 8, 2018).

BizParentz Foundation. "Advance Fee Talent / Krekorian Scam Prevention Act." http://www.bizparentz.org/entertainmentlaws/krekorianact.html (accessed February 14, 2018).

California Massage Therapy Council. "Requirements to Certify." http://www.camtc.org/requirements-to-certify/ (accessed December 6, 2017).

Casting Society of America (CSA). "Who We Aren't." http://www.castingsociety.com/about/faqs#what-is-the-CSA (accessed January 1, 2018).

Curbed Los Angeles. "For Rent in LA." https://la.curbed.com/la-apartments-houses-for-rent (accessed February 9, 2018).

DiGiacomo, Frank. "'Hamilton's' Lin-Manuel Miranda on Finding Originality, Racial Politics (and Why Trump Should See His Show)," *Hollywood Reporter online*. August 12, 2015. https://www.hollywoodreporter.com/features/hamiltons-lin-manuel-miranda-finding-814657

FilmL.A. Inc. "Hollywood at Heart of LA, California & US Economic Backbone." December 13, 2010. https://www.filmla.com/hollywood-heart-california-economic-backbone/

Forbes online. "Los Angeles, CA." https://www.forbes.com/places/ca/los-angeles/ (accessed June 8, 2017).

Garner, Scott:
"Neighborhood Spotlight: Larchmont." *Los Angeles Times online*. Dec. 23, 2006, http://www.latimes.com/business/realestate/hot-property/la-fi-hp-neighborhood-spotlight-larchmont-20161224-story.html
"Neighborhood Spotlight: Hancock Park." *Los Angeles Times online*. April 22, 2016, http://www.latimes.com/business/realestate/hot-property/la-fi-hp-0423-neighborhood-hancock-park-20160423-story.html
"Neighborhood Spotlight: East Hollywood." *Los Angeles Times online*. Sept. 2, 2016. http://www.latimes.com/business/realestate/hot-property/la-fi-hp-neighborhood-spotlight-east-hollywood-20160903-snap-story.html-
Handel, Jonathan. "The SAG-AFTRA Merger Attempt: Why is it Happening Now?" *Backstage.com*. July 12, 2011.https://www.backstage.com/news/the-sag-aftra-merger-attempt-why-is-it-happening-now/ (accessed February 2, 2017)."
Heyt, Eric. "Hidden Talent: The Emergence of Hollywood Agents by Tom Kemper." *Senses of Cinema*.com. December 2009. http://sensesofcinema.com/2009/book-reviews/hidden-talent-the-emergence-of-hollywood-agents-by-tom-kemper/
Horowitz, Simi. "Stockard Channing Reflects on Her Unintended Life as an Actress." *Backstage online*. Oct. 26, 2011. https://www.backstage.com/interview/stockard-channing-reflects-on-her-unintended-life-as-an-actor/ (accessed June 1, 2018).
Hutchinson, Pamela. "The silent-era film stars who risked life and limb doing their own stunts." *The Guardian*.com. September 7, 2015. https://www.theguardian.com/film/filmblog /2015/sep/07/silent-era-film-stars-risked-their-lives-doing-film-stuntsn (accessed October 16, 2017).
Igler, Marc. "North Hollywood Growth Cap Sought." *Los Angeles Times*. Dec. 19, 1985. http://articles.latimes.com/1985-12-19/local/me-30471_1_north-hollywood-residents-assn (accessed July 14, 2017).
Kagan, Ron. "Beware of casting scams." *Backstage online*. August 20, 2015. https://backstage.zendesk.com/hc/en-us/articles/201802099-Beware-of-casting-scams (accessed October 11, 2017).
La Monica, Paul R. "Netflix plans to spend nearly $16 billion on content." *Money.CNN*. online. August 15, 2017. http://money.cnn.com/2017/08/14/investing/netflix-disney-content-costs/index.html (accessed February 5, 2018).
LA Stories. "Stories about Life in Los Angeles." *LAStories*.com http://www.lastories.com/ (accessed March 31, 2017).
Los Angeles Better Business Bureau. "Los Angeles Modeling & Acting." https://www.bbb.org/BBBWeb/Forms/General/ (accessed March 30, 2017).
Los Angeles Police Department. "Valet Businesses and Valet Drivers Need a Permit." http://assets.lapdonline.org/assets/pdf/Valet%20Permit.pdf (accessed December 4, 2017).
Los Angeles Almanac. "Weather." http:/www.laalmanac.com/weather/index.php.
Los Angeles Metropolitan Transportation Authority:
"Facts at a Glance." https://www.metro.net/news/facts-glance/ (accessed December 8, 2017).
"Fare Structure." https://www.metro.net/riding/fares/ (accessed December 8, 2017).
Los Angeles Police Department. "Valet Permits." http://assets.lapdonline.org/assets/pdf/Valet#20Permit.pdf (accessed December 8, 2017).
Los Angeles Times. "Mapping LA." http://maps.latimes.com/neighborhoods/ (accessed May 1, 2017).
Los Angeles Unified School District. *Fingertip Facts*. https://achieve.lausd.net/facts (accessed June 8, 2017).

Los Angeles Yellow Pages. "Temporary Employment Agencies." https://www.yellowpages. com/los-angeles-ca/temporary-employment-agencies (accessed December 4, 2017).

McClintock, Pamela. "Box Office: Get Ready for Hollywood's Shrinking Studio System." *Hollywood Reporter online.* January 4, 2018. https://www.hollywoodreporter.com/news/ box-office-get-ready-hollywoods-shrinking-studio-system-1071457 (accessed March 30, 2007).

Murray, Noel. "Peter Falk—Interview." *The AV Club.com*, August 25, 2004. https://www. avclub.com/peter-falk-1798208368

Nashawaty, Chris. "Steven Spielberg talks about 'Jaws'—the greatest summer movie ever made." *Entertainment Weekly.com.* June 8, 2011. http://ew.com/article/2011/06/08/ steven-spielberg-jaws-interview/ (assessed June 19, 2018).

Nielsen. "For Us By Us? The Mainstream Appeal of Black Content." Nielsen online. February 8, 2017. http://www.nielsen.com/us/en/insights/news/2017/for-us-by-us-the- mainstream-appeal-of-black-content.html

NowCasting. "Ask the Voice Cat." *Actor's Ink.* https://www.nowcasting.com/actorsink/ section.php?sectionID=36 (accessed October 16, 2017).

Now Casting online. "About Now Casting." https://www.nowcasting.com/aboutus.php (accessed August 13, 2018).

Oprah Magazine online. "Oprah Talks to Tom Hanks." September 2001. https://www.oprah. com/omagazine/oprah-interviews-tom-hanks/all (accessed August 19, 2018).

O'Neill, Ann W. "Actress Fired Over Pregancy Wins $5 Million." *Los Angeles Time online.* December 23, 1997. http://articles.latimes.com/1997/dec/23/news/mn-1420

Reisman, Abraham. "Steve Zahn. Seriously." *Vulture.com.* July 13, 2017. http://www.vulture. com/2017/07/planet-of-the-apes-steve-zahn-on-his-farm-and-his-craft.html (accessed October 11, 2017).

Robb, David. "SAG-AFTRA Warns Members About Casting Workshop 'Scams'." *Deadline. com.* July 19, 2016. http://deadline.com/2016/07/casting-workshop-scam-sag-aftra- warns-members-1201788870/ (accessed October 11, 2017).

SAG-AFTRA:
> "Discrimination & Harassment Policy." https://www.sagaftra.org/content/non- discrimination-policy (accessed January 31, 2018).
> *Personal Managers Code of Ethics and Conduct.* http://www.sagaftra.org/files/personal_ manager_code_of_ethics_and_conduct_0.pdf (accessed November 8, 2017).
> "Production Notice & Resources." https://www.sagaftra.org/production-notices- resources-0 (accessed January 30, 2018).
> *Safety Bulletins.* https://www.sagaftra.org/content/safety (accessed January 29, 2018).
> "Voucher Scam." http://www.sagaftra.org/content/voucher-scam (accessed October 19, 2017).
> *Your Relationship with Your Agent.* https://www.sagaftra.org/your-relationship-with- your-agent (accessed November 6, 2017).

SAG-AFTRA Foundation. "Casting Access." https://sagaftra.foundation/performers- programs/casting-access/ (accessed August 13, 2018).

Santa Monica College: Theatre Arts. "About the Department." http://www.smc.edu/ AcademicPrograms/TheatreArts/Pages/default.aspx (accessed January 21, 2017).

Satran, Joe. "How Fairfax Became the Coolest Street in Los Angeles." *Huffington Post.* Feb. 2, 2015. http://www.huffingtonpost.com/2015/02/02/fairfax-los-angeles_n_ 6558672.html (accessed June 24, 2017).

Schleuss, Jon, Doug Smith, and Richard Verrier. "Film set accidents." *Los Angeles Times online*. March 11, 2015. http://spreadsheets.latimes.com/film-set-accidents/ (accessed January 29, 2018).

SelectUSA. *Media and Entertainment Spotlight: The Media and Entertainment Industry in the United States*. https://www.selectusa.gov/media-entertainment-industry-united-states (accessed February 1, 2018).

Spangler, Todd. "Cord-Cutting Explodes: 22 Million United States Adults Will Have Cancelled Cable, Satellite TV by End of 2017." *Variety online*. September 13, 2017. http://variety.com/2017 /biz/news/cord-cutting-2017-estimates-cancel-cable-satellite-tv-1202556594/

Studio City Chamber of Commerce. "About Studio City". http://www.studiocitychamber.com/aboutstudiocity.php (accessed May 29, 2017).

"Successful Actors Talk About Their Training." *Backstage* online. Nov. 9, 2011. https://www.backstage.com/news/successful-actors-talk-about-their-training/ (accessed March 5, 2017).

UCLA: School of Theater, Film and Television. "About the School." http://www.tft.ucla.edu/about/ (accessed January 21, 2017).

Universal City/North Hollywood Chamber of Commerce. "NoHo Arts District." http://noho.org/our-history/ (accessed May 29, 2017).

University of Southern California: School of Dramatic Arts. "Professional Development." http://dramaticarts.usc.edu/programs/professional-development (accessed January 21, 2017).

Audiovisual

Karas, Sandra. *2018: What Can We Expect*. "Online Tax Seminar," 11:41/13:31; Actors Equity Association, https://members.actorsequity.org/resources/vita/2018-online-tax-seminar/ (accessed May 1, 2018).

Legal Agreements

Actors Equity Association. Los Angeles Transitional 99 Seat Transitional Code. http://www.actorsequity.org/agreements/agreements.asp?code=800 (accessed February 23, 2018).

SAG-AFTRA:

    16(g) Instructions: California Agents. https://www.sagaftra.org/16g-franchise-agent-application-ca-2015 (accesssed November 3, 2017).

    1991 Screen Actors Guild Codified Agency Regulations. https://www.sagaftra.org/files/sag/documents/sag_rule_16_g.pdf (accessed November 1, 2017).

    2004 SAG Data Report Overview. https://www.sagaftra.org/content/2004-casting-data-report-overview (accessed January 29, 2017).

    2005 Basic Agreement. https://www.sagaftra.org/files/2005theatricalagreement.pdf (accessed October 11, 2017).

    2007 & 2008 Casting Data Reports. https://www.sagaftra.org/content/studies-and-reports (accessed February 11, 2018).

2012 Music Video Agreement. https://www.sagaftra.org/files/independent_mv_
   agreement_0.pdf (accessed December 28, 2017).
2013 Commercials Contract. "Use of Commercials." https://www.sagaftra.org/
   files/2013commercialscontract_e-book_0.pdf (accessed December 12, 2017).
2014 Basic Agreement. "Air Travel and Flight Insurance." https://www.sagaftra.org/
   files/2014_sag-aftra_cba.pdf (accessed December 13, 2017).
   "Studio Zone," https://www.sagaftra.org /files/2014_sag-aftra_cba.pdf (accessed
      December 13, 2017).
   "Nudity," https://www.sagaftra.org /files/2014_sag-aftra_cba.pdf (accessed
      December 13, 2017).
2014 New Media Agreement. https://www.sagaftra.org/files/2014_sag-aftra_dramatic_
   new_media_agreement_sample_0.pdf (accessed December 28, 2017).
2014 Theatrical and Television Contracts Digest. "Background Actors." https://www.
   sagaftra.org/files/digest_background_actors_la_zones_8_4_0_1.pdf (accessed
   December 28, 2017).
2015 Corporate/Educational and Non-Broadcast Agreement. https://www.sagaftra.org/
   files/2015_corporate_educational_and_non-broadcast_contract_ebook_0.pdf
   (accessed December 8, 2017).
2017 Interactive Media Agreement. https://www.sagaftra.org/files/2017_interactive_
   refbklt.pdf (accessed December 27, 2017).
2017 Theatrical/Television Memorandum of Agreement. https://www.sagaftra.org/
   files/2017_tv-theat_refbklt_final.pdf (accessed December 28, 2017).

Governmental Documents

California Department of Industrial Relations. "Laws Relating to Talent Agencies: Excerpts
   from the California Labor Code. Revised 2009." http://www.dir.ca.gov/dlse/Talent/
   Talent_Laws_Relating_to_Talent_Agencies.pdf (accessed November 2, 2017).
California Department of Alcoholic Beverage Control (ABC). "License Education
   on Alcohol and Drugs (LEAD)." https://www.abc.ca.gov/ (accessed December 4,
   2017).
California Department of Consumer Affairs (CDCA):
   California Tenant Law, "What are your rights," https://caltenantlaw.com/ (accessed
      August 19, 2018).
   "Boards/Bureaus—Consumers." http://www.dca.ca.gov (accessed December 4, 2017).
   "Landlords' and Tenants' Responsibilities for Habitability and Repairs." http://www.dca.
      ca.gov/publications/legal_guides/lt-8.shtml (accessed December 6, 2017).
   "California Tenants." http://www.dca.ca.gov/publications/landlordbook/catenant.pdf
      (accessed December 7, 2017).
   "When You Have Decided to Rent." http://www.dca.ca.gov/publications/landlordbook/
      when-rent.shtml (accessed February 18, 2018).
California Contractors State Licensing Board. "Applicants—Examination Study Guides."
   http://www.cslb.ca.gov/Contractors/Applicants/Examination_Study_Guides/ (accessed
   December 4, 2017).
City of Burbank. "History of Burbank." http://www.burbankca.gov/about-us/burbank-
   history (accessed July 14, 2017).

County of Los Angeles: Consumer and Business Affairs Department of Consumer
Affairs:
"Your Home: Before You Rent." http://dcba.lacounty.gov/wps/portal/dca/main/home/
yourhome/beforeyourent? (accessed December 6, 2017).
"Living in Your Rental Unit." http://dcba.lacounty.gov/wps/portal/dca/main/home/
yourhome/livinginyourrentalunit/ (accessed December 7, 2017).
"Moving Out of Your Rental." http://dcba.lacounty.gov/wps/portal/dca/main/home/
yourhome/movingoutofyourrental/ (accessed December 7, 2017).
Federal Trade Commission: Consumer Information. *Look Out for Modeling Scams.* https://
www.consumer.ftc.gov/articles/0071-look-out-modeling-scams (accessed November 8,
2017).
Housing and Community Investment Department of Los Angeles (HCIDLA):
"Property Owners—RSO Overview." http://hcidla.lacity.org/RSO-Overview (accessed
December 7, 2017).
"What is Covered Under the RSO." http://hcidla.lacity.org/What-is-Covered-under-
the-RSO (accessed December 7, 2017).
Internal Revenue Service:
Publications 463: Travel, Entertainment, Gift, and Automobile Expenses. https://www.irs.
gov/publications/p463 (accessed May 1, 2018).
Publication 529: Performing Artists. http://www.irs.gov/publications/p529/ar02.
html#d0e344 (accessed April 22, 2017).
"Independent Contractor Defined." https://www.irs.gov/businesses/small-businesses-
self-employed/independent-contractor-defined (accessed May 12, 2017).
"Is Your Hobby a For-Profit Endeavor?" https://www.irs.gov/uac/is-your-hobby-a-for-
profit-endeavor (accessed May 12, 2017).
"S-Corporations." https://www.irs.gov/businesses/small-businesses-self-employed/
s-corporations (accessed February 24, 2018).
"Simplified Option for Home Office Deduction." https://www.irs.gov/businesses/
small-businesses-self-employed/simplified-option-for-home-office-deduction
(accessed April 22, 2017).
US Census Bureau: American Factfinder. "2011–2015 American Community Survey
Selected Population Tables." https://factfinder.census.gov/faces/tableservices/jsf/pages/
productview.xhtml?src=CF (accessed July 14, 2017).
US Department of Commerce: International Trade Association. "2017 Top Markets
Report Media and Entertainment." https://www.trade.gov/topmarkets/pdf/Top%20
Markets%20Media%20and%20Entertinment%202017.pdf (accessed February 18,
2018).